Modern Irish Theat.

Cultural History of Literature

Modern Irish Theatre

MARY TROTTER

polity

Copyright © Mary Trotter 2008

The right of Mary Trotter to be identified as Author of this Work has been asserted in accordance with the UK Copyright, Designs and Patents Act 1988.

First published in 2008 by Polity Press

Polity Press
65 Bridge Street
Cambridge CB2 1UR, UK

Polity Press
350 Main Street
Malden, MA 02148, USA

All rights reserved. Except for the quotation of short passages for the purpose of criticism and review, no part of this publication may be reproduced, stored in a retrieval system, or transmitted, in any form or by any means, electronic, mechanical, photocopying, recording or otherwise, without the prior permission of the publisher.

ISBN-13: 978-0-7456-3342-8
ISBN-13: 978-0-7456-3343-5(pb)

A catalogue record for this book is available from the British Library.

Typeset in 11.25 on 13 pt Dante
by SNP Best-set Typesetter Ltd., Hong Kong
Printed and bound in Great Britain by MPG Books Ltd, Bodmin, Cornwall

The publisher has used its best endeavours to ensure that the URLs for external websites referred to in this book are correct and active at the time of going to press. However, the publisher has no responsibility for the websites and can make no guarantee that a site will remain live or that the content is or will remain appropriate.

Every effort has been made to trace all copyright holders, but if any have been inadvertently overlooked the publishers will be pleased to include any necessary credits in any subsequent reprint or edition.

For further information on Polity, visit our website: www.polity.co.uk

Contents

Acknowledgements

This project has benefited from the generosity of a number of institutions and individuals. I began work on this book as a professor at Indiana University – Purdue University Indianapolis (IUPUI). I gratefully acknowledge Indiana University's support of this project through an Arts and Humanities Grant, as well as a Grant-in-Aid for Research from IUPUI. In 2005 I joined the Theatre and Drama faculty at the University of Wisconsin-Madison, where I have had the pleasure of discussing this work with new Theatre and Celtic Studies colleagues, and the opportunity to test some of the concepts in this project with students in the classroom. Start-up funds from the Graduate School and the European Studies Alliance at the University of Wisconsin, along with a research grant from the Vilas fund at the University of Wisconsin helped pay for much needed scholarly materials in support of the project as well as academic travel. I am grateful to the librarians at the Berg Collection at the New York Public Library, the Spencer Library at the University of Kansas, the National Library of Ireland, and the Special Collections at Southern Illinois University and Northwestern University, for research assistance related directly to this project.

I am fortunate indeed to have benefited from the generosity of many scholars around my work, including former and current colleagues at IUPUI and UW; but I do want to single out a few of the many persons who have been particularly supportive of this project. First, I am grateful to Andrea Drugan, Jonathan Skerrett, and the two anonymous reviewers of an early version of this manuscript for their enthusiasm and advice about this book. The good humour and boundless intellect of Irish studies colleagues Susan C. Harris, Liz Cullingford, Helen Burke, and Sarah McKibben have always been an email away; and the friendship and inspiring scholarship of Barbara Clayton, Joan Dean, Sean Farrell, Sandy Pearce, and Scott Boltwood have inevitably kept me serious about what is important, and less serious about what isn't. I am especially grateful to colleagues Ann Archbold, Margot Backus, Gail Brassard, Tracy Davis, Heather DuBrow, Jon Eller, the late Christian Kloesel, Michael Peterson, Susan Sweeney, and Manon van de Water for their intellectual inspiration and their support during life and work transitions. Paige Reynolds's advice and friendship has been invaluable. Finally, my husband and my heart, Robert Kaufman, offered shrewd edits and sensible suggestions throughout the writing of this work, as well as patience and support. I dedicate this book to him.

Timeline of Significant Events in Irish Arts and Politics

1890s

1893	Gaelic League Founded
1894	Oscar Wilde's *The Importance of Being Earnest* performed
1899	Irish Literary Theatre's First Season

1900s

1900	Inghinidhe na hEireann founded
1901	Douglas Hyde's *Casadh an tSugain* performed
1902	W.B. Yeats and Lady Gregory's *Cathleen ni Houlihan* performed
1903	Irish National Theatre Society founded
1904	Abbey Theatre opens as the Irish National Theatre
	Ulster Literary Theatre founded
1906	Theatre of Ireland founded
1907	Riots surrounding *The Playboy of the Western World*
	Cork Dramatic Society founded
1908	Irish Universities Act

1910s

1912	Abbey Theatre's United States tour
1914	Third Home Rule Bill passes
	Start of WWI
1915	Padraic Pearse's *The Master* performed
1916	Easter Rising
1919	George Bernard Shaw's *Heartbreak House* performed
1919–21	Irish War for Independence (Anglo-Irish War)

1920s

1921	George Shiels's *Bedmates* performed
1922	T.C. Murray's *Aftermath* performed

1923   Partition of the Six Counties of Northern Ireland
        Civil War begins (1922–3)
        O'Casey's *Shadow of a Gunman* performed
1924   O'Casey's *Juno and the Paycock* performed
1925   Anew McMaster's touring company established
1926   Riots at the Abbey over *The Plough and the Stars*
1927   The Peacock Stage opens at the Abbey Theatre
1928   Dublin Gate Theatre founded
1929   Dennis Johnston, *The Old Lady Says No!* performed
1929   Sean O'Casey's *The Silver Tassie* rejected by the Abbey

1930s

1930   George Shiels, *The New Gossoon* performed
1931   Mary Manning's *Youth's the Season – ?* performed
1932   Lady Augusta Gregory dies
        Fianna Fail wins General Election, de Valera becomes Taoiseach
            (Prime Minister) of Ireland
1936   Teresa Deevy's *Katie Roche* published in *Best Plays of 1935–6*
        Longford Productions founded
1937   New Constitution ratified in the Irish Free State
1938   Tonia Moisewitch begins designing at the Abbey Theatre
        Douglas Hyde elected first President of Ireland
1939   W.B. Yeats dies
        Paul Vincent Carrol's *The White Steed* performed
        Second World War begins, Ireland declares neutrality

1940s

1940   Ulster Group Theatre founded
        Dublin Airport opened
        Lyric Theatre Company, Dublin founded
1941   German air raids in Belfast
1943   M.J. Molloy's *Old Road* performed at Abbey Theatre
1947   Radio Eireann Players founded
1949   Republic of Ireland Act goes into effect
        O'Casey publishes memoirs, *Inishfallen, Fare Thee Well*

1950s

1950   G.B. Shaw dies
1951   Lyric Players Theatre founded
        Original Abbey Theatre building destroyed in fire

1953	Pike Theatre Club founded
	Samuel Beckett's *En Attendant Godot* performed
1954	Brendan Behan's *The Quare Fellow* performed
1955	Ireland enters the UNO
	Bord Failte (Irish Tourist Board) founded
1959	Sean Lemass elected Taoiseach

1960s

1960	Michael Mac Liammóir's *The Importance of Being Oscar* performed
1961	J.B. Keane's *Many Young Men of Twenty* performed
	Television service in Republic of Ireland
	Aosdana founded
1963	Arts Council of Northern Ireland established
	Belfast Airport opens
1964	Brian Friel's *Philadelphia, Here I Come!* performed
1965	J.B. Keane's *The Field* performed
	Anglo-Irish Free Trade Agreement
1966	New Abbey Theatre building opens
1967	Project Arts Center founded, Dublin
1968	Thomas Murphy's *Famine* performed
1969	Large-scale deployment of British troops in Northern Ireland

1970s

1972	'Bloody sunday' in Derry
1973	Republic of Ireland joins the European Economic Community (EEC)
1975	Druid Theatre, Galway founded
1977	Thomas Kilroy's *Talbot's Box* performed

1980s

1981	Hunger strikes among IRA prisoners in Northern Ireland
	Field Day Theatre Company founded
	Brian Friel's *Translations* performed
1983	Christina Reid's *Tea in a China Cup* performed
	Charabanc Theatre Company founded
1985	Hillsborough Anglo-Irish Agreement
	Frank McGuinness's *Observe the Sons of Ulster* performed
	Anne Devlin's *Ourselves Alone* performed
1989	Dermot Bolger's *A Lament for Arthur Cleary* performed

1990s

1990	Mary Robinson elected President of Ireland
1992	Irish referenda on abortion and divorce
1993	Downing Street Declaration Signed
	Corcadorca Founded
1994	Ceasefire by IRA and Loyalists
	Marina Carr's *The Mai* performed
	Declan O'Kelly's *Asylum! Asylum!* performed
1995	Divorce becomes legal in Republic of Ireland
	Sebastian Barry's *The Steward of Christendom* performed
1996	Jimmy Murphy's *A Picture of Paradise* performed
	Martin McDonagh's *Leenane Trilogy* performed
	Enda Walsh's *Disco Pigs* performed
1998	Good Friday Agreement signed by leaders in London, Belfast and Dublin
	Conor McPherson's *The Weir* performed
	Marina Carr's *By the Bog of Cats* performed
1999	Mark O'Rowe's *Howie the Rookie* performed

2000s

2001	Abbey Theatre Festival celebrates work of Tom Murphy
	McDonagh's *Lieutenant of Inishmore* performed
2002	Marina Carr's *Ariel* performed
2004	Arthur Riordan and Bell Helicopter's *Improbable Frequency* performed
2005	Druid Theatre Company's Druid/Synge Festival
	IRA halts its armed campaign
2007	Protestant and Catholic leaders sign a power-sharing agreement
	Adigun and Doyle's adaptation of *The Playboy of the Western World* performed

Introduction

Theatre is a community activity that requires its producers to draw in the attention and participation of audiences who, through their reaction to the performance, participate actively in the construction of meaning in the theatre event. The nature of theatre, therefore, makes it an important potential site for the imagination and solidification of new community formations. Thus, it is not surprising that when the cultural nationalist movement arose in Ireland in the 1890s with the active purpose of creating a sense of identity and belonging among Irish people outside of British stereotypes or ethnic, religious, or class divisions, theatre quickly was marked as a vehicle for imagining what this anti-colonial Irish community could be. Making and attending theatre was recognized as a means of identifying oneself as part of the nationalist community. The first plays to emerge out of the Irish nationalist movement were humble and amateur affairs, but earnest in purpose. Within a decade, however, the Irish theatre would have an identifiable aesthetic, and professional players to perform it. And, by the 1930s, Irish plays were being performed internationally and inspiring theatre movements interested in ethnicity and identity in the United States, Europe, and Asia. At the same time that Irish theatre was achieving this international notoriety, however, amateur theatre groups across Ireland continued to write and perform plays locally about their communities and their culture. In the second half of the century, when statehood had been achieved in part of the country, but six counties remained connected to the United Kingdom, Irish theatre re-emerged out of what some considered a self-satisfied and conservative aesthetic to address the social and political crises fomenting in both Northern Ireland and the Republic. And in the twenty-first century, Irish theatre's legacy continues, with companies outside Ireland committed to performing works from the Irish dramatic repertoire, and a new generation of playwrights, directors, and performers working inside and outside Ireland's geographical boundaries who identify themselves and their work as part of this cultural tradition.

This book traces the history of Irish drama over the long twentieth century as a communal and community-building art form. At its worst, Irish theatre has offered uncomplicated recitations of dramatic tropes that fit too easily into artistic and ideological clichés. At its best, it has addressed the complexity of Ireland's history, and the diversity of opinions about nationality or identity in ways that provoke its audiences to find new approaches and to think in new ways. But Irish theatre's power as a cultural force, historically as well as in the age of YouTube and DVDs delivered to your door, lies in its ability to engage local and national audiences, to make theatre communities. The commitment to Irish theatre today can be seen in the high degree of government support for both major theatres and small companies since the 1980s, and the number of productions of Irish plays abroad. It can also be seen in the number of people who choose to participate in Irish theatre's production and reception, and the ways in which Irish performance is reinventing itself during these rapidly changing times. This sustained commitment to political performance in Ireland is really the continuation of a century-long conversation among Irish persons from a range of identity backgrounds, living and working both inside and outside Ireland's borders, using theatre as a vehicle for cultural definition and social change.

This book offers an introduction to some of the major trends that have shaped modern Irish theatre's cultural legacy since the 1890s. While it includes close examinations of particular plays and playwrights, these works are put in the context of the companies who performed them, the socio-political events surrounding them, and the artistic, cultural, political, and social communities they represented. By focusing on the institutional role of theatre, rather than on theatre texts, I hope to reveal the dynamic, even symbiotic, relationship between Irish theatre and Irish culture. To facilitate the flow of this argument, the book is divided into four sections, each representing an important historical period in Irish history. Each part begins with a brief introduction highlighting significant political events of the period and outlining major themes. The chapters themselves look at significant developments, controversies, crises and triumphs within Irish theatre during that period, emphasizing how theatre is relating to its historical moment, and how and why theatre companies are producing particular plays.

Part I, 'Performing the Nation, 1891–1916', looks at modern Irish theatre's origins within the cultural nationalist movement, and the array of theatre companies and ideologies that emerged out of that period. The first chapter focuses on the Irish Literary Theatre and the Abbey Theatre, and their centralizing influence on the nationalist theatre movement. The following chapter, however, considers how the high modernist leanings of the Abbey's directors were supplanted by the rise of an Irish realist aesthetic that engaged with local communities and concerns.

Part II, 'War and After, 1916–1948', examines the impact of revolution, Civil War, and their aftermaths on Irish theatre. Chapter 3 looks at the ways the theatre responded almost immediately to the experience of war through the dramatic works of Sean O'Casey, portrayed magnificently by early stars of the theatre, and watched by participants in and witnesses to the fighting. The fourth chapter explores how Irish theatre looked outward as well as inward during the 1930s, both with Irish theatre touring abroad and influencing other theatre movements, and with groups like the Dublin Drama League and the Gate Theatre performing avant-garde work from Europe and America. It also considers how realist playwrights like Teresa Deevy and George Shiels reacted to the growing conservativism, isolationism, and neocolonialism in Ireland, as well as generational differences, with plays addressing the conflict between the imaginative individual and a repressive culture.

Part III, 'Rewriting Tradition, 1948–1980', considers the impact of the establishment of the Irish Republic, economic reforms, European artistic influences, and the rise of sectarian violence on Irish theatre mid-century. Chapter 5 then looks at how Irish theatre in the 1950s and 1960s both continued to develop the Irish realist tradition, while also taking on new forms, influenced by the new revolutions in writing in Europe and North America. Specifically, this chapter considers playwrights and companies who collaborated with innovative theatre activities outside Ireland, like Joan Littlewood's Theatre Workshop in London, the Guthrie Theatre in Minneapolis, and the Berliner Ensemble in East Berlin. This chapter also looks at how theatre in Northern Ireland responded to the crisis of the Troubles in the 1970s, not by creating diversionary, entertaining theatre, but by addressing head on their community's crisis.

Part IV, 'Re-imagining Ireland, 1980–2007', analyses what some consider a second renaissance in Irish theatre as the Field Day Theatre Company, along with other theatre groups, employed community theatre strategies to address the crises surrounding the Troubles in Northern Ireland. The final chapter considers how theatre companies North and South responded to the tremendous economic growth in the Republic, and the diplomatic advances in Northern Ireland, to develop strategies for representing Northern Ireland and the Republic's rapidly shifting demographic, cultural, and economic identities.

It is with some temerity that I offer this book as a contribution to the rich library of Irish theatre monographs that have appeared in recent years. I am especially indebted to the insights of recent book-length histories by Christopher Morash, Lionel Pilkington, Susan C. Harris, Ben Levitas, Paige Reynolds, Karen Vandevelde, Joan Dean, Christopher Murray, and Tom Maguire. The bibliography of this text points to other scholars who have enriched the field and influenced this work with their research in Irish theatre studies and cultural studies. I hope that the reader of this book new to Irish theatre history will find it a useful means for entering into the conversation surrounding Irish theatre and culture, and that those with more advanced backgrounds in the field will find in it new perspectives and questions to address.

Part I

Performing the Nation, 1891–1916

Introduction to Part I

Since the seventeenth century, theatrical performance in Ireland has served as a site of social and political contest at home, and a product of cultural export abroad. Theatre from Ireland dominated anglophone dramatic writing and theatre practice, with many of the great 'English' playwrights and actors, Goldsmith, Sheridan, Macklin, Woffington, Shaw, and Wilde, actually having Irish roots. But Irish theatre did not fully exploit its propagandist potential until the end of the nineteenth century, when a perfect storm of political and cultural events in Ireland led to tremendous shifts in the aesthetics and the purposes of the form. Throughout this period, amid heated artistic and political conflicts, theatre prevailed as a vital mode of entertainment and activism, with the stage becoming a kind of laboratory in which different models of Irish identity and experience could be performed and watched by the very individuals working for an independent Ireland in their everyday lives. A national tradition of great playwriting and acting became a nationalist dramatic movement. That dramatic revolution, working hand in hand with the political efforts of the day, would contribute to Ireland's self-refashioning in the Irish revival, and would come to influence modern drama for the century to come.

While interest in Irish culture had been on the rise in Ireland since the 1870s, and was especially apparent with the founding of the Gaelic Athletic Association in 1884, Irish cultural activities developed an increasingly nationalist dimension in the 1890s, largely in response to a lack of faith in legislative attempts to earn Irish home rule. For years, Charles Stewart Parnell, the head of the Irish Parliamentary Party and one of the greatest statesmen of the Victorian age, fought valiantly in the UK parliament for Irish independence from the United Kingdom, and was even jailed briefly in the early 1880s for his efforts to obtain land reform. But his practically cultic status among the Irish people disappeared when it was learned that he had been having an affair with Katherine O'Shea, the wife of another Irish MP, and was even the father of two of her children.

Parnell went from having complete control over votes by Irish MPs in Westminster to losing his seat in parliament in a matter of months. He died a year later.

For many nationalists, Parnell's death signalled the demise of their hope in a diplomatic solution to Ireland's forced inclusion in the United Kingdom, and they turned their attention to developing a strong sense of national identity and purpose at home. And, indeed, the radical events in Ireland throughout the nineteenth century did put its cultural identity in a state of flux and crisis. In the 1830s, the island held over 8 million people, the majority of whom spoke Irish exclusively. The famine of 1846–9 led to the deaths of approximately 1 million people, and the emigration of millions more, so that by 1891 Ireland held only around 4 million people, with English rather than Irish as the dominant language, and more people living in eastern Ireland, where British influence was strongest, than the more isolated and economically disadvantaged west. The Irish who had moved into the cities, many nationalists feared, were abandoning their Irish heritage for the material comforts and social benefits of 'modern English' ways. In other words, economic and political domination by the English had established a kind of cultural imperialism over the Irish people.

Irish nationalists argued that buying into British cultural norms meant accepting the notion that the Irish were a historically inferior race that required the civilizing influence of Britain. As L. Perry Curtis points out in his book *Apes and Angels: The Irishman in Victorian Caricature*, nineteenth-century Britain was rife with images of the Irish as childlike 'Paddys' in need of the guidance and education of a maternal Britannia, or Fenian devils with simian features, who needed to be forcibly restrained from destroying not only their own nation, but Western civilization. The nationalist movement sought to establish a sense of Irish identity and community to counter these British imperialist stereotypes on economic, political, and social levels. And one of the main means to establish that community was through cultural activism.

One of the inspirations for the Irish revival was Douglas Hyde's speech before the National Literary Society, 'On the Necessity of De-Anglicising Ireland' (1892). The Irish people, Hyde argued, needed to return to and embrace Irish language and customs to rid themselves of the colonial sense of inferiority. 'In order to de-Anglicize ourselves,' Hyde remarked, 'we must at once arrest the decay of the language. We must teach ourselves not to be ashamed of ourselves.' The following year, Hyde founded a non-partisan cultural organization called the Gaelic League, and chapters rapidly spread across Ireland, as well as in its diaspora communities in England, the United States, Australia, and Brazil. The Gaelic League promoted learning the Irish language, and also learning and participating in Irish sport, games, craft, and literature. It also encouraged its members to purchase only Irish goods, thus lessening Ireland's economic dependency on England.

The Gaelic revival thus encouraged its members to self-consciously perform a notion of Irish identity through their choices of dress, speech, and behaviour. To buy an Irish product, or to wear a reproduction of a Tara brooch, or to speak Irish instead of English was to act out an identity counter to that imposed upon the Irish people from England. This notion of the performance of an Irish identity in everyday life as an act of anti-colonial resistance would inform the practices of nationalist theatres – and their audiences – throughout the first years of the Irish dramatic movement.

In fact, the first theatre events of the Irish dramatic movement were directly linked to political groups and events. Irish playwrights like Father Dineen, Alice Milligan, and Padraic Colum began writing drama for Gaelic League festivals. Likewise, nationalists like Maire O'Neill, Sarah Allgood, and Dudley Digges would become theatre actors as part of their political activism. And, while W.B. Yeats, Lady Gregory, George Moore and Edward Martyn may have relied on less-than-nationalist friends for support of the Irish Literary Theatre, the project grew out of the impetus of activities by groups such as the National Literary Society, and the passion about Irish culture shared (albeit in varying degrees) by its founders.

The bicentennial of the Rebellion of 1798 increased popular interest in Irish nationalism, and local groups readily welcomed new recruits. Thus, by the time an alliance of nationalist groups collaborated to perform the revolutionary play *Cathleen ni Houlihan* in 1902, theatre had established itself in Dublin as a legitimate site for nation-building, with groups across Ireland holding play contests and offering Irish and English-language performances as part of their cultural national agenda. Even commercial theatres, like the Queen's Royal Theatre, Dublin, highlighted Irish nationalist melodramas with titles like *Robert Emmet* and *The Famine*, and performances of pro-British plays, or plays with stage Irish stereotypes, were roundly criticized in the nationalist press (de Burca 1983). With the opening of the Irish National Theatre Society, or the Abbey Theatre, in 1904, the theatre's central role in imagining a new Irish state was clear.

Nationalist audiences were deeply engaged in what they were seeing on stage, and were sensitive to the fact that, by going to see a play, they were in fact performing their commitment to the nationalist ideology repre-sented by both the play and the group producing it. And, of course, they sometimes felt as obligated to protest about a play as to approve of it. The Abbey Theatre became a prime target for such protests, thanks to the Anglo-Irish directorate and their British, anti-nationalist patron. Often, complaints against the Abbey reflected not only what was being performed on stage, but also the critics' own nationalist agendas.

Indeed, the range of ideologies and identity positions within the nation-alist community was one of the greatest challenges faced within the nationalist movement. Anglo-Irish, Catholics, Socialists, militants, and liberal nationalists all made up parts of the movement and, while all fought for Ireland's independence, they did not always stand together in the battle. And Unionists, likewise, grew increasingly vocal in their support of Ireland staying within the United Kingdom. Collaborations among nationalists with different points of view were often uneasy, and some-times outright hostility was shown among different factions, as was reflected in the riots surrounding J.M. Synge's *The Playboy of the Western World* (1907), when audience members of the Abbey argued with voices and fists over whether Synge's play was an insult to Irish womanhood and a blaspheme against the idea of a national dramatic movement, or an artistic celebration of the Irish west that deserved at the least a polite and respectful hearing.

At the time of the debut of the *Playboy* in 1907, however, people who did not care for the Abbey certainly had their choice of other theatre com-panies for nationalist entertainment at the time, including Gaelic League performances, the Independent Dramatic Company, the National Players, the Theatre of Ireland, the Ulster Literary Theatre, and the Cork Dramatic Society. But even companies artistically or politically opposed to the Abbey often rented the Abbey Theatre space for their own performances, and collaboration among companies for actors, scripts, and audiences was com-monplace. Also, many of the playwrights of this period got their start in these amateur societies before seeing their works produced at the Abbey. Thanks to the fame of their directors, their international reputation, their physical presence with their own, licensed building in the heart of Dublin, and the comparatively professional quality of their work, the Abbey was already a yardstick against which other companies would measure them-selves. And, as the self-proclaimed national theatre, they also became the lightning rod for controversies about appropriate representations of the Irish people, and appropriate ideological perspectives for an Irish national theatre.

Abbey patron Annie Horniman's cancellation of her subsidy to the Irish National Theatre Society in 1910 created an economic crisis for the self-proclaimed national theatre company, solved largely by the know-how and connections of Lady Gregory, and an increased tour schedule. The Abbey even created a second company that would perform in Dublin while the 'real' company toured England and North America. These tours not only helped keep the company afloat, but also increased the fame of the company and its actors. Many Abbey players, in fact, ended up leaving the company to work in England and the United States.

Theatre controversies, however, were a pale reflection of the growing political conflicts in Ireland in the 1910s. Nationalist activity in Ireland had reached fever pitch. Events like the lockout of members of the Irish General Transport Workers' Union in 1912–13 radicalized many Irish nationalists. In the same year, almost 250,000 Northern Irishmen signed the Ulster Covenant vowing allegiance to the death to the King of England. The Irish Volunteers, a nationalist paramilitary army made up of members of the Irish Republican Brotherhood, began to speak more openly of revolution, and the Irish Citizen Army offered socialist nationalists an opportunity to join in military preparations. The majority of Irish nationalists were following the Irish Parliamentary Party's advice to continue to work through diplomatic strategies. Yet their voices were being edged out by charismatic figures like Padraic Pearse, whose rhetoric of blood sacrifice to renew the nation informed both his speeches and the plays he wrote to be performed by the children studying at his nationalist schools, St Enda's and St Ita's. Pearse would not be the only playwright calling for violent revolution, however. Seven men signed the Proclamation of the Irish Republic on Easter 1916, the start of the military war for independence. Three of those signatories were playwrights.

This section explores the ideological, material, and artistic progress of the modern Irish theatre movement during these years of its tumultuous birth. Chapter 1 traces the establishment of Irish theatre companies as part of the larger cultural nationalist agenda, focusing on the National Theatre Society, or the Abbey Theatre. It concludes with a reading of the riots surrounding the performance of J.M. Synge's *The Playboy of the Western World*, considering the events surrounding that particularly famous theatre scandal as a forum for theatre's role within the nationalist movement. Chapter 2 considers the development of a realist theatre aesthetic across Ireland that came to overshadow, but not obliterate, verse plays and plays written on themes from Irish legend. Realism's rise both in professional and amateur, urban and rural venues, allowed for a multiplicity of voices that sought to express Irish experience at the level of the regional and the personal. The chapter ends, however, with a close look at the use of theatre to promote military insurrection in the months preceding the Easter Rising of 1916. Throughout this period, nationalist theatre's relationship to the social drama of imagining a new nation-state was intimate and often intense. Still, the voices that emerged from the movement spoke not only to the movement itself, but also to the world, influencing theatre practice and writing internationally.

1

Imagining an Aesthetic: Modern Irish Theatre's First Years

In Ireland at the dawn of the twentieth century, a person with cultural nationalist leanings would have a wide range of opportunities to enjoy theatrical entertainments that reflected her activist politics. If she felt a little highbrow, she might attend a performance by the Irish Literary Theatre. If she felt a little lowbrow, she could watch a patriotic melodrama at the Queen's Royal Theatre, Dublin, or some other commercial theatre. Or she could attend an array of performances at nationalist events held by such groups as the Gaelic League, Inghinidhe na hEireann (the Daughters of Erin), or the Celtic Literary Society. As a nationalist, she might even consider it her responsibility to support these activities with her attendance, or to participate as a ticket seller, performer, or playwright. It was out of this rich performance context, with its range of political positions and aesthetic possibilities, that modern Irish theatre emerged.

This chapter traces the development of Irish drama at the turn of the twentieth century by looking at some of the central missions and challenges facing key individuals and groups involved in creating a modern Irish theatre aesthetic, and the diverse ways they went about meeting those goals. The modern Irish dramatic movement in its first years was a consciously political movement, made up of artist/activists wanting to use theatre as a kind of laboratory for imagining an Ireland independent of British control. There was a common interest in creating an image of the Irish people counter to stage Irish stereotypes, and in promoting positive images of the Irish people, their history, and their unique culture. Some were interested in developing dramas in the Irish language. Some wanted to bring avant-garde aesthetics like symbolism and naturalism to the Irish stage. Almost all eventually came to the conclusion that, like other products of the Irish revival's self-help movement, the theatre needed to be made in Ireland, by the Irish, for Irish consumption. Since most previous Irish playwrights and performers, from Richard Sheridan and Charles Macklin to George Bernard Shaw and Tyrone Power, ended up working in London rather than Ireland, the idea of developing a premiere theatre community at home, and about home, was exciting indeed. It also served to counter Britain's imperialist argument that Irish culture was dependent on English influence and support. Yet despite – or perhaps because of – their common purpose, theatres and audiences often fought over what kind of theatre was the best way to proceed. Many of these controversies crystallized in 1904, when W.B. Yeats, Lady Augusta Gregory, and J.M. Synge assumed control of the Irish National Theatre Society and, with the aid of an English patron, turned a formerly democratic nationalist theatre made of individuals from different classes and religious backgrounds into a professional theatre run by Anglo-Irish directors, proclaiming their theatre Ireland's national stage. But debates over the Abbey's legitimacy as a nationalist project or a nationalist institution merely focused the intensity of the discussion surrounding the idea of establishing a new Irish theatre aesthetic that generated such interest within nationalist circles, and inspired such a range of artists to become involved in, and build the foundation, for modern Irish theatre.

The Gaelic League and the Performance of Irish Identity

The Irish revival, or the cultural nationalist movement, resisted English domination through the self-conscious performance of Irish identity in everyday life. Playing Irish games, wearing Irish fashions, buying Irish goods, learning and speaking the Irish language, were all means of subverting British cultural and economic imperialism, while reaffirming Irish civilization as an ancient, unique, sophisticated and – most importantly – autonomous cultural tradition of a people deserving self-rule. This work was not merely putting on a show, but a call to reclaim a culture under real threat after centuries of systematic attempts at British enculturation, as well as the devastating impact of famine and emigration on the Irish population and its psyche only fifty years earlier. P.J. Matthews points out that this 'cultural' activity was indeed 'political' because it was 'revising the imperial narrative of Ireland and relocating the nation at the centre rather than at the periphery of experience' (10). Quoting Irish cultural theorist Luke Gibbons, he remarks: 'To engage in cultural activity in circumstances where one's culture was being effaced or obliterated, or even to assert the existence of a civilization prior to conquest, was to make a political statement, if only by depriving the frontier myth of its power to act as an alibi for colonization' (Matthews 2003: 10).

But while the revival was widespread, it was far from monolithic. In *Imagined Communities*, Benedict Anderson argues that the modern nation-state is built upon a commonly established belief in a shared identity and a common past. In practice, however, individuals and groups otherwise united in an anti-colonial struggle will often clash over the means to achieve or maintain the national community. This was certainly the case in the Irish revival, whose participants included individuals with a range of conflicting histories and identity positions. And this diversity naturally led to energetic conflicts within the movement about how Ireland and Irishness was being represented.

Theatrical performance, an event that is created collaboratively by text, audience, actors, space, and historical/cultural context, was quickly recognized by cultural nationalist organizations as one of the liveliest and most complex means for creating and contesting national identity. By the 1890s theatre generally had established itself across Europe as a site for discussing pertinent social issues.[1] Thus, it is no surprise that theatre quickly became a common product of cultural activism within the revival, with Gaelic League chapters offering performances at feisianna and regularly holding playwriting contests. Timothy McMahon notes how quickly these performances in the Gaelic League, often begun as Irish language teaching tools, became staples of Gaelic League events (2008). By the mid-1890s, nationalist theatre critics assessed performances both within and without the movement against a nationalist yardstick.

Since Gaelic League plays, like all its other cultural products, were designed to rid Ireland of English influence, the first target to be eradicated from the Irish stage was the stereotype of the stage Irishman. These stage Irish stereotypes, Hyde and other Gaelic League leaders argued, needed to be replaced by images of an Irish 'folk' with the qualities upheld by the movement – spiritual, morally upright, healthy and, in order to appear as far removed from British influence as possible, living in an idealized, rural, Irish language-speaking West (Fleming 1995). Realist dramas glorifying the Irish peasants and their way of life emerged as a genre in Irish and English theatre, known as the peasant play, that would serve as the backbone of the modern Irish dramatic movement, and is a genre that continues to influence Irish dramaturgy (albeit often ironically) today. The other tactic was to dramatize a story from pre-Christian, ancient Irish mythology, proving that Ireland had possessed a rich cultural heritage centuries before the encroachment of British imperialism. Since these stories preceded the waves of invasions and plantations that helped form the Irish population in late nineteenth-century Ireland, it was a literary heritage that could be claimed by Irish individuals from all religious and class backgrounds. Also, staging an ancient Irish myth allowed for larger casts (thus more patriotic involvement) and more ornate experimentations in costume and language. P.T. McGinley's *Lizzie and the Tinker* (1901), a peasant farce, needs three actors. Alice Milligan's *The Last Feast of the Fianna* (1900) requires at least a dozen, and could accommodate more.

These early Irish language performances spread across Ireland in the 1890s. Irish language enthusiasts like Fr Dineen, Alice Milligan, and P.T. McGinley began to write dramas in Irish for performance at Gaelic League events. However, the importance of these performances rarely matched their quality since, as Karen Vandevelde points out, very few individuals in Ireland possessed dramatic talent and training together with fluency in the Irish language (2005; 42). Creating theatre with a group of individuals untrained in playwriting, acting, or design is naturally challenging. Asking these amateurs to perform in a language many are just learning to speak makes the task monumental. Thus, the first Irish language plays performed at Gaelic League events were probably applauded with respect, but not too much pleasure. *Fàine an Lae*, a journal in support of the Irish language movement, recommended the following strictures for writing Irish language plays: 'It is not necessary that such a play should be original, probably it would have to be translated. But it should not be long, for three reasons. First, the difficulty of writing; second, the difficulty of learning and speaking the parts; third and principal, the difficulty of inducing the audience to stand it' (Hogan and Kilroy 1975: 56). Yet these dramas served an important role in both the revival generally and the dramatic movement specifically, by giving voice to the Irish language in public forums, thus increasing the general interest in and comprehension of the language, and by helping to establish dramatic performance as a legitimate nationalist enterprise.[2]

While the Gaelic League's populist performance strategies raised interest in both cultural nationalism and theatre throughout Ireland, its ability to flourish into an independent dramatic movement was limited ultimately by a dearth of audience members sophisticated in both theatre and the Irish language, and theatre's auxiliary position to the Gaelic League's goals. A parallel attempt at an Irish dramaturgy emerged in the late 1890s that avoided those limitations by working primarily in English and linking itself with the international avant-garde rather than local nationalist initiatives. However, in the process of their work, this modernist attempt to produce an Irish avant-garde would discover new challenges in developing a national theatre for Ireland.

From Nationalist Theatricality to Anglo-Irish Drama: the Irish Literary Theatre

The first major attempt to create an Irish theatre dealing with nationalist issues but not stemming out of a particular nationalist group was the Irish Literary Theatre (hereafter ILT), conceived by W.B. Yeats, Lady Augusta Gregory, and Edward Martyn in 1897 (with George Moore joining the group slightly later), and operating in Dublin from 1899 until 1901. Yeats was a rising star in the Irish revival in the 1890s, noted as a poet, but just beginning his career as a playwright.[3] Throughout the 1890s, he established nationalist credibility in the Irish revival with his poetry, and also with his activism, being one of the founders of the National Literary Society in 1892. Additionally, he was a disciple of Irish nationalist John O'Leary and joined the Irish Republican Brotherhood. His politics in the 1890s were also deeply influenced by his friend, fellow theosophist and life-long love interest, the radical nationalist Maud Gonne. His most productive collaboration within the Irish revival, however, was his partnership with his friend and patron, Lady Gregory.

Lady Augusta Isabella Persse Gregory, like Yeats, was an Anglo-Irish person with a strong interest in Irish cultural nationalism. Her position as the Protestant widow of the former British governor of Ceylon (now Sri Lanka), and mistress of Coole Park in County Galway made her appear an unlikely revolutionary. But her life experiences were radically different from the stereotype of the conservative Anglo-Irish matron often thrust upon her.[4] She travelled regularly in Europe where she had met many of the great modernist thinkers of the time, and even had an affair with Wilfred Scawen Blunt in the 1880s. She also spoke fluent Irish, and turned her Anglo-Irish sense of noblesse oblige into an early ethnographic project, travelling the Gaeltacht, or Irish-speaking areas of Ireland, capturing folktales and stories in their original tongue and translating (and often bowdlerizing) them for a wider audience.

Edward Martyn also joined the venture. Part of an old Irish Catholic family, Martyn was deeply committed to the nationalist cause. He co-founded Sinn Fein with Arthur Griffith and John Sweetman, and was the organization's first president (1905–8). Martyn was educated in Europe, where he became interested in playwriting: before joining forces with the Irish Literary Theatre, he had already submitted two plays, which had been rejected by an English actor-manager (Hogan and Kilroy 1975: 25). Yet he was also deeply committed to Ireland, and believed that an Irish dramatic movement could do for Ireland what Ibsen and his allies had managed to do for Norway only a few decades before.

As the ILT directors began rehearsals for their first season, they realized they needed a partner with professional theatre experience and called in Martyn's cousin, George Moore. Although a landed Irish gentleman living in England, Moore came from revolutionary Irish Catholic stock. His great uncle was a leader in the Rebellion of 1798, and his father was a British MP for Mayo and one of the founders of the nationalist Catholic Defence Association. Moore, however, had lived in London most of his adult life, pursuing his interest in naturalism through his novels, but also achieving some success as a playwright: one of his dramas, *The Strike at Arlingford*, was produced by the Independent Theatre Company in London.[5]

In its first season, in 1899, the Irish Literary Theatre performed Yeats's drama, *The Countess Cathleen*, a folk play about a landed gentlewoman, who, during a famine in her lands sells her soul to the devil in exchange for food for her starving tenants. Cathleen's soul is saved at the end of the play because of the selflessness of her actions. This early play shows Yeats's already exquisite talent for verse drama, as well as the influence on his work of members of his theosophical circles, like Florence Farr, the London actress and artist who performed the leading role in the ILT performance.

However, as Adrian Frazier has noted, *The Countess Cathleen* also reflects Yeats's early insensitivity to some nationalist sensibilities. Instead of focusing on the historical legacy of the Irish famine and its millions of victims, Yeats glorifies a landlord, a member of the class largely responsible for the national crisis caused by the famine. He also shows Catholics willing to sell their souls to the devil, and, in an earlier version, destroying a shrine (Frazier 1990: 9–17). Yeats's own identity as a member of the Anglo-Irish class, and a theosophist to boot, only added to concerns about his representation of both the famine and of Catholicism. Before the play was even staged, it had raised a furore throughout Dublin, thanks to a widely distributed pamphlet protesting against the play, 'Souls for Gold', by F. Hugh O'Donnell, that accused the play of perpetuating stage Irish stereotypes and denigrating the Catholic Church.

His argument led to Cardinal Logue condemning the play, and to some disturbance during its production. The vociferousness of O'Donnell's attack, as Ben Levitas points out, over exaggerated the offence to Catholic Irish sensibilities (Levitas 2002: 42–5), so the drama ultimately was considered a success. But it was also a precursor to the many attacks on his work in the theatre that Yeats would endure in the decades to come.

Edward Martyn's *The Heather Field*, the other play on the first season's bill, inspired less controversy. Written in the style of Ibsen, but set in Ireland, *The Heather Field* was a more immediately accessible form of modernist dramaturgy than Yeats's play, and was clearly in line with the national theatre aesthetics coming out of Scandinavia and Germany at the time. In Martyn's play, an idealistic, artistic man who owns an estate is crushed by the materialistic demands of his wife of ten years, forcing him to descend into insanity, just as the heather field he has tried to tame into arable farmland returns to its wild, natural state. The domestic drama drew parallels between the man driven insane by his attempt to quash his identity as an artist for the sake of his materialist wife, and the Irish people losing touch with their cultural identity in favour of Anglicization. Both plays were well received, with a slight advantage to Martyn, and were even given a performance in London later that year. But without the publicity surrounding them – the *Countess Cathleen* controversy, the international reviews, the publication of the first number of the ILT journal, *Samhain*, the dinner for literati thrown by the Dublin newspaper *The Daily Express* in honour of the season – these performances would have had much less consequence.

Thus, the first year of the Irish Literary Theatre was not immediately revolutionary, but it did put forward the growing interest in nationalist performance generally, while calling specifically for Irish dramatists to write indigenous plays in the modernist vein. In its second season, the ILT expanded its scope by including *The Last Feast of the Fianna*, a play based on the legend of Oisin, by Belfast-based Alice Milligan. In 1900 Milligan was already established as a writer, editor, and activist within the nationalist movement. She co-edited the nationalist women's journal, *The Shan Van Vocht*, with Ethna Carberry from 1896 to 1900, and had written and directed plays and tableaux for Gaelic League events, and for other nationalist groups. As a highly respected figure in the movement, Milligan and her play served as an important bridge between the Irish Literary Theatre's mostly intellectual audience, and the much larger, more populist, Gaelic League base.

In the third season, the ILT continued to seek the best way to blend European modernist dramaturgies with Irish themes as they were being illustrated within the nationalist movement. Yeats and Moore collaborated on a play from Irish myth, *Diarmuid and Grania*, which, while indeed written with high ambition, flopped in performance. Yeats and Moore had worked on the piece for two years, in a contentious collaboration often requiring the mediation of the judicious Lady Gregory. The play was doomed by such quarrelsome overwriting before the curtain ever rose on it; but its ultimate failure in performance stemmed from its English actors. Yeats had hired the Frank Benson Shakespearean Company who, utterly unfamiliar with Irish (and apparently unschooled by directors Yeats and Moore), mispronounced Irish names. Caoilte, one of the characters in the play, had his name pronounced as 'Wheel chair', 'Cold Tea', and 'Quilty' by different actors (J.C. Trewin, qtd in Hogan and Kilroy 1975: 96).

The success of the season, on the other hand, was a play in Irish by Douglas Hyde, *Casadh an tSugain*, or *The Twisting of the Rope*. Hyde had written the play at Lady Gregory's home, Coole Park, in three days, with the encouragement and help of his hostess. Performed by members of the Gaelic League, including the author, this one act took a comic look at a community's cleverness at maintaining tradition while preserving itself at the same time. In the play, Hanrahan, a wandering poet, enters a house where a party is going on. Following Irish rules of hospitality, he is welcomed into the house; but then he begins to woo Oona, a young woman engaged to another man. Fearing that the poet will seduce Oona away from home, but not wanting to break courtesy by kicking him out of their house, her mother and her fiancé ask Hanrahan to help them twist a rope. Hanrahan begins twisting the rope and, as the rope grows longer, begins to move backwards towards the door. When he crosses the threshold, Oona slams the door against him, to everyone's delight.

The performance of *Casadh an tSugain* broadened both the scope of the Irish Literary Theatre and its audience. Since this season was performed in the large Gaiety Theatre instead of the more intimate Antient Concert Rooms used for the previous two seasons, there were more seats available, and less expensive seats also, many of which were taken by supporters of the Gaelic League performance. When the Gaelic League performers took the stage, therefore, they were greeted with the vocal shouts of encouragement and energetic excitement one would find at a Gaelic League feis – a very different decorum than that expected from the ILT's usual audience, that tended to obey the codes of respectful and appreciative silence for middle-class and upper-class audiences of the modern commercial theatre. Stephen Gwynn wrote of the performance: 'I never was in an audience so amusing to be among; there was magnetism in the air' ('The Irish Literary Theatre and Its Affinities', *Fortnightly Review* (1901): 1055–8, qtd in Hogan and Kilroy 1975: 114). James H. Cousins, who would later write plays for the Irish theatre, called the play in performance, 'A simple story; but its dressing and dialogue and the energy and delight of the actors were irresistible, and a scene of ungovernable enthusiasm followed, in which I too was carried away' (Cousins 1988: 2). Indeed the performance of *Casadh an tSugain* made it apparent that an indigenous, heterogeneous theatre audience beyond the nationalist intelligentsia was prepared and eager to see a modern Irish theatre prosper for political purposes. But Irish texts written with 'high ambition' were not enough. Like all Irish items consumed by participants in the movement, it needed to be made only of Irish materials, and by Irish labour.

Enter the Irish Actor

The markedly different audience responses to *Diarmuid and Grania* and *Casadh an tSugain* made it absolutely clear that the Irish dramatic movement could not move forward in English or in Irish until it had a body of trained Irish actors to perform its plays. Yeats and Gregory found those actors with the aid of the director of *Casadh an tSugain*, William G. ('Willie') Fay. Fay and his brother, Frank, were well known in Dublin theatre circles: Willie as a director and teacher; Frank as a critic. In 1902, Willie Fay organized the Irish National Dramatic Company, made up of actors from Inghinidhe na hEireann, the Ormond Dramatic Society, and the Celtic Literary Society. The group agreed to perform a mythic drama by George Russell (Æ), entitled *Deirdre*, with a one-act play Yeats wrote in collaboration with Lady Gregory, *Cathleen ni Houlihan*, as an afterpiece. The performance of *Cathleen ni Houlihan* at the Antient Concert Rooms would become one of the most important events in Irish theatre history.

Set in Killalla on the eve of the Rebellion of 1798,[6] *Cathleen ni Houlihan* tells of a young man who sacrifices his life on the eve of his wedding to fight for Irish freedom. The play, set in a peasant kitchen, begins with a happy domestic scene – the Gillane family preparing for their son Michael's wedding. The bride's dowry and Michael's wedding clothes are laid out on the kitchen table, symbolizing the economic transaction underpinning the marriage. Michael's mother, Bridget, shows joy at the economic windfall the marriage will bring to the family after years of struggle: she even ponders the expensive possibility that their second son will go to seminary to become a priest. Then a poor old woman wandering the roads enters the house, and tells the family she is heading to find friends who are going to help her get back her 'beautiful fields'. When she tells them her name is 'Cathleen, the daughter of Houlihan', Michael recognizes the name from a song, and begins to be mesmerized by the woman, and asks her what he can do to help her. The old woman then describes the death and destruction to come in the impending battle, but also the glory awaiting those who die in her service:

> Old Woman: It is a hard service they take that help me. Many that are red-cheeked now will be pale-cheeked; many that have been free to walk the hills and the bogs and the rushes will be sent to walk the hard streets in far countries: many a good plan will be broken; many that have gathered money will not stay to spend it; many a child will be born and there will be no father at its christening to give it a name. They that have red cheeks will have pale cheeks for my sake, and for all that, they will think they are well paid.
>
> (*She goes out; her voice is heard outside singing.*)
>
> They shall be remembered for ever,
> They shall be alive for ever,
> They shall be speaking for ever,
> The people shall hear them for ever.
> (Yeats 1966a: 229)

As Michael begins to follow her, Bridget tries to distract him with his wedding clothes, and Delia begs him to stay: yet Michael rushes out to join the other young men following Cathleen to meet the French ships in the bay. After he leaves, Michael's little brother, Patrick, who entered the house after Cathleen left, is asked by his father if he saw an old woman on the road. Patrick replies, 'I did not, but I saw a young girl, and she had the walk of a queen' (1966a: 231).

The text of *Cathleen ni Houlihan* brilliantly employs particular tropes that by this time had already become established in Irish nationalist theatre – the idealized rural family with the characters' love of nation and link to a spirituality and tradition that supersedes materialism or personal desire, the representation of Irish folk culture, and a crystal-clear anti-colonial message. But what truly captured the audience for the play that night in April 1902 was the involvement of so many recognized activists and organizations in the performance. In both *Cathleen ni Houlihan* and *Deirdre*, the audience saw actors they recognized as activists, like Maire Nic

Shiubhlaigh, Dudley Digges, and Æ. Thus, the actor's body carried a triple signification in performance: character being played, actor playing the character, and activist taking on the task of acting as both political and artistic labour. In applauding the actors, therefore, the audience acknowledged the activist/actors' offstage as well as onstage work, and the audience's appreciation of the actor/activists' characters was highlighted by the resonances of their knowledge of the actor/activists' real-life 'character' within the nationalist movement (Trotter 2001). This phenomenological resonance was especially apparent in the most brilliant casting in the play – or in perhaps any play in Irish theatre history: the casting of Maud Gonne as Cathleen ni Houlihan.

Maud Gonne was an extraordinary woman in an extraordinary time. She was actually not Irish by birth, but moved to Ireland as a child when her father, a British soldier, was stationed there. She rapidly adopted the nationalist cause of her new home, and, in an age when there were no significant spaces for women in the public sphere not born into the position, she became a radical and notoriously public activist. Gonne was six feet tall, beautiful, and with a good supply of intelligence and money, and she used these resources to help her break both civic laws and cultural decorum. In the early 1890s, she protested at the sites of tenant evictions in the west of Ireland, gaining her an almost saintly reputation in that region. In Dublin, when Queen Victoria visited in 1898 and her neighbours displayed Union Jacks outside their homes in her honour, Gonne hung a black petticoat outside her window. Gonne's skills were administrative as well as spectacular. In the late 1880s she lived in France and published *L'Irlande Libre*, a nationalist newspaper, with her lover (and the father of her daughter, Iseult) Lucien Millevoye.[7] She regularly wrote articles and gave speeches about Irish nationalism, and in 1900 founded *Inghinidhe na hEireann*, or the Daughters of Erin.

When Gonne appeared on stage as the poor old woman calling the men of Ireland to die for her protection and freedom, they naturally heard the echoes of her years of similar calls to Ireland's men and women in her political activism. 'I have never since seen an audience so moved as when Madam MacBride (Gonne) . . . spoke the closing words as she turned away from the cottage door,' Seumas O'Sullivan recalled (1988: 12). In her autobiography, fellow actor Maire Nic Shiubhlaigh commented: 'She was the very personification of the character she played on stage' (19). At the end of the performance, the audience sprang to their feet for the last event on the bill, the singing of 'A Nation Once Again'.

In many ways, the performances of *Deirdre* and *Cathleen ni Houlihan* in the Antient Concert Rooms defined the direction of the Irish dramatic movement for the next decade. It was a utopian moment of collaboration among leading individuals and groups with diverse political goals and aesthetic sensibilities, and it was entirely Irish. And, riding on the excitement of the event, its participants agreed to shift their energies from creating nationalist performances to establishing a national theatre.

A National Stage: The Irish National Theatre Society

In 1903, the coalition of actors, writers, and theatre enthusiasts engaged in or inspired by the successful collaborative production of *Cathleen ni Houlihan*, joined forces to form the Irish National Theatre Society (hereafter INTS). Originally, the group was based on the cooperative principles common among most Irish nationalist groups of the time, with all members having an equal vote in artistic and administrative decisions. The actors, under the training of the Fay brothers and made up of nationalist activists who were deeply respected by the nationalist movement, served as the theatre's bedrock.

In its first months, the company's egalitarian promise showed in its choice of plays with a range of styles, and its performing at the Samhain Festival sponsored by the populist, cultural nationalist umbrella organization, Cumann na nGaedheal. Within nine months, however, Yeats strengthened his hold on the company, moving from serving as a figurehead president of a democratic political performance troupe into artistic director of a hierarchically structured theatre company. The change in leadership, likewise, led to a change in aesthetics, with Yeats and the other directors – Lady Gregory and J.M. Synge – pressing for an artistic agenda that reflected their own, highbrow aesthetics and a philosophy of good art over politics.

Yeats's Early Dramas: A Dialogue of Self and State

While the INTS must have anticipated more plays in line with *Cathleen ni Houlihan*, Yeats quickly turned to dramas based on Irish legends in his plays, staging what he saw as the antithetical relationship between the bourgeois, materialist mentality of the British state, and the spiritual ideals of the Celtic spirit. These dramas were influenced not only by Yeats's interest in Irish myth and legend and his exposure to legendary dramas by Irish nationalist authors like Alice Milligan, but also, and perhaps more strongly, by his own occult interests, and his background in European theatre of the *fin de siècle* (Flannery, Jeffares, Harper).

These diverse influences inform Yeats's legendary drama for the INTS, *On Baile's Strand* (1904). This play is based upon a myth of the Irish warrior hero Cuchulain, in which Cuchulain is challenged to a duel by his son, the daughter of Aoife, a warrior queen from Scotland. Neither father nor son are aware of their relationship – the boy was born after Cuchulain left Scotland, unaware of Aoife's pregnancy – and Cuchulain ends up learning of his son's identity only after he has killed him in battle. Yeats politicizes the tragedy by beginning the play with Cuchulain taking an oath of fealty to King Concobar. Cuchulain's allegiance to Concobar obligates him to fight his son, even though he intuitively knows that he should not take up the duel. By agreeing to obey Concobar, Cuchulain not only loses the choice to follow his own instinct and wisdom, but he also kills his son, thus destroying, in Yeats's logic, the heroic lineage upheld by his bloodline.

Yeats juxtaposes the high tragedy of the main plot with a comic shadow plot of a pair of tramps – the Blind Man and the Fool – who arrive at the castle seeking food and shelter. As they overhear the events of the play, the Blind Man, who had visited Scotland in his youth, figures out that the stranger is actually Cuchulain's son, but does not interfere. The Fool, however, unintentionally reveals the young man's paternity to Cuchulain after the warrior has killed his child in battle. Cuchulain, in his grief, falls into a rage and rushes offstage to the beach where he begins to battle the waves, thinking he is fighting Concobar. The Fool reports to the Blind Man that the people of the community are running to the beach to witness the event, and that the waves, representing the inexorable force of time, are triumphing over the hero. 'There, he is down! He is up again. He is going out in the deep water. There is a big wave. He has killed kings and giants, but the waves have mastered him, the waves have mastered him!' (Yeats 1966d: 524). The Blind Man's response to the tragedy, however, is to urge the Fool to help him steal bread out of the ovens of the people witnessing the tragedy on the beach. 'The ovens will be full,' he says. 'We will put our hands into the ovens' (525).

In the original legends, Cuchulain is a saucy, impulsive, youthful figure. Yeats's Cuchulain, however, is more serious – a man belonging to a dying tradition of honour who pledges his fealty to a weaker and more politically minded leader. And, in making that commitment, he goes against his own instinct and sense of honour, thus unwittingly killing his only son. The death of Cuchulain's son represents for Yeats the supplanting of a higher cultural code with Conchobar's modern, materialist, and more politically expedient way of life. The Blind Man responds to the tragedy in a modern, materialist way, by stealing the staff of life from the hearths of the people, impoverishing them of their physical nourishment at the moment that they lose the last bastion of an older, higher way of life. A nationalist audience would be encouraged to read *On Baile's Strand* from at least two points of view. First, by dramatizing Irish legend, Yeats's play valorizes ancient Irish literature as a field worth study, translation, and adaptation, coming down finally on the nationalist side of the political controversy that had raged at Trinity College a few years before. Second, Cuchulain's pledge to support an inferior leader echoes Yeats's concerns that the Irish people were giving up their superior way of life for the economic and personal comforts of modernization, which were linked politically to England.

Synge and Gregory's Ethnographic Parables

While the INTS performed Yeats's mythopoetic dramas throughout his lifetime, such plays would quickly be supplanted by realist works by such dramatists as Lady Gregory and J.M. Synge.[8] The Anglo-Irish Synge came from a wealthy family and studied languages at Trinity College Dublin, as well as universities in Europe, including the Sorbonne. He also studied music at the Royal Irish Academy, which helps explain the wonderfully complex sounds and cadences common in his dialogue. Unsure how to use his talents, he visited, at Yeats's suggestion, the Aran Islands in the summer of 1898, and spent the next five years living among and gathering information about the people of that community. Based on those experiences, Synge wrote his first two plays, *Riders to the Sea* and *The Shadow in the Glen*, in 1902, and shared them both with W.B. Yeats and Lady Gregory. Synge's work was embraced by Yeats and Gregory, who made him a fellow director of the reorganized INTS in 1904, and he held that position until his untimely death from Hodgkin's disease in 1909.

Both fluent Irish speakers who had spent time gathering stories and other cultural data in the Gaeltacht, Synge and Gregory translated the idioms of the Irish language into an English language dialect designed to catch the aural and imagistic qualities of the Irish tongue. Gregory's 'Kiltartan' dialect and Synge's elaborate turns of phrase are far from literal translations, of course, and Gregory's language is often criticized for its sing-song simplicity that often drifts closer to British melodrama than Irish modernism; but it is notable that both playwrights try to make a language for the stage that, being neither 'proper English' nor 'real Irish', captures the spirit of Irish language and thought, while also illustrating the dualities and duplicities inherent in the life experiences of many of their characters, who must negotiate maintaining their Irish identity, customs and beliefs within a colonial system that imposes a different, imperialist ontology, represented by English language and English law.

In Gregory's *Spreading the News* (1904), for example, a removable magistrate, whose last post was in the Adaman Islands (another island, but one with a very different culture), arrives in a western Ireland village prepared to wipe out the 'agrarian crime . . . boycotting . . . [and] maiming of cattle' ([1904] 1995b: 312) he assumes are common in the neighbourhood. At the start of the play, the magistrate sums up his first image of the Fair Green of the village in two words: 'No system' (312). He is unable to see the customs of his new home, nor does he seek them out. Instead, by imposing his own system of law and order on the village, he disrupts the balance of the community. Between the magistrate's questioning, and the community's love of talk, the story of a man trying to return a hayfork to its rightful owner turns into an assumed conspiracy involving false identity, adultery and murder. While Gregory's farce appears at first to make fun of the gullibility of the villagers, it is really the magistrate's inflexible suspicion that leads to anarchy within the community, and a breakdown in identity for its citizens.

Gregory's one-act peasant comedies, like *Spreading the News*, were vital to the success of the INTS in its first years. The sheer number and speed with which Gregory wrote these plays, while also completing other important writing projects[9] and serving as director of the theatre, is astounding and, some say, indicative of a gender bias within the movement that devalued her work, so that she sacrificed development of her talent as a playwright in service to the immediate needs of the theatre. Although Gregory stated that she 'had been forced to write comedy because it was what was wanted for our theatre, to put on at the end of the verse plays' (1913: 538), it is a sign of her talent that she fulfilled this duty so well and so prolifically. Synge's work, on the other hand, garnered a great deal more respect from the critics, but his images of the harshness and hypocrisies of rural Irish life often led to criticism, most famously with his 1907 drama, *The Playboy of the Western World* (1907), discussed below.

Acting at the INTS

To accommodate the range of work that the INTS's relatively inexperienced performers were addressing, W.G. Fay worked with the actors to found a style that would undo the melodramatic gestures common among new actors. Fay called for stillness in his actors' bodies, urging them instead to draw the audience in with their eyes. Joseph Holloway would later call this style 'the art of staring into space'. He also emphasized vocal training with the actors, making them excellent vehicles for verse drama and for the complex cadences of Synge's plays. The INTS actors quickly gained acclaim for this 'simple and homely style' (*Daily Express*, quoted in Morash 2002: 140), which suited well their small stages and simple sets. In fact, the INTS came to pride itself in offering an ethnographic authenticity in its stagings of the rural west, with such touches as importing props and costumes like real Aran Island pampooties for the actors to wear, or learning about such rituals as the funeral keen from peasants still engaging in such traditional practices.[10] A decade later, when the Abbey players toured the United States, it would influence the acting styles of the little theatre movement. In Ireland, however, in future decades the simple staging of the peasant cottage was an easy set design, often seen to the point of cliché.

For his own plays, Yeats developed a scenic strategy informed by French symbolism, using few design pieces and focusing on only a few colours, and employing abstract designs. Influenced by his collaborators Sturge Moore and Edward Gordon Craig, as well as by the influence of his own family of visual artists, Yeats understood that his simplicity of design worked as a necessary counter to the imaginative world evinced by language in his plays. Regarding the design for the 1903 production of Yeats's *The Hour-Glass*, Richard Allen Cave notes that:

> The techniques espoused by [British actor-manager Henry] Irving and his like were to Yeats and his companions emblematic of all that defined the decadence of English culture with its fixation on materialism, whereas the staging of *The Hour-Glass* pursued a studied simplicity . . . What Irving chose to see as 'otherworldly' and so an excuse for theatrical trickery, Yeats accepted as the intrusion of a different dimension of reality into human affairs. Yeats chose to see the difference of mind-set apparent here as proof of cultural difference between England and Ireland, and this fuelled his

determination to offer an alternative to the theatrical fare currently being performed on Dublin stages which was in large measure provided by English touring companies promoting tales akin to those evident in Irving's work. Yeats sought radical reforms (of acting style, movement, vocal delivery, stage directing, and all the elements that constitute design), and for him this means a refined simplicity, a conscious pursuit of austerity as an aesthetic, cultural and political imperative. (2004: 96)

Will the Revolution be Subsidized? The Abbey Theatre and the Theatre of Ireland

Yeats did make a calculated compromise to his scenographic ideals, however, when he signed on Annie Horniman to design costumes for his INTS plays. Horniman was the heir to a large tea company fortune from Manchester, England, and no friend to Irish nationalism; but she had been deeply enamoured of Yeats since meeting him as a fellow theosophist in London in the early 1890s.[11] While made of rich materials and based on archaeological evidence, Horniman's costumes were widely criticized by the actors, the press, and Yeats himself. Still, the experience helped convince Horniman to purchase a permanent space for the INTS players, and to cover their expenses for several years. With the aid of architect and avid theatregoer Joseph Holloway, a building in the city centre was transformed into the Abbey Theatre. But along with Horniman's patronage came strict rules for the theatre, especially her strident 'no politics' policy. Indeed, her contempt for the Irish actors, whom she treated dismissively as workers rather than artists, while also being contemptuous of their nationality and nationalism, would be a source of serious friction within the company for years.[12]

The Faustian bargain was sealed in 1904, when the INTS performed for the first time in what was to become their eponymous home, the Abbey Theatre. The change in venue, however, led to a change in the company's financial and administrative needs, and Yeats went on a crusade 'to end democracy in the theatre' (qtd in Frazier 1990: 117) by putting the actors on salary and leaving the artistic and ideological decision-making to himself, Gregory, and Synge. Yeats achieved his goal in late 1905, turning the democratically run group into the Irish National Theatre Society Ltd, a limited liability company. Angered by their shift in identity from full contributors to salaried workers, a large group of the original performers, including Maire Nic Schiubhlaigh, her brother Ponsias Nic Shiubhlaigh, George Nesbitt, and Helen Laird, quit the company to create their own group, the Theatre of Ireland (Cluithcheoiri na hEireann), in 1906. Other members of the company included Edward Martyn (who had been excluded from the INDC), James Cousins, and Padraic Pearse.

While never offering a real challenge to the subsidized, building-owning Abbey in material terms, the Theatre of Ireland did challenge the Abbey's self-proclaimed authority as national house. The company declared as its mission: 'to produce plays in Irish and English. Believing that drama can be of inestimable value in moulding and giving expression to the thought of the people, the Theatre aims at giving free and full dramatic utterance to everything that makes for the upbuilding of an enlightened and vigorous humanity in Ireland' (Cluithcheoiri na hEireann 1906: 3). As the Abbey claimed an apolitical stance with an emphasis on art over democracy, the Theatre of Ireland offered a more democratic bill of fare with a clearly political goal – plus they touted their ability to perform in Irish as well as English.

Many critics who had grown annoyed by the Abbey's insistence on art over politics found much to praise in the Theatre of Ireland, and were not shy in using reviews of the company's work as a stick for thrashing the Abbey. Sinn Dicat remarked that 'Cluithcheoiri na hEireann has come apparently just at the right time . . . and there is an audience not only willing but eager to listen to and appreciate good plays, and beginning to get a little weary of the vagaries of the National Theatre Society, Limited' (*Sinn Fein* 15 December 1906: 3).[13] Ironically, the very thing that set them above the Abbey in the eyes of many nationalists – their amateur status, and their commitment outside the theatre to other nationalist groups – led to their downfall, as the quality of both the performances and their finances began to disintegrate. They disbanded, ultimately, in 1912.

In January of 1907, however, much of the Irish nationalist community agreed with Sinn Dicat, for the Theatre of Ireland played to full houses while the Abbey was struggling to attract audiences. But the Abbey would steal the limelight again with one of the most pivotal events in twentieth-century Irish theatre: the riots and controversy surrounding J.M. Synge's *The Playboy of the Western World*.

A Drift of Mayo Girls . . .

A national theatre, according to Lauren Kruger, is a site of 'cultural legitimation', expected – if not called – to represent a particular image or idea of the nation in line with the ethos of the national culture. The theatre's output exists in a dialectical relationship with the state it represents, informing, and being informed by, the nation's ideas about and for itself. By 1906, the cultural agenda of the Irish nationalist movement and the Gaelic revival were clear, and included the valorization of Ireland's ancient, pre-colonial past, the idealization of rural Ireland, and strict adherence to behavioural codes and representations of Irish life that countered British stereotypes of the Irish as lazy, violent, overly emotional or sexually licentious. The Abbey Theatre, however, in the eyes of many in the nationalist movement, wished to claim the authority as the theatrical site of cultural legitimation within the nationalist movement, but it did not want to play by the movement's rules, and even undermined – often on a world stage – the counter-hegemonic representations of Irish culture the movement was trying to uplift. With Annie Horniman's subsidy, Yeats, Gregory, and Synge did not need to worry much about the movement's opinion of their work. As Yeats said in his curtain speech on the opening night of the Abbey Theatre building, 'We can ask ourselves, first, does it please us? And then does it please you?' (Yeats's Speech on the Opening Night of the Abbey, 1904, n.p.). And, since it was the Abbey and not the Gaelic League feisianna that were being featured in English, French, and American newspapers, it was Yeats's vision, not that of the larger movement, that was being broadcast as the mirror up to Irish culture.

A telling example of this conflict occurred around the first performance of J.M. Synge's play, *The Shadow of the Glen*, in 1903. *The Shadow of the Glen* is based on what Synge claimed to be a story he heard on the Aran islands (Roche 1994: 147), about a young woman, Nora Burke, trapped in a loveless marriage with a manipulative, older man, Dan. As the play begins, Nora is holding vigil over her husband's seemingly dead body, when a tramp wandering by asks for shelter from the bad weather. Nora lets him in the house and he keeps watch with her until she leaves to meet Michael Dara, a neighbouring farmer. When she leaves, Dan reveals that he has only been pretending to be dead to test his wife's faithfulness. Hearing Nora's return, he jumps back on his 'bier', and swears the tramp to secrecy. Nora returns with Michael Dara who proposes marriage to Nora; she rejects him, but not before first remarking on the horrors of growing old. At this, Dan sits up and orders Nora out of the house. Michael refuses to help Nora, but the tramp offers to take her on the roads with him. Nora decides to follow the tramp but, before leaving, offers her husband a malediction:

You think it's a grand thing you're after doing your letting on to be dead, but what is it at all? What way would a woman live in a lonesome place the like of this place, and she not making a talk with the men passing? What way will yourself live from this day, with none to care for you? What is it you'll have now but a black life, Daniel Burke, and it's not long, I'm telling you, till you'll be lying again under that sheet, and you dead, surely (Synge [1903] 1982b: 57)

The play ends with Nora and the tramp going out of the house, while Dan and Michael, ignoring Dan's threats against Michael moments before, share a drink of whiskey.

The play quickly raised the hackles of factions of the nationalist movement, infuriated by the play's matter-of-fact, gritty depictions of rural poverty, loveless and violent marriage, and female sexuality that were a far cry from the whitewashed peasants found in the typical Gaelic League folk play. Many of the protests do appear to have been overly sensitive, and even to deny the social problems Synge's short drama brought to the fore. While exasperating to the Abbey directors, this response to Synge's play showed that as long as the INTS called itself the national theatre, the nationalist movement would insist on having its say at the theatre, even if it would not always get its way.

By the time *The Playboy of the Western World* (1907) arrived, many in the nationalist movement felt they had a great deal to say about the Abbey Theatre, and Synge's three-act comedy was the match that lit a shortened fuse. Synge's play describes a western Ireland community of passionate women and meek or drunken men. Pegeen Mike, the daughter of the drunken town publican, is engaged to her second cousin, Shawn Keogh, a young farmer with a timidity and religious conservatism that won't allow him to marry Pegeen until he gets a 'special dispensation' from Rome. When Christy Mahon, a scrawny boy, arrives at the public house and reveals that he is a fugitive after killing his father, the community makes him a hero, and Pegeen falls in love with him.

The attention of the town, especially the village girls, Pegeen, and the Widow Quin, a strong and lusty woman who killed one of her four dead husbands by hitting him with a rusty shovel so that he contracted tetanus, causes Christy to perceive himself differently, and he quickly transforms into the confident hero the village perceives him to be. When his father, who was not murdered by his son but only given a bad bump on the head, comes to the town to bring Christy home, however, Christy transforms from a hero into a liar and object of mockery. When he attempts to kill his father a second time, the village sees him as a murderer. As Pegeen remarks, 'there's a great gap between a gallous story and a dirty deed' ([1907] 1982a: 169), and her infatuation is transformed by the proximity of Christy's violence. But when Christy's father reappears, still not killed, the villagers release Christy, and he leaves the community transformed from a weak and timid boy dominated by his father into a confident and passionate figure. When his father asks him to leave with him, Christy replies: 'Go with you, is it! I will then, like a gallant captain with his heathen slave. Go on now and I'll see you from this day stewing my oatmeal and washing my spuds, for I'm master of all fights now' (173). As he leaves, however, Pegeen realizes that his loss leaves her no option but a return to her former way of life and marriage to Shawn. In the last line of the play, Pegeen cries, 'Oh my grief, I've lost him surely. I've lost the only playboy of the western world' (173).

Today, *The Playboy of the Western World*, with its exquisite dialogue, complex characterizations, well-constructed comic plots, and illustrations of the power of language and imagination to transform, is considered a masterpiece of the Irish canon. But even before its first performance in 1907, the Abbey knew they were dealing with a controversial play, and banned spectators – even Abbey Theatre habitué Joseph Holloway – from rehearsals. On opening night the play went on without incident until the final act, when the audience, already troubled by what images of Irish life they were seeing, responded to Christy's line, as spoken by the actor playing the role, W.G. Fay, 'It's Pegeen I'm seeking only, and what'd I care if you brought me a drift of Mayo girls, standing in their shifts itself maybe, from this place to the eastern world?' (Morash 2002: 132),[14] with hisses and boos. At the next performance, about forty of the eighty audience members, aware of the offence of the play, started to disrupt the performance at the rise of the curtain. By the third performance, the action was performed onstage in dumb-show over the noisy crowd, and the onstage event was overshadowed by the performances of the audience members, including outraged nationalists, drunken Trinity College students, a man with a bugle, and a man from Galway who started the evening 'offering to fight anyone in the pit' (Morash 2002:134). Yeats and Gregory called in the police, and had several members of the audience arrested. The arrested parties were given a small fine or excused, although the presiding judge did note that only protesters of the drama, and not equally rowdy supporters, were the ones picked out by Gregory and Yeats to be arrested for disturbing the peace (Hogan et al. 1978: 140).

The riots surrounding *The Playboy of the Western World* made the Abbey enemies, and its box office would remain weak for years afterwards. But, ultimately, the riots proved Oscar Wilde's adage that the only thing worse than being talked about is not being talked about. The attention paid to the play, and the passionate nature of the ensuing protest, reflected the degree of investment the nationalist movement was placing in its national theatre, and in theatrical representation of Irish culture generally. In a little over a decade, the Irish National Theatre Society, the Ulster Literary Theatre, the Theatre of Ireland, the Gaelic League, and the other nationalist theatres had laid the foundation for a political theatre intimately engaged with the nationalist movement's questions about Ireland's present conditions and future possibilities. The next chapter of this text looks more closely at the dramatic genres this movement was beginning to develop, their mark on modern theatre, and their role in the nationalist imagining of an Irish insurrection.

2

Realisms and Regionalisms

One of the most remarkable aspects of the modern Irish theatre movement was its ability to create such innovative and exciting theatre work while remaining so deeply engaged in Irish nationalist politics and activism. From the founding of the Gaelic League in 1893, performance of one's politics through everyday life choices was a central tenet of the Irish revival. Nationalist theatrical performance grew out of this sense of political performativity and, even when the Irish Literary Theatre sought to create a dramaturgy that promoted good art over politics, the theatre's nationalist audience remained deeply invested in the performance's imagining and representing of the nation. Indeed, few theatre movements that are so clearly political have managed to produce such talented and influential artists in such a short amount of time. In a little over a decade, playwrights like Yeats, Gregory, and Synge had written plays still produced and studied internationally today; W.G. Fay had developed a style of acting that would influence theatre and film acting into the 1930s, as well as cultivating new theatres in the USA, England, and Scotland; and actors like Dudley Digges and Sara Allgood were well on their way to international careers. These individual achievements, however, like the Abbey Theatre project in which their participants were involved, were only part of the wellspring of nationalist theatre interest across Ireland in the early 1900s.

While the previous chapter looked at the modern Irish theatre's foundations through the lens of the establishment of the Abbey, and a national Dublin aesthetic, this chapter examines how the nationalist theatre movement built upon its professional successes in Dublin to inspire new Irish dramas across the nation, especially in Belfast and Cork. It also overviews the influence of Irish expatriate playwrights Oscar Wilde and Bernard Shaw, whose dramas critiqued British assumptions about both Ireland and itself, on Irish realist playwrights. By the 1910s, Irish theatre had settled rather securely into the realist mode. Realism's relative simplicity to produce and accessibility to audiences allowed inexperienced playwrights

and performers to present on the stage authentic and idiosyncratic representations of the diversity of Irish life. The idealized, Gaelic dialect- speaking peasant from the Irish west who had dominated the first years of
modern Irish theatre was being replaced by not only Dublin accents, but
also the voices of the midlands, Kerry, Cork, and Belfast. In 1938, as part
of a lecture series celebrating the Abbey's achievements in its first decades,
Andrew E. Malone noted:

> The doors of the Abbey Theatre hardly had been opened ere its poetic
> portals were invaded by the realists, led by Padraic Colum, Lady Gregory,
> and William Boyle. The work of conquest proved to be deliciously easy,
> and in a little while the realists were in complete command of the Irish
> drama. The pioneering realists – the vanguard of the conquering army –
> had been fascinated by the language and speech of the people of rural
> Ireland; the rhythmic language which had captivated everybody when it
> was used in the plays of Synge. It was, however, the presentation of actual
> conditions in the social and political life of the country, with pressing
> problems and strongly marked characters, that appealed most strongly to
> those young writers who derived their originating impulse to write plays
> from the Abbey Theatre. (1939: 93)

Instead of imagining an idealized past, many Irish realist playwrights
attempted to present the personal and political challenges of the present,
such as poverty, emigration, and sectarianism, and their roots in British
imperialist policies. By examining the leading Irish realist playwrights in
the context of the theatres or schools out of which they developed, this
chapter hopes to reveal both the diversity of Irish experiences unveiled in
the theatre of the period, as well as the range of theatres at work in establishing an Irish voice onstage. At the same time these theatres were thriv-
ing, however, the realism of Irish politics grew increasingly heated. This
chapter closes, therefore, with an examination of theatre's relationship to
growing calls for violent revolution in the years immediately preceding the
Easter Rising.

In light of the explosion of new artistic modes of political theatre
that engulfed Europe and the United States after the First World War,
from Dada to Brecht, it is easy to dismiss realism as a weak, bourgeois
theatrical mode that ignores systemic political concerns in favour of
sentimental examinations of individual concerns. However, as addressed
above, performing counter-hegemonic representations of early twentieth-
century Ireland and the Irish in any form was a vital political act.
The stageability of the dramas allowed them to be performed by
the most amateur of groups. Their development of psychologically

complex characters hastened the death of the stage Irishman in Ireland. And their emphasis on regional voices and concerns created a more complex picture of contemporary Ireland than the idealized peasants or pre-Christian heroes that populated many plays in the previous decade.

Realism and the Irish Expatriate: Wilde and Shaw

At the same time as the Irish revival was calling for the imagining of a national community in Ireland through the edification and promotion of aspects of Irish culture, many Irish artists were working and living in London, the economic, political and, to a large extent, cultural capital of the British Empire. None of these Irish artists working in London at the turn of the twentieth century segregated themselves from the cosmopolitan milieu of London that attracted them to that city in the first place, yet they all seemed poignantly aware of their difference from their English colleagues, and engaged that difference in particular ways in their writing. Ironically, some of Yeats's most romantic imaginings of the Irish landscape, like 'The Lake Isle of Innisfree', were written while he was in London, allowing Yeats to take on the persona of the exile longing for the natural beauty of his homeland while abroad. Others used their insider/outsider position within the London elite to comment upon British politics and culture with a coolness and objectivity that would have been much more difficult for their London-born colleagues. The ease with which playwrights Wilde and Shaw managed to critique London society while being celebrated by it, to out-English the English with their facility with language, makes their own Irish identity, and the Irish influence on their work, much less obvious than that of Gaelic League writers of the period. To their contemporaries on both sides of the Irish Sea, however, they spoke, and they wrote, with an Irish accent, and their influence on their homeland's dramatic output would be profound.

Oscar Wilde's double-cross

Of the Irish nineteenth-century playwrights working outside the country, Oscar Wilde, the aesthete, darling of the London elite, and satirist of the mores of the English upper crust, seems the most surprising to many, since his life was in so many ways an act of self-invention. He was born Oscar Fingal O'Flaherty Wells Wilde in Dublin in 1854, into a well-off Anglo-Irish family firmly embedded into the Dublin elite. His father was a noted eye surgeon. His mother was a famous Irish writer with nationalist leanings, who took the pen name Speranza. From his earliest childhood, he was granted both a superb formal education, and an even more special informal one, thanks to his parents and their friends. Unlike most children during this era, Oscar was allowed to sit at his parents' dinner table as a child, although he was not allowed to talk. The banter he heard among the Irish elite at those dinners may well have helped to shape his ear for epigrams.

After some study at Trinity College Dublin, Wilde matriculated to Oxford, where he studied with Walter Pater, and became a leader in the aesthetic movement of art. As an aesthete, Wilde would gain fame for his intelligent, thoughtful, and humorous writings in the aesthetic mode – from his children's stories, to his essays and lectures for mature audiences. After graduating he quickly earned a reputation as a lecturer, reviewer, and writer, and became a favourite guest within London society. He was such a notorious celebrity in England, in fact, that he was even parodied in a Gilbert and Sullivan opera.

The Aesthetic Movement celebrated the notion of art for art's sake, and argued that one could counter the dehumanizing effect of the industrialized world by creating one's own reality through art. As Wilde put it in his critical dialogue, 'The Decay of Lying', 'Life imitates Art far more than Art imitates Life. This results not merely from Life's imitative instinct, but from the fact that the self-conscious aim of Life is to find expression, and that Art offers it certain beautiful forms through which it may realize that energy' (1994a: 239). While at first appearing absurd, Wilde's remarks actually offer an insightful opinion on the notion of perception, and the role of the artist, and culture generally, in the conceiving of an agreed-upon 'real'. Wilde in fact treated his own persona as a work of art, and would display his aesthetic sensibilities in his self-conscious, everyday performance of self, including his velvet waistcoats, his green buttonholes, and his bon mots. When arriving in the United States for a lecture tour, for example, Wilde announced to the customs agent, 'I have nothing to declare but my genius.'

The decadence espoused by the aesthetic movement had social overtones, for it challenged the seriousness, moral doggedness, and sense of absolute truth that pervaded Victorian society and its social policies, and threatened to reveal the hypocrisies belying those absolutes, from imperialism, to poverty, to the fact that England had more prostitutes in the nineteenth century than any other nation in Europe. Phrases like 'wickedness is a myth invented by good people to account for the curious attractiveness of others', or 'Ambition is the last refuge of failure' (1994a: 572), question Victorian surety, with their call for a decadent dismissal of a positivist moral framework that merely maintains the culture's rigid social and economic orders. The dandy men in Wilde's social comedies, like the eponymous character of his short novel, *The Picture of Dorian Gray*, challenged English imperial absolutes in their paradoxical, witty ways, showing the anxiety belying Britain's upper class, and the arbitrary ways its rules may be rethought and rewritten to maintain the status quo.

The spirit of Wilde's work shows most splendidly in his masterpiece, *The Importance of Being Earnest*. Along with being an almost perfectly constructed comedy, the play takes 'the art of lying' to the comic extreme. In the first Act, two bachelors, Jack Worthing and Algernon Moncrieff, learn that each avoids their societal responsibilities by caring for an 'invented' friend. Algernon escapes the tedious parties of his aunt, Lady Bracknell, by going to the country to visit his non-existent sick friend, 'Bunbury'. Jack leaves the tedium of country life and responsibility of being his niece's ward to visit London, where he must look after his non-existent wicked brother, Ernest. Adding to the connections and complications in these men's friendship, Jack is in love with Algernon's cousin, Gwendolyn; and, in Act II, Algernon falls in love with Jack's ward, Cecily. Their feelings are reciprocated, but before they can marry, their potential fiancées require them to fulfil particular preconceived ideals – most importantly, that they be named Ernest. There is also the impediment of Lady Bracknell, who, as Algernon's and Gwendolyn's closest relative, must approve of the matches. At first she protests, but when she learns that the adopted Algernon's true parents are in fact relatives of her own, and that Cecily has no aristocratic title but is very, very rich, she accepts the matches. And, to add to the serendipity of the news of Jack's true parentage, it is revealed that he was indeed christened with the name Ernest. Thus, Wilde's dandy bachelors, like their determined fiancées, find that with the right manoeuvring, and 'earnest' effort of imagination and invention, they can make their lives imitate their social desires. Lady Bracknell reveals this belief in Act I, when she learns that Jack owns a house on the 'unfashionable side' of the street in Belgrave Square, but remarks 'that could easily be altered' (1994b; 369). Jack naively counters, 'Do you mean the fashion, or the side?' Lady Bracknell replies: '(*sternly*) Both, if necessary, I presume' (369). Life imitates art for Lady Bracknell, and Jack and Algernon become ready to marry and take their place in society when they join Lady Bracknell in her belief, giving up a double life for a life they can change at will. 'Gwendolyn, it is a terrible thing for a man to find out suddenly that all his life he has been speaking nothing but the truth,' Jack confesses to his bride. 'Can you forgive me?' The worldly Gwendolyn, her mother's daughter, replies, 'I can. For I feel that you are sure to change' (418).

While some might consider Wilde's London fame a sign that he had turned his back on Ireland, in fact he kept in intimate contact with Ireland, and identified himself as an Irishman. He also kept close alliances with other 'Celtic' writers in London, and was known to point out his national difference from the English in matters of art. When his French play, *Salome*, was about to be censored on the English stage, Wilde told his friend Robert Ross, in an interview for the *Pall Mall Budget*, that, 'If the Censor refuses *Salome*, I shall leave England to settle in France where I shall take out letters of naturalization. I will not consent to call myself a citizen of a country that shows such narrowness in artistic judgement. I am not English. I am Irish which is quite another thing' (qtd in Ellman 1987: 372). While these words are coming from a provoked author, they still reflect Wilde's lack of allegiance to his British passport, and his sense of not only his aesthetic sensibilities, but of his very self as Irish and other.[1] And this difference was clear to both his English and Irish colleagues.

In her introduction to her edition of his selected writings, for instance, Isobel Murray points out how, for his Irish colleagues, at least, Wilde's work was playing a subversive and dangerous game with the British self-image. She quotes Wilde's Irish contemporary G.B. Shaw, who wrote:

> there is nothing to the world quite so exquisitely comic as an Englishman's seriousness. It becomes tragic, perhaps, when the Englishman acts on it; but that occurs too seldom to be taken into account, a fact which intensifies the humour of the situation, the total result being the Englishman utterly unconscious of his real self, Mr. Wilde keenly observant of it and playing on the self-unconsciousness with irresistible humour, and finally, of course, the Englishman annoyed with himself for being amused at his own expense, and for being unable to convict Mr. Wilde of what seems an obvious mis-understanding of human nature. He is shocked, too, at the danger to the foundations of society when seriousness is publicly laughed at. (Beckson, qtd in Murray 1997: ix)

Shaw wrote these lines, of course, with the benefit of hindsight: he saw how quickly the English aristocracy turned on their 'allowed fool' during

Wilde's lawsuit against one of their own – the Marquess of Queensberry, author of the rules for boxing, among other accomplishments, and father of Wilde's lover, Lord Alfred Douglas – for calling him a sodomite. Wilde lost. Homosexuality was a crime in England at the time. Information revealed in the trial ultimately led to Wilde's conviction of sodomy, with a sentence of two years' hard labour in Reading gaol. When he was released from prison, he was abandoned by many of his former friends, and died almost penniless in Paris in 1900.

When asked why he did not live in Ireland, Wilde replied, 'I live in London for its artistic life and opportunities. There is no lack of culture in Ireland, but it is nearly all absorbed in politics. Had I remained there my career would have been a political one' (Mikhail 1979: 63). In retrospect, Wilde's artistic and personal legacies became deeply political in their own ways, challenging Victorian social and artistic norms, and revealing its hypocrisies around such issues as class, race, and sexuality.

G.B. Shaw, anti-imperialism, and the stage Englishman

Another noted Irish playwright working in London in the 1890s was George Bernard Shaw. Born within a few years of Oscar Wilde in Dublin, both emigrated to London, broke into the business of writing in England through journalism and reviewing, and became noted playwrights in the 1890s. Yet their backgrounds were quite different, as were the ways they used their art to address class, race, and English imperialism. Shaw was born into an Anglo-Irish family in economic decline. After spending his late teens living with his alcoholic father and working as a clerk and a cashier (the family's finances made advanced education for Bernard out of the question), Shaw moved to London in his early twenties, eager to begin the education and career unachievable in Dublin under his father's roof.[2] He was also fortunate to have his potential recognized by the likes of the playwright William Archer, who helped him attain a job as a reviewer, and Granville Barker, who produced Shaw's first play, *Widowers' Houses*, at the Independent Theatre Company in 1892. Shaw seized his opportunities, becoming one of the most prolific and energetic critics, playwrights, and political activists up until his death in 1950.[3]

Like Wilde's, Shaw's London fame in the 1890s was based not only on his literary genius, but his performative strategies. His first notoriety arose from political speeches supporting 'outrageous' ideas, like socialism, vegetarianism, anti-vivisectionism, and educational reform, and his wit, energy, and Irish brogue made it easy for some to find him more entertaining than effective. He cultivated an ironic self-image as a wise Paddy. 'His fame as an entertainer was global: his influence in England minimal,' Kiberd remarks. As Shaw himself commented, 'Being an Irishman, I do not always see things as an Englishman would. Consequently, my most serious and blunt statements raise a laugh and create the impression that I am intentionally jesting' (Kiberd 2001: 345). Still, Shaw's decades of devoted work on the issues of socialism, feminism, and anti-imperialism were recognized. He won the Nobel Prize for Literature in 1926, and his dramas continue to influence contemporary dramaturgy.

Shaw's most obvious statement about Ireland is found in the play *John Bull's Other Island* – a comedy that simultaneously parodies the gap between the romantic notions of Irishness held in England, and critiques the imperial system that perpetuates such mollifying assumptions of the impact of English cultural and economic presence on Irish society. Shaw actually wrote it for performance by the Irish National Theatre Society; yet Yeats rejected the play, citing staging problems, and so its first performance was at the Court Theatre in London in 1904. Shaw would later write, in a 1906 preface to the play, a remark intimating that its London rather than Dublin venue may have permitted it a more critical hearing: 'It was uncongenial to the whole spirit of the neo-Gaelic movement, which is bent on creating a new Ireland after its own ideal, whereas my play is a very uncompromising presentment of the real old Ireland' (Shaw, 'Preface', 1962a: 443). Indeed, *John Bull's Other Island* offers one of the earliest dramatized intellectual, economically grounded critiques of Ireland's and England's imperialist relationship, deconstructing assumptions about that relationship held on either side of the Irish Sea.

The central characters of Shaw's play are two businessmen living in London: an Englishman, Tom Broadbent, and his Irish partner, Tim Doyle. The two are civil engineers involved in the urban development and modernization of territories outside England. Broadbent informs Doyle that he has business taking over some properties in Rosscullen, Doyle's home in Ireland. A very reluctant Doyle thus joins Broadbent on the trip, returning home to see friends and face a woman who has been waiting for him after eighteen years away in England. Joining them are two servant characters – Hodson, their English butler, and Haffigan, a man Broadbent pays to join them to serve as a kind of cultural ambassador, although Doyle informs him that he is actually a Glaswegian playing the part of the stage Irishman to earn money for drink.

While Wilde's comedies featured English dandies who seemed to care more about buttonholes than business, the English Tom Broadbent is quite busy indeed; and, in his patronizing attitude towards Ireland and the Irish, shockingly unaware of the impact his development of Roscullen will have on the community and its people. In fact, he sees his business trip as a civilizing mission: 'I am an Englishman and a Liberal; and now that South Africa has been enslaved and destroyed, there is no country left to me to take an interest in but Ireland. Mind: I don't say that an Englishman has not other duties. He has a duty to Finland and a duty to Macedonia. But what sane man can deny that an Englishman's first duty is his duty to Ireland?' (507).

Once he gets to Ireland Broadbent comically goes native – or what he assumes to be native – as he projects his Manichean fantasies of the Irish as a passionate and sentimental people on his experience there. By the end of the play, Broadbent has become a comic fixture of Roscullen. He will marry the woman who has been waiting for Doyle for eighteen years (a symbolic uniting of the imperialist, male energy of Broadbent with the feminized colonized community represented in the female Nora), will run for parliament as a Home Ruler, and, along with Doyle, will buy the land out from under most of its citizens, thus turning the area into a profitable enterprise for himself in the name of progress. Father Keegan, a defrocked priest, predicts the results of Doyle's and Broadbent's schemes, which will bankrupt many locals and force them to emigrate until:

> at last this poor desolate countryside becomes a busy mint in which we shall all slave to make money for you, with our Polytechnic to teach us how to do it efficiently, and our library to fuddle the few imaginations your distillery will spare, and our repaired Round Tower with admission sixpence, and refreshments and penny-in-the-slot mutoscopes to make it interesting, then no doubt your English and American shareholders will spend all the money we make for them very efficiently in shooting and hunting, in operations for cancer and appendicitis, in glutton and gambling; and you will devote what they save to fresh land development schemes. (Shaw 1962a: 608)

Indeed, as Kathleen Ochshorn points out, 'in *John Bull's Other Island*, Shaw manages to define and ridicule colonialism; anticipate the nature of a postcolonial Ireland; and imply the difficulties of a free trade, neocolonial economy, where individual and national interests are subverted by the all-powerful forces of development and transnational commerce' (Ochshorn 2006: 181).

Although the Abbey did not produce the play Shaw wrote for them, the Abbey put another of his dramas to good political use in 1907, by producing in Dublin Shaw's *The Shewing-Up of Blanco Posnet*, a play that had been censored by the Lord Chamberlain in England, thus asserting the Irish stage's freedom from English censorship (Laurence and Grene 1993: xv). In 1915, he offered the Abbey a new play, *O'Flaherty V.C.*, which is a fierce and provocative argument against nationalism and war. Again, the Abbey balked at the play, and the Irish authorities refused to allow it to be put on during such delicate political times. Daniel Laurence and Nicholas Grene note that 'Sir Matthew Nathan, the Under Secretary at the Castle, wrote Shaw a very sympathetic letter in which he said that in the light of likely demonstrations in which "the fine lesson of the play would be smothered", "the production of the play should be postponed till a time when it will be recording some of the humour and pathos of a past rather than of a present national crisis"' (1993: xix). Thus, while Shaw's work came to be performed often in Ireland, none of his dramas premiered there.

This does not seem to have been a grave concern for Shaw, who disliked Dublin – or at least found his visits back painful (his last visit to Ireland was in 1923, thirty-seven years before his death). He still supported Irish arts and artists, befriending the likes of Sean O'Casey and co-founding with W.B. Yeats the Irish Academy of Letters in 1932 (O'Flaherty 2004: 134). But even though he eschewed Irish nationalist politics, Shaw's work reflected his sympathy to the land of his birth, which he knew so intimately, and which had shaped his understanding of both the delusions and perils of imperialism and neocolonialism in the modern world. His theatre, in return, would offer an important and influential model for talking politics on the modern Irish stage.

Realism at the Abbey

Some of the earliest realists in the movement got their start at the Irish National Theatre Society. Fred Ryan's *The Laying of the Foundations* (1902), an urban drama with a socialist subtext, dealing with government corruption and life in Dublin's slums, was one of the first dramas to be performed by the Abbey's precursor, the Irish National Dramatic Company. Once the INTS established itself, Lady Gregory and J.M. Synge, as described in the previous chapter, established realism as a major element within the INTS's future theatrical canon.

Playwright Padraic Colum, one of the original members of the INTS, was familiar with both Gaelic League and conventional theatre audiences: his poetry and plays gained the attention of both the populist Cumann na nGaedheal and the more elite Yeats and George Russell (Diviney 1997: 69). His work with the Fays as an actor led to the natural transition towards working with the INTS, and he was an active member of the society until seceding from the group to join the Theatre of Ireland in 1906. The Abbey continued to produce Colum's plays, even as he served as secretary of the Theatre of Ireland, thanks to their quality and popularity.

Colum's most famous play, *The Land* (1905), addresses one of the pre-occupations of Irish realism at the start of the twentieth century, emigration, with a detailed, historically specific examination of rural life in the Irish midlands. Set shortly after the land wars of the 1890s,[4] the play describes two old farmers, Martin Douras and Murtagh Cosgar, who find at the end of their lives that, in holding on to their land for so long, they have lost their opportunity to leave it to the most capable of their children, who have since emigrated to America. Now, in their old age, each has two children left at home. Ideally, they will join their farms by marrying their most ambitious children – Murtagh's son, Matt, and Martin's daughter, Ellen – to each other. Instead, Matt chooses to emigrate to America, where Ellen will join him after finishing her education. Instead of Matt and Ellen, the land will be inherited by Murtagh's unimaginative daughter, Sally, and Martin's less intelligent son, Cornelius, since they are the only children who have not left home. At the close of the play, the audience is torn between celebrating the two happy marriages and grieving Ellen and Martin's decision to leave their community at the moment when the landlords' hold over the property is finally being loosed. The final words are given to Cornelius, who tactlessly urges his father, who is heartbroken by Martin's decision to emigrate, to convince the group of young émigrés not to leave: '"Men of Ballykillduff," you might say, "stay on the land and you'll be saved body and soul; you'll be saved in the man and in the nation. The nation men of Ballykillduff, do you ever think of it at all? Do you ever think of the Irish nation that is waiting all this time to be born?" (*He becomes more excited; he is seen to be struggling with words)*' (Colum 1990: 110).

While Colum's play celebrates the political triumph of the Wyndham Land Act, it also illustrates the struggle between family duty and personal ambition in rural Ireland, especially in light of the suffocating traditions of Irish familism.[5] Colum remarked about the play, 'In *The Land* I tried to show that it was not altogether an economic necessity that was driving young men and women out of the rural Irish districts; the lack of life and the lack of freedom there had much to do with emigration' (Colum, 'Introduction,' *Three Plays*, 1916). Colum's remark points out that Irish realism sought not only to reject external views of Irish culture, like the stage Irishman, but also to offer introspective examinations of the Irish experience.

Colum's sombre tales of rural life in the midlands can be juxtaposed with George Fitzmaurice's black comic explorations of country life in County Kerry. Rich in dialect and fantastic in imagery, Fitzmaurice's comedies expose the moral and material prejudices of rural life, with characters repressing their real desires beneath a veneer of respectability, to tragicomic ends.

The Pie Dish (1908) for example, examines parodically the tension between the realist theatre's fascination with the relationship between the individual and society, and the eccentric's tenuous relationship to the larger, socially conformist community. In this play, Leum, an old man at death's door, does not worry about his children or his soul so much as an uncompleted pie dish that he began years before. While his daughters, Johanna and Margaret, and his priest worry that he cares more for his pie-dish project than his last rites, Leum replies: 'Twenty years at my pie-dish, twenty years! And thirty years before that thinking of it, but I neglecting to give under making it all that time with diversions coming between me and it. But it's fifty years the pie-dish is in my brain, and isn't it great work if I don't get time to finish it in the heel?' (Fitzmaurice 1969: 55). Leum falls into death throes and, when praying to God does not alleviate his pain for him to continue work on his pie-dish, he offers his soul to the devil: 'Let the devil himself give me time, then, let him give me time to finish my pie-dish, and it's his I'll be for ever more, body and soul! [*He shakes. The pie-dish falls and breaks. He screams and falls back on chair*]' (56). Leum dies, and the priest declares '. . . 'tis likely he is damned!' (56). The responses to Leum's tragicomic death are varied. Johanna worries about the family's status in the community, declaring 'it's disgraced surely we'll be over him during the duration of time through the length and breadth of Europe' (56). The priest, taking up a piece of the broken pie-dish, remarks on the vanity of Leum's quest. Margaret, however, feels remorse that she did not support her father and his dreams more in his lifetime. ' ''Tisn't damned he is, and no sin on him but what he did in the heel. But it's dead he is, and where was the good in my being too hard and bitter with him in his latter end! [*throwing herself on her knees*] May the Lord have mercy on his soul!' (56).

Later Fitzmaurice plays, like *The Magic Glasses* (1913), move into a more fantastic realm, but continue to celebrate the imaginative spirit over bourgeois social norms. Indeed, like the Abbey playwrights Yeats and Synge, Fitzmaurice's plays exposed the imagination and passion extant in Irish life, even if marginalized by modern morality and material expectations. And, like the plays of the directors, his work is almost poetic in its language, as Fitzmaurice (who grew up in an Irish-speaking household in Kerry) masterfully captured County Kerry's rich and idiosyncratic dialect (Slaughter 1969: ix). Despite his early promise with the Abbey, Fitzmaurice's later work was not accepted by the theatre, although *The Country Dressmaker* (1907) was revived often. While Austin Clarke claimed that Fitzmaurice's break from the theatre was due to jealousy of Fitzmaurice's work on the part of Yeats (Clarke 1967: vii), it is more likely that his dark and complicated tragicomedies diverged too far from the broad comic repertoire the financially burdened theatre cultivated in the 1910s.

The master of broad comedy among the Abbey realists was William Boyle, whose satires of life in the Irish midlands became favourites among Abbey audiences. His first play, *The Building Fund* (1905), satirizes the gap between socially proscribed senses of moral obligation, and the self-interest that causes people to hold on to or disrupt those norms. In the play, a miserly woman named Mrs Grogan lives on a farm with middle-aged son Shane and adult granddaughter, Sheila. Having been kept on a short tether with no prospects for personal financial gain, Shane has grown as miserly as his mother, and bides his time until the land will be his. Sheila, whose mother was disowned by Mrs Grogan, has arrived at the twilight of her grandmother's years in hope of reconciliation and a possible inheritance. Mrs Grogan is suspicious of her offspring's motives toward her, and chooses to leave all of her money and property to the church building fund, although she never went to church, leaving her family penniless. Thus, her act of generosity to the community is really a spiteful act against her children – especially her son, who had worked for her for years – and a selfish attempt to save her own soul. Hearing the news, Shane and Sheila stop competing and join forces, realizing that they might still get a portion of the property if they appear appropriately pious before the priest.

Considering its cynical take on family and religious values, it is surprising that this drama, which Robert Welch calls an 'odd, nasty little play,' (1999: 37) was greeted so warmly, while Synge's attacks on similar issues were condemned. Overall, it appears that the accessibility of Boyle's language, compared with Synge's poetic recreations of Gaelic cadences into English, and the opportunities for broad and obvious stage business played by the likes of W.G. Fay, led audiences to connect to Boyle's work as harmless Irish entertainment, but entertainment with an authentic Irish accent.[6]

The Abbey rounded out its repertoire of regional voices with the aid of Northern Irish playwright, St John Ervine. Born in Belfast, Ervine moved to London at the age of seventeen where, shadowing Shaw's footsteps somewhat, he joined the Fabian Society and began writing for newspapers. His 1911 play *Mixed Marriage* was produced at the Abbey, beginning what would become a contentious relationship, since Ervine did not bother to hide his contempt for the ideals of the theatre nor the lack of discipline he perceived in the actors.[7] *Mixed Marriage* offered a radical examination of life in working-class sectarian Belfast that ultimately claimed that sectarian violence was informed as much by class, or even personal conflict, as by religion or nationalist politics. He also claims in the drama that sectarian violence is a hyper-masculine response to urban social conditions, and represents the women in his drama as counterpoints to violent masculinity, thus objectifying even as he idealizes them as peacekeepers. At the end of the drama, Nora, the Catholic woman whose marriage to the Protestant Hugh helped set up a wave of unrest, runs into the street as a group of soldiers fire into a growing mob. Mortally wounded, she tells her husband, 'Don't be cryin', Hugh. It wus right t' shoot me. It wus my fault. A'm quaren glad' (St John Ervine [1911] 1988a: 63). *Mixed Marriage* anticipates the political and gender politics found in O'Casey's Dublin trilogy a few years later, mixing an awareness of the socioeconomic factors that inform sectarian politics in urban spaces, with an essentializing symbolism that juxtaposes male violence in the public sphere with representations of female obedience, nurturing, and peace in the home.

In his masterwork, *John Ferguson* (1915), Ervine turns to economic violence in the country, as a family's attempts to resist eviction lead to the rape of the daughter of the household, and the arrest of the son wrongly accused of killing his sister's rapist. As in *Mixed Marriage*, family devotion and sacrifice is supreme, and it is when accident or loss of nerve hinder these traits that tragedy ensues. Hannah Ferguson's refusal to marry James Caesar to save the family farm leads indirectly to her rape by Caesar. Likewise, Andrew disobeys his father when he goes out to avenge his sister's violation, causing his father to go after him and end up murdering Caesar, although Andrew will confess to the crime to save his father. At the end of the drama, the family finds itself broken ultimately by its failure to bend ideals to economic necessity, while the play questions a social system that would allow an upright family like the Fergusons to get into such a situation in the first place. Ervine was not interested in performing an idealized Ireland, or in dramatizing poignant satires of Ireland's colonial condition. Despite his heavy use of the family as a microcosm of the state, and essentializing of gender norms, Ervine was one of the first major playwrights of the Irish theatre movement to address seriously the economic and social conditions of Northern Irish life.

The Theatre of Ireland's Urban Realism

While the INTS continued to establish a realist dramatic and acting aesthetic on the Abbey stage, its rival theatre, Cluithcheoiri na hEireann, or the Theatre of Ireland, was offering different reflections on Irish life. The Theatre of Ireland was established by some of the leaders of the original INTS in 1906 in protest to the radical shifts in INTS governance, which denied the performers a say in the artistic choices of the theatre and obligated them to perform the roles given to them by the directors. The Theatre of Ireland included not only some of the INTS's best performers at that time, but also many of its best Irish speakers, and their ability to perform plays in Irish put the Abbey at a political disadvantage. Even more important than their theatre capabilities for many nationalists of the time, however, was their activism within the movement beyond their work in the theatre. To attend a performance by the Theatre of Ireland was to return to the model of the Irish National Dramatic Company's performance of *Cathleen ni Houlihan* only a few years earlier, in which the player's identity as a nationalist activist had a presence and force grounding the performance of the character he or she played. By joining the Theatre of Ireland, the playwrights and players who left the INTS for the Theatre of Ireland committed to put the mission of their theatre beyond the possibility of earning a professional career. Padraic Colum joined the Theatre of Ireland, and offered them a translation of *The Land, An Talamh*, which they performed in 1906 (Vandevelde 2005; 209). Along with Irish realism, the Theatre of Ireland offered looks at urban life in Ireland not offered at the Abbey, most famously in the work of Seumas O'Kelly. O'Kelly was 'an ardent nationalist who was active in the Gaelic League and the Sinn Fein movements' throughout his life (O'Grady 1997: 271), and who channelled his politics into his livelihood as a journalist and author.[8]

O'Kelly's 1907 one-act, *The Matchmakers*, helped the Theatre of Ireland secure its footing as a forum for original work. Ultimately, this very funny and actable play became a favourite of amateur societies, appearing in every county in Ireland (O'Grady 1997: 271) within a few years of its Theatre of Ireland debut. His 1909 play, *The Shuiler's Child*, however, gave him a lasting mark in Irish drama, and the Theatre of Ireland their most important success. The drama describes a middle-class family, the O'Heas, who adopts a young boy out of the workhouse. The boy's biological mother, Moll Woods, is a shuiler, or woman of the roads. She stops by the O'Hea home seeking alms, and discovers her child there. Nina O'Hea, the child's foster-mother, suddenly finds herself trapped in her own kitchen between the child's biological mother and the government inspector who is visiting to ensure that the home is appropriate for the child. Stirred by the sight of her son, Moll returns to the workhouse and demands that her son be returned to her. Obligated by law, the authorities return the child to Moll; but she then returns the child to the O'Heas, realizing that they will provide a better life for her son than she is able. Although Moll has given her son away to be adopted, she is arrested for abandoning the child years before. Yet she leaves of her own accord, no longer cursing her misfortune, but blessing the O'Heas for rescuing and raising her child.

O'Kelly's tragedy of maternal love and sacrifice was dedicated to the actress who played the leading role, Maire Nic Shiubhlaigh, who brilliantly performed the character of the fiery and physical shuiler, Moll Woods. Other nationalist activists in the cast whom audiences would quickly recognize included Con Markiewicz, Irish nationalist author, founder of the Fianna Fail, and member of Cumann na mBann, who played the inspector from the government board. Markiewicz performed regularly in political plays in pre-revolutionary Ireland, including starring with the Irish Dramatic Company. A member of a wealthy Anglo-Irish family, the Gore-Booths, Markiewicz's refined accent must have been enjoyed by the audience, seeing the aristocrat-turned-socialist playing the role of the classist and unsympathetic board inspector. Indeed, it was the Theatre of Ireland's ability to hold on to the ideal of theatrical performance as one among many modes of public activism for its actors that made the theatre such a vital one for its nationalist audiences.

As discussed in the previous chapter, the Theatre of Ireland in its heyday offered audiences some of the best amateur performances in Ireland, many of which may have rivalled the INTS in quality. It also offered a venue for Dublin playwrights who were either frustrated by the INTS's no-politics policy, or favoured an aesthetic that did not suit the taste of the directors. Although both O'Kelly's and Colum's work would be produced by the INTS in the 1910s, working with the Theatre of Ireland provided both playwrights with an important milestone in their careers. And the Theatre of Ireland provided Dublin with an urban, activist-driven approach to Irish nationalist theatre.

The Cork Realists

While Dublin was acknowledged as the centre of nationalist theatre activity in the early years of the Irish theatre movement, by 1910 the Cork Dramatic Society became one of the leading sources for new dramas. 'Cork realism', with its frank tragic and comic approaches to economic and social anxieties within the region's tight-knit community, deeply influenced theatre across the rest of the country.[9]

According to Cork playwright and Abbey theatre manager and director Lennox Robinson, the move towards a new, Irish realist dramaturgy in his hometown was inspired by a tour by the Abbey players there in 1907. Describing his epiphany, Robinson remarked in his autobiography, *Curtain Up*, that, 'It came on me as a flash, as a revelation.[10] Play-material could be found outside one's own door, at one's own fireside' (1942: 18). By 1909, the Cork Dramatic Society was offering, along with legendary dramas in the Gaelic League vein, new plays designed to capture Cork's voice and spirit for the Irish national repertoire.

Lennox Robinson, who would go on to become one of the most influential individuals in Irish theatre, responded to the call for an Irish voice onstage by turning a story he had written with his sister into a play, titled *The Clancy Name* (1908). In this drama, a woman whose son was involved in a murder tries desperately to stop her son from confessing on his deathbed to his involvement in the crime. When her son dies, she does not mourn his death, but rejoices that he has not revealed his secret and 'the Clancy name' remains intact. Likewise, in his comedy of some years later, *The Whiteheaded Boy* (1916), a family desperately tries to cover up the family's favoured son, Denis's, failure at Trinity College from their community, and ends up ruining the futures of the other members of the family to maintain the image of his success. First, they decide to send Denis to Canada to be a labourer, but they tell their neighbours he has an excellent job waiting for him, fearing the mockery of the town: 'Great laughing the neighbours will be having at us, and all the talk we made about his cleverness for the last twenty years,' Denis's aunt warns the family (Robinson [1916] 1982b: 83). His sister, Babe, agrees: 'People to laugh at me – 'twould make me mad' (83).

His fiancée's father, thinking his daughter is being abandoned in favour of a successful future in Canada, insists that Denis marry his daughter, or he will sue the family. But when Delia and Denis do marry secretly, and Denis begins to work as a day labourer, both the bride's and the groom's family beg Denis to take a comfortable job in one of his future father-in-law's businesses, with £320 thrown into the bargain. 'The truth's a dangerous thing to be saying in a little town like Ballycolman,' (93) Denis's Aunt Emily remarks. Perhaps, but the family finds lies more expensive.

Robinson adds to the sardonic wit of the play by having the stage directions, which are actually Shavian commentary on the action, spoken aloud in performance. When Donough, a character engaged to one of Denis's sisters, appears onstage, the narrator remarks through the spoken stage directions: '(*He's not much to look at, is he? A simple poor fellow, it's a wonder he had the spunk to think of getting married at all. JANE could have done better for herself, but she thinks the world of the little man . . .*)' (68). In this way, the Narrator both guides the audience's response to the events onstage, and reflects the very kinds of remarks about themselves and their actions the characters fear and avoid from the wider community. Thus, Robinson's play works on two levels – as a light-hearted look at small-town life in County Cork, and as an ironic commentary on the psychic distortions and economic peril put upon a family who, like Mrs Clancy in Robinson's early play, is willing to sacrifice the future of four siblings to maintain the illusion of success showered upon the favoured son.

Robinson's Cork realist colleague, T.C. Murray, examined this theme from a purely tragic perspective in his 1912 play, *Maurice Harte*. As in *The Whiteheaded Boy*, this drama offers the tragedy of a family investing its hopes and money in a single child, only to have that investment fall apart. In this case, farmers Michael and Ellen Harte have sacrificed for years to send their son, Maurice, to seminary to become a priest. It would be unusual in 1912 Ireland for a priest to come from a farming background, but the family has made the sacrifice because of Maurice's proven intellectual capacity, as well as the encouragement of Father Mangan, the parish priest. After over eight years of study, however, Maurice realizes that he does not have the vocation and, when he returns home to share the information with his family, he learns that they have gone deeply into debt to pay his tuition. Thus, Maurice is torn between ruining his family by not being ordained, and performing a sacrilege in taking vows without being called by God. He suffers a nervous breakdown and, in the last scene, the family prepares to take in Maurice to nurse him back to health, knowing that their prospects for the future are as broken down as Michael's nerves. At the close of the play, Mrs Harte cries to herself, 'My God! My God! My God!' while '(*the priest looks at her with a pained sense of his own helplessness. The curtain falls very slowly*)' (Murray [1912] 1998: 99).

In Robinson's dramas, it is usually family pride that causes economic or social downfall. Murray's drama, however, offers a more deeply ironic and classically tragic situation. He characterizes the Harte family as robust and loving people, who make the sacrifice for their son both for his benefit and also out of a sense of wonder regarding the Church. In one of her more prideful moments, Mrs Harte remarks of her son's ordination, 'And I often say to myself, whenever the death'll come after, 'twont be so hard at all. 'Twould be a great joy thinking of him saying the Mass for your soul, and all the priests and they chanting the great Latin, the same as if 'twas over one o' themselves . . .' (63). Father Mangan, the family priest who convinced the Hartes to send Maurice to university, on the other hand, is ineffectual in dealing with both Maurice's spiritual crisis and its devastating effects on the family. In fact, his failure to act or intervene merely increases the ultimate anguish for the family. Murray does not paint Mangan as a malicious or self-serving character, however. Rather, Mangan's naivety in urging Maurice's enrolment in seminary, and his fear of assisting Maurice and the family with the consequences of that action, reflect the priest's absence of spiritual introspection or ability to face a crisis beyond his control, but not his help. Maurice's inability to fulfil the social duties of a priest without feeling the requisite spiritual vocation – a matter he could easily have lied about – merely foregrounds the gap between Mangan's ease with his social position in the community as priest, and his failure to live up to that role in a moment of extraordinary crisis, when he can only right the social status quo by disrupting it. It is not just

Maurice, but his family and his priest, who are trapped by conflicting social and religious expectations that can only be reconciled through a compromise of ideals.

The realist tragedies and tragicomic plays that came from Cork certainly reflect the aesthetic strategies that one would expect in early naturalism, such as well-made play structures that focus on the individual torn between individual desire and the expectations of an oppressive society, and props used to move the plot forward in ironic and dramatic ways. In *The Whiteheaded Boy*, an enigmatic telegram arrives ahead of Denis, which the family interprets as meaning either that Denis has taken up gambling again, or that he has failed his university exams – both disastrous offences, but comic as the family discusses which terrible outcome they would prefer. In *Maurice Harte*, a more heartbreaking use of props is used when Mrs Harte reveals to her son, Owen, a second account book, showing the debt the family is truly in, and revealing to her son that, thanks to Maurice's failure to be ordained, Owen will be too poor to marry. Ibsen has inspired Irish realism from its earliest days. In Cork, however, Irish realists found a shrewd and powerful adaptation of the form to describe the stultifying social experiences the dramatists found in the county's small-town life; and, like Ibsen, show that these problems are not natural or caused exclusively by individual will, but the result of larger sociopolitical systems. This recognizable Irish theme made Cork realist dramas good draws for theatre companies like the Abbey on tour. And they were embraced by audiences across Ireland as nationalist plays not only because of their modernist representation of Irish life, but also because of their authorship by individuals who, although having their work produced at the Abbey Theatre, were perceived to be outside the circles of the Abbey's Anglo-Irish elite. Indeed, this may be one of the reasons why Yeats hired the relatively inexperienced Robinson to serve as Abbey manager in 1909.[11]

Northern Voices

One of the most overlooked of the realist movements during this period was the shrewd and often satirical voice of the North emerging from playwrights working with the Ulster Literary Theatre, which became an important site for Northern Irish Protestants and Catholics to address national identity amid and despite their region's legacy of sectarianism.

The group was founded after Bulmer Hobson and David Parker, nationalists from Ulster interested in creating an Irish theatre movement in Belfast, travelled to Dublin in 1902, excited by the nationalist theatre developments there, to spend a few days with members of the Irish National Dramatic Company and gain advice and permission to perform some of their plays. Hobson recalled:

> Everybody was most cordial and helpful except Yeats – haughty and aloof . . . we wanted to put on in Belfast Yeats's *Cathleen ni Houlihan* and [James] Cousins's *The Racing Lug*. [INDC actors] Dudley Digges and Maire Quin promised to come and act in our first production. But Yeats refused permission. When Maire reported this to Maud Gonne, Maud said 'Don't mind Willie. He wrote the play for me and gave it to me. It is mine and you can put it on whenever you want to.' So we put on *Cathleen ni Houlihan* and *The Racing Lug* [in November 1902] with Dudley Digges and Maire Quin as our leading actors. Annoyed by Yeats we decided to write our own plays – and we did. (Qtd in Bell 1972: 2)

By December of 1904, the Ulster Literary Theatre (hereafter ULT), as their company would name itself, was performing its own plays with its own actors. While the theatre took several cues from the movement in Dublin, the ULT foresaw a different mission than that espoused by the INTS. 'We recognize at the outset that our art of the drama will be different from that other Irish drama which speaks from the stage of the Irish National Theatre in Dublin,' W.B. Reynolds wrote. 'At present we can only say that our talent is more satiric than poetic. That will probably remain the broad difference between the Ulster and Leinster schools. But when our genius arrives, as he must sooner or later, there is no accounting for what extraordinary tendency he may display' (qtd in Bell 1972: 7).

Indeed, the Ulster 'genius' was offering its talents to a very different, Protestant majority audience, with a very different relationship to theatre and to nationalist politics from their neighbours in the South. For instance, the ULT had to deal with a Protestant suspicion of theatre. The founders of the ULT took stage names, in part to protect their family names and careers. Politically, the ULT sought to promote an Irish nationalism that did not evoke memories of the western peasant, a culturally foreign figure for most Northern Irish,[12] but instead 'to remind audiences of the United Irishmen and of a time when the Protestant settlers identified themselves as Irish', and, beyond that, to confront the serious political and cultural divides within Ulster, that often devolved into religious and cultural discrimination. (Lyons 2000: 41). By arguing for 'a distinct Ulster identity, but one that was pluralist rather than monolithic' (Vandevelde 2005: 122), the ULT sought to become a forum for open discussion of Irish nationalism and Ulster's place in it. The regional voice developed by the Ulster Literary Theatre and its offspring would come to affect profoundly Irish theatre not only in the North, but also across the island.

Its first production, aided by Irish National Dramatic Company actors Maire Quinn and Dudley Digges, was a performance of *Cathleen ni Houlihan*. It also started almost immediately to publish its own journal, titled *Uladh*, the Irish word for Ulster.[13] However, unlike Yeats's *Beltaine* and *Samhain*, the Irish Literary Theatre and Irish National Theatre Society journals that set down the artistic and political mission of the Irish theatre society almost exclusively from Yeats's point of view, *Uladh* provided a more diverse and democratic reflection on the theatre it served, showing how the project was truly a work in progress, with leading members of the group politely offering sometimes conflicting ideas about what their theatre should indeed represent.

In the first issue, W.B. Reynolds did offer an editorial that outlined some of the generally agreed-upon goals of the group. They hoped to help define and cultivate a distinctively Northern Irish dramaturgy, and to promote Northern Irish arts generally, for they feared, Reynolds claimed, 'for the young men in that, if they do not find an outlet in Ulster, they will either go away, or gravitate upon the sloblands of American or English magazine work, which is purely commercial and has no pretention to literature whatsoever' (in Danaher 1988: 6). Reynolds also vowed that the journal would 'be non-sectarian and non-political; each article will be signed by the writer as an expression of his own individual views; other views may be put forward in another number . . . Our contributors are mostly young men, of all sects and all grades of political opinion' (In Danaher 1988: 6). In other words, the Ulster Literary Theatre was less interested in countering British stereotypes of Irishness than in developing a regional theatre and literary scene that would create an audience for high art and literature within Belfast; and they were willing for the work they produced to develop into that voice, rather than to seek out works that followed their pre-set rules. As 'Connla', or James Cousins, remarked in the journal, 'If the product be really good, it will then be time enough to philosophise, to compare and classify; our identity and our differences will be simultaneously manifest' (Danaher 1988: 7).[14] Yet, considering the group's goal of reflecting Ulster life onstage, combined with the limited theatre experience of its members, and the theatre models from Dublin, it is not surprising that realism became a trademark form of the movement.

One of the most successful of the realists to emerge from the group was Rutherford Mayne. Born Samuel Waddell in Tokyo, Japan, in 1878 to Presbyterian missionary parents, Mayne energetically supported the Ulster Literary Theatre and Ulster Theatre as an actor and playwright, and even served as a board member of the institution during the many years he lived and worked as a surveyor in Dublin. He achieved an international reputation as a playwright. Mayne's first play, *The Turn of the Road* (1906), reflects the camaraderie of the ULT's members in its early days. Mayne thanked fellow member and playwright Lewis Purcell for his guidance in the writing of the play; the talented Fred Morrow directed, and Mayne and his future wife acted in the play. Set in a country kitchen in County Down, the drama tells of a young man torn between his desire to become a musician, and the sense of responsibility he feels to take on a more secure career. The play was well received in Belfast and Dublin, where it played at the Abbey. Joseph Holloway remarked in his diary of 'the enthusiastic audience, which was the largest I have seen at the Abbey since *The Playboy* row' (Holloway 1967: 92).

Mayne's next play, *The Drone* (1908), as Wolfgang Zach points out, 'not only became the most successful of all the plays staged by the Ulster Theatre but one of the most popular Irish plays of the first half of the twentieth century' (2000: xiii). The play describes the relationship between John Murray, a widowed farmer, and his brother Daniel, a would-be inventor who has been living off the generosity of his brother for years. Growing weary of Daniel's dependence, and tired of a household being run to ruin by his daughter Mary, John proposes marriage to Sarah McMinn, a no-nonsense spinster who requires Mary to show her the family china and silver immediately after John proposes. Daniel senses Sarah's threat to his livelihood and tries to undermine the courtship at the same time as Sarah tries to expose Daniel's fraud. Daniel amusingly wins John's trust, but fears a breach of contract lawsuit. Daniel settles the suit out of court by selling John one of his useless inventions, with some help from machinations by Mary. At the end of the play, Mary is engaged to a young farmer, John is free of Sarah, and Daniel and John return to their former situation.

While *The Turn of the Road* looked at the conflict between steady work and a creative career from a more serious perspective, *The Drone* laughs at the excesses of the Ulster Protestant work ethic. John chases after hard work and security, investing in his brother's claims of hard work (and perhaps putting family over common sense), and proposing to a woman not for love, but because she 'would be just as nice and saving a woman as I could get' (Mayne [1908] 2000b: 51). But he is a bad investor who is easily influenced and does not look at the long-term value of his investments, with a brother drinking and smoking away his savings, and a wife more interested in running a household than taking a husband. When Sarah's brother is bought off from suing John with Daniel's worthless bellows, however, John's faith in his brother becomes imaginatively justified. Through fast talking and creative bookkeeping, it appears that Daniel has not destroyed his brother's marriage plans to save his own skin, but that he has given John his freedom and saved him £1,000. Daniel avoids shame and bankruptcy, and John avoids admitting his brother's shiftlessness as the brothers return to the relationship they have maintained for years. At the curtain, John says to his brother, '(*with a sigh of intense relief and gratitude*) Dan, I've said it before, and I'll say it again, you've a great head on you, Daniel' (89).

The Ulster Literary Theatre's strong satirical voice often bordered on the acerbic and disrespectful. In the same year that Synge's *Playboy of the Western World* caused riots at the Abbey, Gerald MacNamara, in collaboration with Lewis Purcell, performed *Suzanne and the Sovereigns*, a burlesque of the fight between King James and King William, culminating with the Battle of the Boyne. The Battle of the Boyne is one of the most sacred historical events in the Orange tradition; and, in 1900, as now, the anniversary was marked with marches, bonfires, and other performative gestures marking Protestant supremacy in the region. In this burlesque, we do not see the battle, but we hear it described like a rugby match. To further the parody, the kings in *Suzanne and the Sovereigns* do not fight for Ireland, but for a middle-class woman with whom both have fallen in love. In fact, William is cajoled into going to Ireland only when he learns that one of the Irish delegates sent to urge him to fight for sovereignty of the country is the father of Suzanne. At the end of the drama, William, as in history, has won the day, but not Suzanne, who has run off with William's portrait painter. The play closes with James comforting the distraught William, and a fairy holding an olive branch over their heads before giving the epilogue: 'And now before the curtain fall,/A bright New Year to one and all,/And if you're pleased, you ought, by right/To come again tomorrow night' (MacNamara: [1907] 1988a: 54).

As Karen Vandevelde has pointed out, the ULT's status as an amateur theatre rather than a national theatre, along with their equal mocking of both sides of the sectarian divide, allowed them a high degree of artistic freedom, and a favourable response from a diverse audience. In addition, by working in the tradition of the burlesque and the panto, and performing during the Christmas season, generally a period of theatrical licence, the playwrights had further licence to mock some of the shibboleths of Northern Irish culture.[15] The drama became a favourite at the ULT, and was performed by the company for many years following in Belfast and Dublin.[16] Within the Southern counties, however, some plays about the legacies of British conquest were looking not to inspire laughter, but to evoke violent social change.

Part II

War and After, 1916–1948

Introduction to Part II

In the years between the Easter Rising and the end of the Civil War the work of imagining the Irish nation exploded into waves of violent protest and war. By 1916, nationalist opinion about the surest path to Irish nationhood ranged from 'Home Rulers', willing to wait for the UK to fulfil its 1914 promise to give Ireland Home Rule as a commonwealth, to physical force Republicans demanding immediate and bloody war to wrest the nation away from imperial rule. And, of course, many Irish were ready to fight with equal furore for Ireland to remain a part of the United Kingdom, especially Northern Irish Protestants who, inflamed by the passionate rhetoric of figures like Edward Carson, were among the 250,000 Unionists who signed the Ulster Covenant in 1912, pledging fealty to the British Crown.

Increasing the complexity of this political landscape, Europe from 1914 was in the throes of what would come to be called 'the Great War' – a conflict predicted to be a mere skirmish, which became a war of attrition that cost millions of lives. With all of Europe at war, militant Irish nationalists saw, in Roger Casement's words, that 'Ireland's opportunity is England's adversity' (Foster 1989: 479),[1] and urged that it was the ideal time to strike against and gain independence from a nation whose armed forces were already strained. Actually, Ireland was deeply involved in the war, with hundreds of thousands of Irish soldiers in British uniform. These soldiers included Irishmen who, already members of the United Kingdom's armed forces, found themselves on the battlefront – Home Rulers who signed up, assuming that Home Rule would be granted once the war ended, and Loyalists who enlisted in support of the Crown. Lady Gregory's only son, Robert, died serving in the RAF.[2] But when the UK started moving towards imposing conscription in Ireland, the nationalists felt that it was time to take action.

On Easter Monday, 18 April 1916, about 1,000 members of the Irish Republican Brotherhood, the socialist-nationalist Irish Citizen Army, and the feminist-nationalist Cumann na mBan reported for duty at sites around

Dublin and other major Irish cities, and began their long-anticipated insurrection. Their numbers were greatly decreased thanks to the rising being called off and then called back on the day before, and the uprising was quickly quelled in other parts of Ireland.[3] But in Dublin, the fighting lasted for days, razed much of the city centre, and cost hundreds of lives.[4]

Many of the nationalist artists/activists who had helped found the Irish dramatic movement were actively engaged in the Easter Rising. Playwrights like Padraic Colum fought in the ranks. Actor and founding member of the Irish Dramatic Company Constance Markiewicz led a group of soldiers holding off the British in Stephen's Green. While Markiewicz was probably the only woman actually to engage in combat, other women, like Abbey star and Theatre of Ireland leader Maire Nic Shiubhlaigh, offered support to the soldiers who had overtaken Jacob's biscuit factory.[5] And it is believed that the first casualty of the insurrection was Irish actor Sean Fallon. Supporters of the theatre who had previously used performance for their own political ends, like Padraic Pearse, Thomas MacDonagh and James Connolly, were leaders of the event, and were later executed for their deeds.

The battle in Dublin lasted eight days and resulted in death and destruction throughout the city. The leaders of the insurrection were vilified at first by much of the population but, in the wake of their executions, a growing sympathy for them and their work emerged. By 1918, the IRA had established a shadow government, the Dail Eireann, including police and law courts, and encouraged Irish citizens to turn to their authority instead of the British-controlled government. In 1919 the Irish War for Independence began. Thanks to such factors as committed nationalists, the tactical genius of Irish Republican Army leader Michael Collins and the political savvy of future Taoiseach Eamon de Valera, and England's exhaustion after the First World War, the English agreed to negotiate terms for independence with the IRA in 1921.

The fighting ended with a compromising treaty that kept the six majority Protestant counties in Ireland as part of the British Empire.[6] The British diplomats responsible for the negotiations, including David Lloyd George and Winston Churchill, made it clear that rejection of the treaty would mean years of 'terrible war',[7] tying the hands of the Irish delegation. The treaty split Irish nationalists and led to a civil war between those who chose to support the treaty (Free Staters), and those who rejected it (Irregulars or Die-hards). Guerrilla warfare spread throughout Ireland, with bombings and curfews in urban areas and, throughout the county, the burning of Anglo-Irish 'big houses', the estates of Anglo-Irish landlords which had become representations of Anglo-Irish class privilege. The Civil War ended in an uneasy compromise in 1922 that left the question of the six counties of Northern Ireland indefinitely on the table. Skirmishes between the two sides continued well into 1923.

The first leaders of the new Irish Republic who took office in 1923 reflected a range of ideologies, including socialism and feminism, as well as a sizeable contingent of Anglo-Irish, including W.B. Yeats. Over time, however, the growing strength of de Valera's Fianna Fail party began to lead the country down an increasingly conservative moral and economic path, despite de Valera's radical political roots. The Irish Free State developed an ideology that glorified rural Irish life, but restricted much technological and industrial development, made Irish the official language of the nation and a mandatory course for all schoolchildren, and legislated a morality reflecting the ultramontane doctrines of the Irish Catholic Church. Joyce's *Ulysses*, like information about contraception, was not allowed in the country. And, after the passing of the Irish Republic's Constitution in 1937 and its adoption in 1939, morality was legislated to the point that a woman was not allowed to hold a civic post after she married.

The Republic of Ireland asserted its sovereignty and isolationist policy at the start of the Second World War by declaring neutrality. While some citizens of the Irish Free State held on to the notion that England's difficulty was Ireland's opportunity, especially militant nationalists who recalled Ireland's seeking help from Germany in the previous war, and while some Irish held ideals that were sympathetic to the goals of fascism, most in fact supported the Allies surreptitiously.[8] Ireland did experience severe shortages during the war years, and there were isolated incidents of bombs falling on the Republic; but overall it did not experience the devastation accrued by its neighbours. Northern Ireland, and especially Belfast, experienced tremendous damage during German air raids, and suffered both civilian and military casualties during the war.

The legacy of war and the Irish Free State's deeply conservative social policies of the 1920s to the early 1950s have led some theatre scholars to consider this period an artistic wasteland, skipping from O'Casey's Dublin trilogy to Brian Friel's *Philadelphia, Here I Come!* in the bat of an eye. It is true that Ireland's larger theatres, especially the Abbey, with its government subsidy, moved away from experiment and towards a kind of sentimental realism in their work, re-staging classic texts from the first years of the Irish dramatic movement, along with hundreds of formulaic and forgettable renditions of life in rural Ireland. The actors, many of whom found themselves performing the same kinds of characters in the same kinds of plays for years, grew guilty of hamming it up for the crowd, and breaking the flow of a play with a gesture or comic aside.[9] But this is not the entire story.

While it is true that performance in mid-twentieth-century Ireland often served to reify a vision of Irish culture espoused by the conservative Fianna Fail government, theatre also functioned as a site of resistance from what some felt was a suffocating moral code. A terrific body of scholarship is emerging that recalls a rich legacy of theatrical and paratheatrical events occurring across Ireland during these years, such as the experimental dramas at Dublin's Pike Theatre, Belfast's Lyric Theatre, and other venues that show that curious writers, actors, and audiences were interested in pushing the artistic envelope in both Northern Ireland and in the Republic.[10] Some of these works were designed to support Fianna Fail's ideologies. Many works, however, were designed to test them.

In this section, we will see the argument about the Irish stage shift from how to imagine an Irish culture resistant to hegemonic stereotype to how to represent a new nation-state. The question of whether the image would be neocolonial or postcolonial, rural or urban, glorifying the wars that created the nation or challenging the ideologies that led them, would become the new site of contest. Indeed, just as the theatre during the Gaelic revival was a site for imagining a nation yet to be born, the Irish theatre of the 1920s to 1950s challenged the survival or manipulation of those founding myths in the new Republic and Northern Ireland, addressing frankly how class, gender, sexuality, and modernization were being redefined to serve the needs of the new nation.

The Abbey Becomes Institution, 1916–1929

In 1922, at the height of the Civil War, Sara Allgood, former Abbey star pursuing a professional acting career in London, wrote a friendly letter to her former employer, Lady Gregory. In her letter, Allgood wrote of her deep concern for Lady Gregory's health amid the dangers of the Civil War and her sadness for her 'poor country' (Allgood). Also in this letter, she offered to come back to the Abbey, 'if an appropriate salary could be found'. Allgood wanted to do her bit for Ireland, but she expected to be paid to do it. This anecdote reflects the strange position in which Ireland's self-declared national theatre found itself in the midst of the Irish revolutions of the 1910s and 1920s, and the kinds of ideological and economic negotiations with which the theatre (like most national theatres) dealt in its early years. The Abbey struggled to be the artistic voice of the nation, but its bills had to be paid. And, just as it had done in the years of Annie Horniman's subsidy, the theatre was forced to weigh its artistic ideals against the need to satisfy the expectations of its patrons. By the year Allgood wrote Gregory her letter, the Abbey had survived almost twenty years as a nationalist institution that provided a site for creating a counter-aesthetic to the colonial stereotypes of Ireland found on British and American stages, and that work had earned it an international reputation.[1] It had helped to develop a body of important dramatic literature that would influence such modernist performance experiments as the little theatre movement in the United States. It had also served as the training ground for actors like Allgood, Bridget Dempsey, and Dudley Digges, who would move from Dublin to London, New York, and Hollywood (See Grene 2006 and Barton 2006). And one of its co-founders, the instrumental W.G. Fay, had moved on to direct and teach in the United States and Great Britain, and had even become instrumental in the development of a Scottish theatre movement. But, in Dublin, the diurnal struggle to get bums on seats and pay the gas bill usually overshadowed its international success. In 1924 Lady Gregory noted that the theatre had lost £4,000 in the previous ten years, despite dozens of benefits and fundraisers (Welch 1999:

118). Still, despite its struggles, Gregory and Lennox Robinson, the manager of the theatre since 1917, read scores of new plays a year (vetting the best for consideration by W.B. Yeats), seeking a drama that would push their profit margin into a size more appropriate for the theatre's growing fame.

This chapter examines some of the key economic and ideological negotiations the Abbey pursued from 1916 to 1929, as it moved away from its original goal to be the voice of a few, to an increasingly democratically organized institution that made room for an array of aesthetic points of view. In fact, by the end of the 1920s, the Irish National Theatre Society was directly or indirectly involved with a network of stages that allowed for the development of a range of dramaturgical goals, and nurtured an array of theatrical forms. Sean O'Casey's realist Dublin trilogy is the most famous – and perhaps most emblematic – product of the Abbey in the 1920s, but the Abbey also continued to foster playwrights like St John Ervine and Lennox Robinson, as well as new voices like Dennis Johnston, and to create opportunities for professional acting and dance training in Dublin. These diverse initiatives and opportunities made the Abbey a magnet for new Irish plays and aspiring playwrights and actors. But the institutional identity they accrued through their government subsidy in 1925, and the inclusion of political appointees like George O'Brien and Ernest Blythe on the theatre board, made them the artistic instrument of the Irish Free State, and a magnet for criticism on all sides. Before looking into how Irish theatre in the 1920s responded to revolutionary war, however, this chapter will begin by looking at some of the dramaturgical developments in the 1910s that contributed to the militant revolutionary rhetoric of 1916, and that came to inform later plays addressing the nation at war.

The Revolution Will Be Dramatized

So far, this book has looked almost exclusively at theatre that emerged from the brand of cultural nationalism espoused by groups like the Irish Literary Theatre and the Gaelic League in the early 1890s – a theatre ultimately more concerned with expressing truthful images of Irish life or utopian images of a free Irish state than with inspiring violent revolution. The fight for independence they promoted was more cultural than militant and, in the South at least, reflected the constitutional nationalism of the Irish Parliamentary Party by showing political and economic struggles as 'internecine' events, rather than remarking on their roots in British imperialism (Pilkington 2001: 73). But throughout the first decades of the Irish revival, a strain of theatre calling for violent revolt had also contributed to the theatre movement, and in the years leading up to the Easter Rising of 1916, the military insurrection that spurred the country towards the war for independence, performance promoting violent revolution became more visible and urgent.[2]

   This style of theatre was encouraged by individuals and groups opposed to the growing complacency they sensed in Ireland in the face of the urgent demands of the First World War. In 1914, the British parliament passed the third Home Rule bill, which was to give Ireland limited self-governance. However, the bill held two stipulations: that it would not take effect until after the conflict that had just started in Europe was over, and that the issue of the status of the Protestant-majority counties in Northern Ireland would remain under consideration. As the war escalated and Irish men in British military uniforms began to die by the thousands in the trenches, the question of Irish nationalism at home came to be overlooked by some parts of the population, but grew white hot in the eyes of others. The non-partisan Gaelic League was enveloped by the highly politicized umbrella group, Cumann na nGaedheal, in 1913, with Padraic Pearse as president. Anxiety over their future led to Unionists forming the Ulster Volunteer Force, countered in the South by the founding of the Irish Volunteers and the Socialist Irish Citizen Army. The rhetoric of blood sacrifice for Irish freedom that had flowed through the nationalist movement for years reached fever pitch, and could be witnessed in the newspapers, at the speaker's podium, and on the nationalist stage.

   Actor/activists who had seen the power of performance to inspire social change within the movement for years began to pursue more and more aggressive theatrical messages to reflect the rising militancy within the movement. Publication and performance of these plays helped inspire the nationalist movement's militant minority to take up arms on Easter Monday 1916. But what added to the potency of these aesthetic works was their very close alliance to political activism in the nationalist movement. Authors of these plays, such as Thomas MacDonagh, James Connolly, and Padraic Pearse, were leaders of the nationalist movement.[3] There is a great difference between producing a play calling for blood sacrifice to restore the nation and taking over public buildings with military force. Yet in the case of playwrights like Pearse, Connolly, and MacDonagh, theatre created a vehicle for promoting their political goals. The participants in their theatres were themselves nationalist activists who, in embodying these dramas, created for themselves an even stronger nationalist commitment. And, while some of these revolutionary pieces were performed at the Abbey or other cultural nationalist venues, others were performed in spaces identified with – or involved in – militant nationalist ideals, like the Hardwicke Street Theatre, where the Irish Volunteers drilled when the theatre was not in use (Feeney 1984: 131); St Enda's School for boys, where Pearse and other educator/activists taught the children of the movement about their Irish heritage (Trotter 2001); or the Irish Socialists' Liberty Hall, where labour unions and nationalist groups regularly met. Thus, it is not surprising that, in recollections of the surprising events on the morning of Easter Monday 1916, many thought that the event unfolding was a preparation for a theatrical performance before realizing the hugely important revolutionary event about to unfold. Joseph Holloway, when seeing a copy of the Proclamation of the Irish Republic posted on the streets of Dublin the morning of the Easter Rising, thought at first that it was a stage bill for a play (Morash 2002). And at Liberty Hall, where a group of Irish Volunteers were readying ammunition, someone casually asked Con Markiewicz, one of the soldiers, if they were rehearsing a play for children (Moran 2005: 15).

The 'Rebel Plays' of the 1910s, like those of the previous decade, tend to read more like agit-prop or melodrama than psychological realism. In James Connolly's *Under Which Flag?* (1916), a melodrama that James Moran points out owes much to Boucicault (2005), a soldier must choose what nation to obey – his homeland, or the land whose government pays his salary. In Thomas MacDonagh's *When the Dawn is Come* (1908), set 'fifty years in the future', a group of Irish soldiers plot an insurrection, and one of their members dies spying against the enemy. The best crafted of those written by the movement's leaders, however, are those written by the leader of the Easter Rising, Padraic Pearse, whose dramas employed the Gaelic League and early ILT strategies of promoting a contemporary, anti-imperialist ideology by mytho-poeticizing Ireland's ancient past.

Pearse was a schoolmaster and a poet as well as a revolutionary. His school, St Enda's School for boys,[4] boasted a faculty of nationalist leaders – Mary Maguire Colum, the wife of playwright Padraic Colum, taught at St Enda's. In many ways, Pearse's school formed a kind of ideal nationalist community for the boys who attended. Their dress, language (Irish was the primary language at the school), games, and extracurricular activities all constellated around Pearse's notion of an Irish culture uncorrupted by

British imperialism. Irish arts were, naturally, a large part of the curriculum, and Pearse wrote several religious dramas and adaptations of Irish mythological stories for his students to perform on campus and in the community – the students even performed a Passion Play in Irish at the Abbey Theatre in 1911. In performing these plays, the boys effectively enacted an idealized image of Irish life and culture that complemented the nationalist notions that informed their lessons and everyday experiences at the school.

The rhetoric of Pearse's plays, like many of his political speeches (most famously, his Graveside Panegyric for O'Donovan Rossa in 1916), spoke of the need for blood sacrifice to revive the nation. The saviour who sacrifices for the nation in these dramas tended to be a beautiful and pure youth who, Christ-like, saves his community through faith and fighting, while the older men around him hesitate to take action. In his 1910 drama, *The King* (*An Ri*), for example, a young boy named Gilla na Naomh ('the Servant of the Saints') sacrifices himself to absolve his country of its evil king and free the people. His 1916 play, *The Singer*, most clearly personifies the idea of the revolutionary as a Christ figure, and foreshadows Pearse's thoughts about the upcoming insurrection. In the play, MacDara, a singer, teacher, and poet, returns to his home village after years wandering the roads. Since his poetry was too incendiary to be published, and his politics too controversial for a school to hire him, MacDara has inspired followers of the revolution with his speeches throughout the countryside. Now that he has returned home, he learns that his community is preparing to fight the Gall.

At the end of the drama, when he learns that his brother Colm has gone into battle with only fifteen other men since the elders held back most of the men because of the terrible odds against them, MacDara admonishes them for their lack of faith and fear to fight in what he considers a holy battle: 'It is for your own souls' sakes I would have had the fourscore go, and not for Colm's sake, or for the battle's sake, for the battle is won whether you go or not' (Pearse 1960: 43). When he learns that his brother has died in battle, MacDara declares that he will face the enemy alone: 'The fifteen were too many. Old men, you did not do your work well enough. You should have kept all back but one. One man can free a people as one Man redeemed the world. I will take no pike, I will go into the battle with bare hands. I will stand up before the Gall as Christ hung naked before men on the tree!' (43–4). MacDara then strides out of his mother's house, *'pulling off his clothes as he goes'* (44), while his mother and his sweetheart crouch, grieving, by the fire. This last image of *The Singer* points out how powerfully Pearse's dramas could draw on the nationalist feeling and training of his audience. As MacDara strips off his clothes to meet the enemy, he emulates Christ who 'hung naked before men on the tree', but also evokes the tradition of Irish warriors going into battle naked to show their fearlessness towards their enemy. Finally, the sight on stage of the handsome youth's disrobing body elicits a sensual response that represents what Susan Harris has called the 'erotics of sacrifice' (2002): like Yeats and Gregory's *Cathleen ni Houlihan*, Pearse's play links the consummation of the nation's destiny through blood sacrifice to sexual consummation, thus underlining both the 'naturalness' and the urgency for the sacrifice.

Pearse had planned to produce the play at St Enda's the week before the insurrection, but the performance was called off lest it tip off the government of the Irish Republican Brotherhood's plans. At the end of 1916, the play was performed at St Enda's, however, with the cast Pearse had chosen before the Rising and his ensuing death by firing squad (Moran 2005: 25), and in the years following became a staple of amateur theatre performance and the Irish Free State's course curriculum. Ultimately, the dramas by the revolutionaries of 1916 would not dominate the future aesthetics of the Irish dramatic movement, but their rhetoric and themes, especially in light of the Easter Rising, would influence and be commented on by Irish playwrights and producers in the following decades.

Rites of Inheritance: The Abbey in Wartime

While born out of spectacular pageants and verse dramas in the 1890s, by 1916 the Abbey's aesthetic identity as a realist stage was secure: its repertoire consisted almost entirely of realist fare, with a strong showing of G.B. Shaw, as well as some of its most popular playwrights, including descendants of the 'Cork realist' school like Lennox Robinson and T.C. Murray, and Northern Irish writers like Brinsley MacNamara, St John Ervine, Dorothy Macardle, and George Shiels. There were notable non-realist exceptions, like Yeats's *The Player Queen* (1919), Lady Gregory's wonder play, *The Dragon* (1919), and Lord Dunsany's orientalist fantasies, like *The Tents of the Arabs* (1920); but, for the most part, the Abbey was a house of realist drama.

In his 1919 essay, 'A People's Theatre: An Open Letter to Lady Gregory', Yeats signalled his acquiescence to the Abbey's dominant aesthetic, although he called its success 'a discouragement and a defeat', and announced that his own, poetic, drama would seek other, more elite, audiences. Yet the politician and pragmatist in Yeats saw the value of Irish realism, and approved of its goal of encouraging audiences to examine themselves and their role in the burgeoning nation-state with 'objective modern eyes'.[5] In the words of Lionel Pilkington, 'Yeats's support for the Abbey's "dogged realism" at the same time as his advocacy of an alternative and elite poetic theatre is less of an irony than a consistent ideological position: a recognition that the realism of the Abbey Theatre was vital to an agenda of modernization and state preparation. Hence Yeats's belief that while a modernist and international drama was indeed desirable in Ireland, it was also crucial that this be established within an institution separate from the Abbey, "the centre of Irish truth"' (Pilkington 2001: 83). The elitist divide between the international and the national that Yeats espoused in writing, however, was not always as exclusive in practice as he claimed.

For instance, Yeats supported the initiative of Lennox Robinson and others to found the Dublin Drama League, an 'amateur' theatre group committed to performing European and avant-garde dramas. The company included many Abbey Theatre members, and performed avant-garde theatre on the stage of the Abbey when the Abbey company was not performing. Christopher Morash remarks that the Dublin Drama League 'in effect became a sort of phantom image of what the Abbey might have been – a democratically run, flexible organisation presenting the best of European modernist theatre to a select audience' (2002: 180). 'In its active decade (1919–1929) it produced 66 plays written originally in eleven languages by thirty-six authors from fifteen countries, using nearly twenty directors and over half-a-dozen designers' (Clark and Ferrar 1979: 14). It also allowed Abbey actors to expand their acting repertoire: participants from the Abbey included Sara Allgood, Lennox Robinson, Shelah Richards, Arthur Shields, and Barry Fitzgerald.

At the same time, Yeats was finding his truly ideal theatre audience in London drawing rooms, performing his plays for dancers for strictly invited audiences. In a newspaper description of one of these performances – a 1916 production of *At the Hawk's Well* at the home of Lady Cunard – Yeats boasts that he refused a photographer and reporter entrance to the event. After chasing and compromising for funding for the Abbey for years, Yeats clearly took a palpable delight in shunning the press, who were as nonplussed by Yeats's refusal of the publicity as he was sure they would be by his play.

While the Dublin Drama League offered a high standard of performance of continental fare for elite Irish audiences, it was not the first theatre to offer avant-garde work in Dublin. The Irish Theatre, led by Edward Martyn, produced avant-garde plays in Dublin from 1914 until 1920, by European playwrights like Chekhov, Strindberg, and Ibsen, as well as the work of Irish playwrights such as Edward Martyn and Thomas MacDonagh. The theatre was an act of artistic commitment for Martyn, but that did not stop him from making it at least once a vehicle for revenge against his old collaborators in the Irish Literary Theatre. One of the Irish Theatre's first plays, *The Dream Physician* (1914), was a comedy by Edward Martyn mocking the theosophic beliefs of Yeats and George Moore's high modern airs (Eakin and Case 1995). A much smaller budget and lower production values made its performances rougher than those at the Abbey, but the stage did feature performers such as Maire Nic Shiubhlaigh, Una O'Connor, and Nell Byrne.[6]

While these amateur theatre events flourished, the Abbey continued to fight both a slow box office and the hostility of nationalists who were in disagreement with the Abbey's aesthetics or politics at home. And, as the Abbey found itself caught in real cross-fire during the Civil War, with city curfews curtailing profits to the point that in 1923 the bank refused to cash Abbey Theatre cheques, the challenges to maintain the theatre increased even more. Thanks to its perseverance, the theatre stayed open, and sought new voices for acting and writing for the stage. As the life of the nation was changing under crisis, so the theatre needed a new voice to reflect that crisis. And, even if it might not solve the crisis on the streets, perhaps it could assist in alleviating the crisis in the box office. The Abbey found that voice in Sean O'Casey.

O'Casey's Mirror up to War

On 12 April 1923, Sean O'Casey, a socialist and aspiring dramatist, received his first opening night at the Abbey with *The Shadow of a Gunman*. O'Casey was born in 1880 to a lower middle-class Protestant Dublin family. As a child, he nearly lost his eyesight to an infection common in the slum areas of Dublin where he lived, and his eyes would trouble him for the rest of his life. Considering the clash between O'Casey's intellectual curiosity and the class prejudices that kept him from pursuing them, it is not surprising that he became a socialist in his teens, or that his involvement in the nationalist movement leant not towards the romantic nationalist politics of the Irish Republican Volunteers, but Connolly's

Irish Citizen Army. He responded to his impressions of Irish culture and politics through performance, helping found an amateur theatre company in Dublin.

His work with this theatre led to an interest in playwriting, and in 1919 he offered his first play to the Abbey Theatre. The early plays he submitted – *The Harvest Festival, The Crimson in the Tricolour, Profit and Loss*, and *The Frost in Flower* – were not accepted; but feedback on his work, especially that provided by Lady Gregory, inspired O'Casey to continue with his writing (Welch 1999: 83), and that encouragement led to his submission of *The Shadow of a Gunman* in 1923 – a play that ultimately would reshape the aesthetics of the Irish stage. In *The Shadow of a Gunman*, O'Casey offered the Abbey audience an acerbic look at Dublin during the war for independence; but what stirred its audiences the most was its brave look at the impact of the war for independence not only on the nation, but on the everyday lives of Dublin's working class. O'Casey was not the first Irish dramatist to explore urban tenement life, or the impact of violence on its inhabitants. Seumas O'Kelly's plays, like *The Shuiler's Child* (1904), and Padraic Colum's *The Saxon Shillin'* (1903), had already exposed audiences to city life two decades before, as did more recent plays by playwrights such as Terence MacSwiney and Kennneth Sarr.[7] But O'Casey's *The Shadow of a Gunman* and his future plays captured better than those of his predecessors the inherent contradictions between ideology and experience, rhetoric and reality, in wartime; and they did so with a dark humour that revealed how he saw class and religion instilling their own kinds of violence in Dublin's working class. The Cork realists may have approached social issues by looking back at Ibsen. O'Casey's play looked forward to Brecht.

This difference in approach is most apparent, as mentioned above, in O'Casey's choice of setting. Instead of the peasant cottage of the rural west, which had become an iconic space in Irish theatre by this time, O'Casey sets his play in a Dublin tenement. Dublin tenements in the early twentieth century were made up of formerly stately townhouses that had been given up by their original, upmarket clientele, and taken over by dozens of individuals and families. Kevin C. Kearns noted that, in the 1920s, 'Dublin's overall density of 38.5 persons per acre was nearly twice that of the twenty largest cities in Great Britain . . . In the worst tenement localities there were 800 people per acre and as many as a hundred occupants in a single house. Here it was common to find fifteen to twenty persons in one room and eight sleeping in a bed' (Kearns 2000: 12). The Abbey Theatre, by the way, was a mere stone's throw from some of the most notorious tenements in Dublin. The tenement setting enabled O'Casey to focus not just on a small nuclear family, but to represent a social network made out of individuals with a range of backgrounds, ideologies, and levels of poverty – allowing for more complicated societal arguments from the characters. Ultimately, O'Casey's setting, and the response to the setting by the characters who inhabit it, expose the playwright's opinion of the rift between the ideals of nationalism and the pragmatics of need.

Set in 1920, during the war for independence, the play opens on a room in a tenement house shared by Donal Davoren, a struggling thirty-year-old poet, and his friend Seumas Shields, a pedlar. The men's (especially Davoren's) relative youth, independence, and appearance of education cause their neighbours to admire them and offer them a deference they do not necessarily deserve. This is especially the case for the pretty and idealistic Minnie Powell, an orphaned young woman who falls in love with Donal when he allows her to assume that he is in fact a member of the Irish Republican Army. While Seumas berates Donal for allowing Minnie to think so, Donal replies, 'But Minnie is attracted to the idea, and I am attracted to Minnie. And what danger can there be in the shadow of a gunman?' (O'Casey [1923] 1998b: 32).

Donal may think playing the shadow of a gunman to please a young woman is harmless flirtation, but the shadow of a real gunman – a bag of bombs left in Donal's and Seumas's room by a real IRA man – has dire consequences. The men discover the bag just as the house is about to be raided by the Black and Tans, an auxiliary army fighting for the British in Ireland during the War for Independence. If caught with the bag, Donal and Seumas will be shot. Minnie, a 'woman of action', immediately takes the bag to her room. She is arrested by the soldiers and taken away in a truck, and then shot in the street during an ambush by the IRA.

Minnie's death occurs offstage, while we witness Donal, Seumas, and other residents of the tenement huddling in the house, listening to the gunfire outside, then to the report of her death from passers-by. Donal immediately responds to the news with a speech bemoaning Minnie's fate and his own cowardice: 'Ah me, alas! Pain, pain, pain ever, for ever! It's terrible to think that little Minnie is dead, but still more terrible to think that Shields and Davoren are alive! O Donal Davoren, shame is your portion now till the silver cord is loosened and the golden bowl be broken. Oh, Davoren, Donal Davoren, poet and poltroon, poltroon and poet!' (62). While ending a play about a martyr with a keen by the survivor closest to that character goes back as far as Lady Gregory's *The Gaol Gate* (1906) and Synge's *Riders to the Sea* (1907), O'Casey sets this traditional ending askew. First, instead of a woman bemoaning the fate of a male martyr, here it is a man keening for a woman. Second, the keen is designed to praise the martyr and further the story of his death and, consequently, his beliefs. Donal's keen is empty of political rhetoric, and quickly turns from mourning Minnie to Donal's narcissistic grief over his failure to act. The man who left the bag of bombs in Donal's and Seumas's room may have been a committed soldier who died for a national cause, but O'Casey shows Minnie's death as personally heroic in its selfless attempt to rescue the lives of her two friends, but politically futile.

The Shadow of a Gunman was an immediate success, and the Abbey had its first sold-out houses in years. Audiences and critics were glad to see Frank McCormick returned to Dublin from Hollywood and playing the leading role of Seumas Shields, and, while there were quibbles about the plot, critics also praised the realism of the piece, and O'Casey's ability to capture the sense of disillusionment instilled by the war for independence and the Civil War. P.S. O'Hegarty wrote in *The Irish Statesman*:

> It is a gramophone record of the Dublin accent and the Dublin tenement and the Dublin poor, all illumined by the Terror and sharpened and defined by it. It is not the whole terror, I agree, because it does not give, and does not attempt to give, the heroic side of it, the way life felt to the men on the run and to those who helped them. But it does give what life looked like to the common people of Dublin, between the devil of the Auxiliary's pistol and incendiary bomb and the deep sea of the Irish Volunteer's home-made bomb. That is why it draws a crowd. It tells everybody what they thought while the two armies shot up each other and made their life hideous for people who wanted to go about their business or live a normal human life. It gets back at the heroes. It is a play of disillusion for people who have been disillusioned, and can take their disillusionment without bitterness. (Hogan and Burnham 1992: 147)

O'Hegarty's review marks the tremendous change in attitude about both revolution and representation that one would find in Dublin during these last months of the Irish Civil War. The realism of the drama drew in audiences, aware that tenement houses like the one on the stage were literally a stone's throw away from the theatre in which they sat. Likewise, the play's tight plot construction and use of significant props (the bag of bombs, a piece of paper with Minnie's and Donal's names on it) were perfect for the Abbey stage and the actors on it. It is also noteworthy that

the theatergoers were not afraid to take a critical look at the diurnal violence in the streets during the war for independence, even while similar
violence was under way as part of the Civil War.

The experience of seeing the first production of O'Casey's play in a
theatre in the heart of a still war-battered city must have been uncanny.
By 1923, Dubliners were ready to critique the wars of revolution they
had undergone. Few Irish had been left untouched by these years of
civil unrest, and this difficult separation from the century-long, forced
relationship with England in the United Kingdom. Like the Dubliners
in the audience, the Abbey actors had endured the threats and trials of
urban warfare while going about their business for years. The theatre
had even had a bullet shot through a window of its café. The Abbey
stage, an artistic centre for Irish theatre set in the physical heart of the
city centre, mere blocks from the General Post Office where the Irish
Republic was declared in 1916, as well near the slums in which O'Casey's
play was set, was the perfect site for such an exploration. To use
twenty-first-century performance terms, it was practically site-specific
performance.

Few modern theatre performances blur so thoroughly the line between
the events onstage and those immediately outside the theatre. Lady
Gregory noted that, during the final rehearsal of O'Casey's play, an IRA
soldier was helping an actor playing a 'Black and Tan' with his uniform
and showing him how to hold his gun. Likewise, soldiers ducked into
the theatre to attend performances while on duty, leaving their guns at
the box office. These anecdotes reflect the fine line between military and
civilian experience in Dublin at the time, showing to what extent the
war was part of civilians' everyday life. In this kind of atmosphere, the
Abbey stage became a liminal space where the inner and outer frames
of performance collapsed. The Abbey audience watched characters living
through, and dying in, a war that surrounded their homes, while they
were sitting inside a theatre that was itself in the heart of a guerrilla
war zone.

Ironically, while the performance of the play mirrored for its first audiences the immediacy of military violence within Dublin, the play itself
challenges the glorification of war as a kind of romantic theatre by showing
the absurdity of such a stance, as well as the real costs of military struggle.
The Shadow of a Gunman deftly explores the theatricality of war, as the
characters perform their varying degrees of patriotism, bravery, and
romanticism against the background of the very real violence in the streets.
Donal, a writer who often quotes the romantic poet, Percy Bysshe Shelley

(not, it should be noted, Irish revolutionary romantics), is happy to take on the cloak of intrigue connected to being an IRA man in order to impress a girl. The woman whom he is trying to impress, however, loses her own life by being caught up in the romance of Donal's ruse, when she takes real action against a real threat to protect a man who is only pretending to be politically involved. As P.S. O'Hegarty remarks, this is not the heroic side of war, but the side of pride and desire for personal gain that leads to futile sacrifices. While Minnie dies in the street, Donal is as trapped in his head as he is in the tenement. The characters' working-class status allowed the Abbey's audience not to take the message of the play too personally, and to distance themselves to some degree from the characters' oversimplified and ultimately tragic response to the real violence surrounding them. However, O'Casey would make such a stance more difficult in his later plays, in which the critique of Dublin's capitalist class structure became more overt.

In 1924, O'Casey followed up the success of *The Shadow of a Gunman* with his most famous play, and perhaps the most famous play in the Irish dramatic canon, *Juno and the Paycock*. Set in a Dublin tenement in 1922, during the Civil War, the play swerves from farce, to black comedy, to tragedy in its telling the story of Juno Boyle, the matriarch of a working-class family living in the Dublin tenements, and her struggle to keep her family together as it is torn apart not only by the Civil War, but also by the stresses of a workers' strike, alcoholism, claustrophobic living conditions, religious hypocrisy, and middle-class pretence.

The play opens on a two-room tenancy, in which Juno, 'Captain' Jack Boyle, and their two grown children eke out a living amid the chaos of the Civil War. O'Casey presents Captain Boyle very much in the stereotypical style of the stage Irishman. He is a braggart who drinks too much, shuns work, and runs around town with a parasitic sidekick, Joxer Daly, a man willing to listen to Boyle's stories as long as his buddy is buying the drinks. The Boyles' two children reflect the ideological movements that, in O'Casey's eyes, helped shape their generation. Mary is a factory worker and faithful member of the union, who reads Ibsen. Her brother, Johnny, followed the path of the nationalist movement as a soldier for the die-hards. He took a shot to the hip in the Easter Rebellion and lost his arm in the war for independence. But during the Civil War he has become blacklisted by his fellow comrades since he informed on a fellow soldier and neighbour from the tenement, who was executed by the Free Staters based on Johnny's information. The family is oblivious to Johnny's situation, although he spends much of the play in a state of terror, hiding in the back room of the tenement, and constantly checking that the candle under the picture of the statue of the sacred heart remains lit. Juno, the centre of the family, and of the play, constantly struggles to keep the home and family together, despite the fact that no one in the house is bringing in wages.

While Boyle and Joxer offer vaudevillian comic bits in the first Act, Juno's exasperation and exhaustion offer a counterpoint. For instance, when Johnny boasts of his wounds in the wars for Irish freedom, 'I'd do it agen ma; I'd do it agen; for a priniple's a principle', Juno replies, 'Ah, you lost your best principle, me boy, when you lost your arm; them's the only sort o' principles that's any good to a workin' man' (O'Casey [1924] 1998a: 31). Juno's suspicion of idealism and sacrifice is rooted in her own experiences of poverty: and those experiences of working-class deprivation likewise lead her to be too deferent to those with more money or education than she.

This becomes apparent at the end of Act I when Charles Bentham, a schoolteacher, arrives to inform the family that they have inherited a small fortune from a distant cousin. Without the stresses of poverty, the family dynamic automatically falls into one of middle-class, patriarchal authority, with the head of the household assuming his position as the moral head of the family, giving up drink and Joxer for bourgeois respectability. No longer expected to do manual labour, Boyle takes on the persona of a sober paterfamilias. Juno moves from goading her husband to work to deferring to his wishes. Johnny sees the money as an opportunity to escape the tenement and the war, and Mary quickly forgets her commitment to the workers' strike. The Act ends with a kind of tableau, as Boyle takes Juno's hand and declares melodramatically that 'I'm a new man from this out' (35). If O'Casey were writing a popular Victorian temperance drama,[8] this would be the end of the play. But while O'Casey loved the popular stage, he offers no melodramatic happy ending. Instead, the Boyles' economic windfall exposes the inherent hypocrisies in a capitalist system that equates economic security with morality and, by the conclusion of the play, it also illustrates the social and cultural as well as economic impediments to class mobility.

In Act II the stage moves from showing a kind of Ibsenesque realism of working-class life to a farce of middle-class pretence. After only two days, the Boyles have filled their house with furniture *'of a vulgar nature'* (36), and huge ornamentations like vases and photographs, all bought on credit. There is room for little more, yet Juno finds room for the *pièce de resistance*, a gramophone. Soon, the Boyles are hosting a party with neighbours, and with Bentham, whom we learn is now courting Mary, to her parents' delight. Mary has abandoned her previous suitor, Jerry, a union leader.

The party stops abruptly when Juno hears Mrs Tancred, the mother of the young man Johnny informed against, coming down the stairs of the tenement to bring her dead son's body to the church. Mrs Tancred enters the apartment, grieving the death of her only child. A neighbour tries to comfort her, remarking that 'he died a noble death, an' we'll bury him like a king,' to which Mrs Tancred replies, 'An' I'll go on livin' like a pauper. Ah, what's the pains I suffered bringin' him into the world to carry him to his cradle, to the pains I'm sufferin' now, carryin' him out o' the world to bring him to his grave!' (53). Once Mrs Tancred leaves, however, the party quickly returns to its comic joviality until most of the group head to the street to watch Tancred's funeral procession, leaving Johnny alone in the house.

At this point, a young man enters and orders Johnny to attend a Battalion Staff meeting. Johnny knows that to attend the meeting is to attend his own execution, but when he pleads with the soldier, 'Haven't I done enough for Ireland?', the young soldier replies, 'Boyle, no man can do enough for Ireland!' (59). The two unexpected guests, Mrs Tancred and the soldier, play important roles in the Act that echo one of the first classics of the Irish dramatic movement, *Cathleen ni Houlihan*. Both characters, like Cathleen, are agents in the war for Irish freedom, who enter a festive household to call its inhabitants into the public sphere to become involved in the national struggle. Mrs Tancred, however, is a poor old woman who does not call the Irish to fight, but to grieve for those who have fought. The soldier, on the other hand, is a soldier demanding blood sacrifice, but instead of being 'remembered for ever', like the men who follow Cathleen ni Houlihan in the Irish legend, Johnny's will be the anonymous death of a traitor to his comrade.

In the third Act, the tenement flat, like the Boyles' dreams of middle-class respectability, deconstructs before the audience's eyes. It is discovered that, since Bentham wrote in the will that the inheritance should go to the deceased's cousin, meaning Boyle, but did not mention Boyle by name, dozens of relatives claiming to be cousins had contested the will, and any inheritance was going to be absorbed in solicitors' fees. The breakdown of the family dream is echoed in the breakdown of their home, as first odds and ends, and then larger items, begin to be repossessed. At one point, men are in the flat to take away the furniture – the last remnants of the Boyle spending spree – when two Irregulars enter and drag Johnny away to be executed for informing on Tancred. The repo-men put their hands up and put their faces to the wall, while the Irregulars repossess their disgraced comrade with the same business-like acumen. The curtain then closes and rises again on an almost-empty stage (most of the furniture has now been removed), with Mary and Juno huddled together onstage waiting for word of the disappeared Johnny. When they learn that he has indeed been executed by the Irregulars, Juno begins her keen for her child in a speech that echoes Mrs Tancred's grief for her own son in Act II, and that becomes ultimately a call for reconciliation among Diehards and Free Staters, rather than a traditional celebration of the soldier's sacrifice for Ireland.

After Juno and Mary exit the stage, there is a proto-Beckettian pause before a drunken Boyle and Joxer stumble into the flat, mumbling random verses of war songs and nationalist rhetoric, too intoxicated to be aware that the Boyle home is empty of its usual material and human inhabitants. By removing almost all signs of the family from the space, O'Casey in a sense deconstructs both the set and the national and class ideologies that set represented for its audience. For over twenty years, Irish audiences had learned to read the domestic stage setting, and the family inhabiting the space, as metaphorical of the Irish nation and its people. In Yeats and Gregory's *Cathleeen ni Houlihan*, the curtain closes on a family who has learned that the sacrifice of their son has resurrected the spirit of Ireland. In Synge's *Riders to the Sea*, a mother comes to terms with the grief and hardships to come as she realizes that she has lost her last son to the waves, accepting her tragic fate. O'Casey sees no opportunity for redemption in the mistakes and sacrifices made by the Boyle family. Johnny's death is grieved, but goes unnoticed by most of the community. Instead of a keen or a final word of wisdom, the drunken men are unaware of the domestic devastations around them. Instead of redemption, the curtain falls on Boyle declaring, 'I'm telling you . . . Joxer . . . th' whole worl's . . . in a terr . . . ible state o' . . . chassis!' (86).

The work O'Casey was offering the Abbey differed surprisingly from the other kinds of theatre in the repertoire during these years. The great realists that had come to the Abbey in the 1910s, like Robinson, Murray, Ervine, and Mayne, continued to offer new plays in the repertory. But the only other major drama at the Abbey to confront the Civil War head on was Lennox Robinson's 1926 play, *The Big House*.

Set at a country estate during the Civil War, *The Big House: Four Scenes in its Life* considers an Anglo-Irish family trying to determine their social space in the Irish Free State. The head of the family, St Leger Alcock, and

his English wife try to hold on to the traditions of their class – a combi-
nation of entitlement and *noblesse oblige* that keeps them on the periphery
of the larger community. Alcock is a second son who became the reluctant and timid head of the estate (he has not taken the key to the wine
cellar away from his butler, Atkins, even though he has drunk all the best
wine) when his brother broke his neck riding his horse. Mrs Alcock finds
her life, and the Irish persons around her, absurd. Exasperated by having
to accept a local visitor, and by her drunken butler, Mrs Alcock
remarks:

> I'm a Hampshire woman, a respectable Hampshire woman, in exile, with
> a drunken Irish butler, and now I've got to go and talk to a 'lad of the
> O'Flynns.' Even after living here for twenty years I won't understand half
> of what he says. I suppose he wants a bottle of medicine for his old grand-
> mother, or he wants to sell me a rabbit he's poached a hundred yards from
> our own front-door. (*Half vexed, half amused, she goes out.*) (Robinson [1926]
> 1982a: 149)

Their adult daughter, Katie, works hard to integrate herself as an equal in
the community but is frustrated by her failure to bridge the 'them' and 'us'
feeling' (167) that makes her tolerated but never truly accepted. Her sense
of otherness is confirmed when she learns that a servant she felt would
confide in her has in fact 'betrayed' the family by aiding the IRA, and giving
them access to the house so they can burn it down.

Like O'Casey, Robinson treats his setting of the space symbolically,
almost giving it the status of a character in the play. The big house, like
the tenement, was identified with a demographic in Irish culture very different from that of the rural peasant cottage.[9] Christopher Murray has
remarked that 'Just as O'Casey was writing of the destruction of the tenement community through the 1916 rebellion, the Black-and-Tan campaign
of 1920 and the Civil War of 1922–3, in his three great Dublin plays, so
Robinson was truthfully recording the assault on a Protestant segment of
Irish society which took place about the same time' (Murray 1982: 17). In
the first scene, set on Armistice Day in 1918, the family learns that Ulick,
the oldest son, has died fighting in the war. The second scene moves to
1921, and we see the family trying to hold on to its position, but considering moving to England. In the third scene, set in 1923, they are burned out
of their home by the IRA, who are tipped off by a maid who has been with
the family for years. And in the fourth scene, set the day after scene three,
Katie decides to stay in Ireland despite the destruction of her physical
home, and find a new role and identity for herself while contributing to
the building of the new nation. As the last image of the play, Katie, alone

in the garden of her burned-out ancestral home, senses the ghost of her dead brother and, feeling his approval of her decision, '*she raises her face as if she is being kissed*' (198). Robinson's play shows sympathy for the landed Anglo-Irish that is surprising for a theatre that often downplayed its Anglo-Irish roots. The drama asks its audience to sympathize with this family who, despite their legacy of class privilege, feels misunderstood by their neighbours, and betrayed by their servants, but cannot imagine another kind of home.

National Theatre Becomes 'National Asset'

O'Casey's plays, with their immediate response to history within Ireland and their ensuing international acclaim; the solid dramatic work of realists like Shiels, Robinson, and Murray; the peasant dramas and translations of classic plays into an Irish idiom by Lady Gregory; and the avant-garde experiments of Yeats cemented the reputation of the Abbey as a site for nation-building which it had been cultivating for over twenty years. And in 1925, the year of the INTS's 'coming of age', the Cumann na nGaedheal government acknowledged the Abbey's potential to serve the new state by granting it an annual subsidy of £850. The directors had spent a great deal of energy negotiating with the new government about the Abbey's potential role in the new nation; and had previously been turned down. Yet, as Lionel Pilkington asserts, by 1925 the Cumann na nGaedheal government recognized that the Abbey had supported its policies and points of view both publicly and via their choices of plays, which tended to be critical of anti-treaty activities, and could serve the new state.

In terms of cultural identity, the Abbey was useful to the new government. Its Anglo-Irish directorate lent an image of unity to the new nation-state; yet, at the same time, the Abbey had incorporated performances by An Comhar Dramuiochta, an Irish language theatre group, into the Abbey repertoire, thus aiding the new government's mission towards de-Anglicization.[10] Two years later, the government raised the theatre's subsidy to £1,000, and the Abbey was able to pay its actors a salary year-round for the first time in its history.

Of course, a new patron also meant new strings. When Annie Horniman agreed to subsidize the Abbey in 1904, she insisted on a policy of 'no politics'. Now that the national government was its main contributor, state politics would factor into Abbey decisions. Some of the expectations of the subsidy were dealt with proactively by Gregory, Yeats, and

Robinson. In his proposal for support, for example, Robinson wrote that the Abbey directors 'would give special performances on such occasions as the government would require' (Hogan and Burnham 1992: 98). And, when they received the funds, they were public and effusive in their thanks. In fact, when the subsidy was announced on 8 August 1925, Yeats wished to give a public thanks from the stage to Ernest Blythe, Ireland's Director of Finance, followed by supper for Blythe and his wife onstage (Welch 1999: 93–4). But the Abbey was now part of the Irish Free State bureaucracy, and would ultimately find it even more difficult to evade the government's requests – especially with a government representative on the Abbey board – than it had ignoring Annie Horniman's angry letters from Manchester. And, as the government was growing increasingly anxious about representations of morality and sexuality, concerns about the Abbey repertoire popped up almost immediately. Robert Welch notes:

> O'Brien's nervousness manifested itself immediately over Robinson's next play at the Abbbey, *The White Blackbird* (12 October 1925), when it was considered by the Board of directors. In the play William, played by F.J. McCormick, expresses an inclination to marry his half-sister Bella, the liveliest of his mother's second family, the Naynoes. The play also features a prostitute who unsuccessfully tries to seduce this kindly but timorous young man. O'Brien took advice about its content from legal friends of his at the Kingstown Club, a move which outraged Robinson. Eventually O'Brien agreed to allow the play to go on, for fear of raising suspiscions of over-zealous government interference at so early a stage in the new arrangements. (1999: 94)

In less than a year, the Abbey's state-subsidized identity would receive a true test with the opening of O'Casey's *The Plough and the Stars* (1926), mere months after the tenth anniversary of the Easter Rebellion. While *The Shadow of a Gunman* bravely examined the effects of war on Dublin's poor while the country was still at war, the critique of the war came out of the mouths of broadly drawn sons and daughters of tenement life. *Juno* went further in its war critique by including representatives of life beyond the tenement, like the middle-class English Bentham, the upwardly mobile union leader Jerry Devine, and even Irish nationalist soldiers. Yet reviews were positive, due in large part to the excellent performances by Sara Allgood and Barry Fitzgerald as Juno and Jack; and Eileen Crowe and F.J. McCormick as Mary and Joxer. However, in O'Casey's third play, many in the audience would determine that his critique of the nation had gone too far.

First, O'Casey set this drama during Easter 1916, the sacred start of the twentieth-century military fight for independence. Ten years after the event the insurgency and its leaders were held in near-saintly reverence by much of the population, so for O'Casey to challenge the righteousness of their struggle was daring indeed. Also, while O'Casey returned to a tenement flat as his main setting, he also took the play into the streets of Dublin amid the fighting, and showed a much larger ideological array of characters, including Irish Citizen Army and British soldiers, a socialist, an Anglo-Irish alcoholic woman with a son fighting in Europe, a young woman opposed to her husband's involvement in the Rebellion, a consumptive girl, a prostitute, and an unnamed speaker, who remains offstage and is called 'Figure in the Window', but is obviously the leader of the Rebellion, Padraic Pearse.

While O'Casey does not attack the idea of independence from England, he does challenge the way the Rebellion went about it, with a rhetoric of blood sacrifice that O'Casey believed played on masculinist and class anxieties among many of the soldiers involved. This opinion is illustrated best through the central couple in the play, Jack and Nora Clitheroe. Nora is an energetic woman who wants to create a secure life for her family, although her spending and middle-class tastes lead to animosity against her among other women in the tenement, who feel she is too full of 'notions of upperosity' (O'Casey [1926] 1998c: 67), especially when she asks to have a lock put on her door, thus separating herself physically as well as socially from her neighbours.

Her husband, Jack, is a bricklayer by trade, but also a soldier in the Irish Citizen Army. O'Casey describes him as '*a tall well-made fellow*' whose face '*has none of the strength of Nora's. It is a face in which is the desire for authority, without the power to attain it*' (81). Although Nora seems the weaker figure in her desperate attempts to keep her husband from going to battle, she voices O'Casey's opinion that most of the soldiers of the Easter Rebellion fought out of fear of appearing cowards rather than love for Ireland.

Another strong female figure in the play is Bessie Burgess, a Protestant tenant of the tenement, whose son is fighting in Europe as part of the British army. She mocks the soldiers ruthlessly during the battle, and is quick to join in the looting of shops amid the chaos of the war, but takes Nora into her home when she returns hysterical from the battle lines where she tried to find her husband and miscarries her pregnancy. Bessie dies from a sniper's bullet while pulling the delirious Nora away from a window. Again, O'Casey presents the women in the play as pragmatists who make calculated choices and sacrifices in response to the war, while the men ultimately fight out of fear. When Mrs Gogan remarks that the soldiers are not cowards, Nora replies:

> (*with denunciatory anger*) I tell you they're afraid to say they're afraid! . . . Oh, I saw it, I saw it, Mrs Gogan glowin' in all their eyes . . . An' in the middle o' the sthreet was something' nuddled up in a horrible, tangled heap . . . His face was jammed again th'stones, an' his arm was twisted around his back . . . An' every twist of his body was a cry against th' terrible thing that had happened to him . . . An' I saw they were afraid to look at it . . . An' some o' them laughed at me, but th' laugh was a frightened one . . . An' some o' them shouted at me, but th' shout had in it th' shiver o' fear . . . I tell you they were afraid, afraid, afraid! (123)

O'Casey's most theatrical illustration of the divide between the rhetoric of war and the experience of war appeared in Act II, in which O'Casey juxtaposes a political rally and conversation inside a pub. The Act begins with a prostitute, Rosie Redmond, complaining that the rally is bad for her business. 'You'd think they were th' glorious company of the saints, an' th' noble army of martyrs thrampin' through th' streets of paradise. They're all thinkin' of higher things than a girl's garthers' (96). Slowly, different characters wander into the pub while, from a window, one can see the profile of 'the speaker', and hear his words rallying the crowd. The speaker can be heard delivering famous lines from speeches by Padraic Pearse, the leader of the Rebellion. Throughout the Act O'Casey juxtaposes the rhetoric of blood sacrifice spoken at the rally outside the pub to the earthier conversations inside the pub; and there is a weird clash between the two rhetorics when Jack Clitheroe and two other soldiers enter the pub carrying the Plough and the Stars (a socialist flag) and the Irish tricolour. O'Casey describes them as '*in a state of emotional excitement. Their faces are flushed and their eyes sparkle; they speak rapidly, as if unaware of the meaning of what they said. They have been mesmerized by the fervency of the speeches*' (114). They drink, vowing to die for the independence of Ireland, then rush out again when a bugle blows the Assembly. The scene ends with Rosie and Fluther leaving the pub together at the same time that the army begins to mobilize.

The first audiences to see *The Plough and the Stars* approved of the drama but, within a week, the Abbey confronted a public controversy over the representation of the soldiers of 1916, led by women who had high credentials as being related to heroes of the Uprising (or having fought in the Uprising itself).[11] *The Irish Times* reported that: 'When the lights went up at the end of the second act everyone could see many women who are prominently identified with Republican demonstrations in the city. Shocking epithets were hurled at Miss Ria Mooney while she played Rosie Redmond in pantomime, but the wrath of the interrupters was for the most part directed against the political significance of the play, its brutal exposition of what took place in the homes of the rank and file of the Citizen Army, while the leaders were making speeches about freedom in the abstract' (Hogan and Burnham 1992: 295).

By the start of the third Act, when Nora remarks that the soldiers are fighting not for love of country, but for fear of being called cowards, around a dozen women stormed the stage, and chaos ensued. The curtain was lowered, the crowd cleared, and Yeats took the stage, accusing the audience of shaming itself, and calling O'Casey the new J.M. Synge. By the time Yeats finished his speech the police had entered the building and the disturbance had died down to several women who continued protests from the audience, until removed by the police.

This 'women's row', as the *Irish Times* called it, was dismissed as feminine hysterics by many. Since one of their main criticisms of the drama was the presence of a prostitute in the play (despite the large number of Dublin prostitutes working the streets around the theatre even as the play was being produced), and the tricolour being dragged into the pub in Act II, it was easy to dismiss their protest as the 'hysterics' of overly pious Republican women. The demonstrators, however, saw their protest as a performance intervention. As citizens of the Irish Free State, they did not want to see the makers of Irish independence recorded this way on the national stage: 'The Free State Government is subsidizing the Abbey to malign Pearse and Connolly,' Hanna Sheehy-Skeffington declared during the protest. 'We have not come here as rowdies. We came here to make a protest against the defamation of the men of Easter Week' (Hogan and Burnham 1992: 300). In this, the tenth anniversary of the Uprising, the protest called for some kind of more respectful memory of the revolution and its leaders, rather than the parody of 'the speaker' in Act II, or the characterization by Nora in the play that the soldiers are merely vain cowards, appearing on the national stage as the only version of the story. Hearkening back to the riots surrounding *The Playboy of the Western World*, it was not just the message, but the messenger.

Likewise, the protesters were frustrated by the representations of women in the play, as they were reduced to sexual beings designed to shock the pious sensibilities of Catholic conservatives, or stereotypes that essentialized women as wives or mothers. As keeper of the family hearth, Nora, like Juno, is a protector of the domestic sphere who is forced to abandon that space due to the deforming pressures of war and poverty. Like a Victorian 'true woman', her power lies in her place as wife and mother, and her actions are driven not by ideology or intellect, but by a desire to maintain the family unit. This reduction of woman to womb was oddly exploited as well as protested by the 'widows and mothers' of 1916, but its protest reflected growing concerns among many women in Ireland about the way they were being pushed out of public life in the increasingly conservative Irish Free State.[12]

In a letter to the *Irish Independent*, Sheehy-Skeffington remarked that 'the outrage was directed against a "supposedly national theatre" that had "helped to make Easter Week, and that now in its subsidized, sleek old age jeers at its former enthusiasms"' (Murray 2004: 176). Less than a year after receiving the subsidy, the Abbey had already been identified as a site for constructing not only imaginings of what the nation might be, but authoritative records of its past and present. Just as the *Playboy* riots howled at the offence of what were read as negative stereotypes appearing on a nationalist stage with international press, so Sheehy-Skeffington and the other protesters expressed their frustration that the most visible state remembrance of the Rising was a critique of its ideological failures on the national stage. O'Casey's plays were a mirror up to war: the protesters feared that it would become not just a mirror, but a record.

O'Casey and the Abbey ultimately gained great cultural capital from the controversy surrounding *The Plough and the Stars*; for the event helped move the aesthetic of Ireland's main theatre more firmly into the ideological mainstream. In the coming years, the Abbey would take fewer and fewer risks with its repertoire. In 1928, it turned down O'Casey's expressionist drama about the First World War, *The Silver Tassie*. This naturally shocked O'Casey, who had assumed the Abbey would embrace his play despite its non-Irish subject. After all, the Macmillan Press had already agreed to publish it. O'Casey was so certain of its production, in fact, that he had already written to Lennox Robinson with suggestions for casting the play.[13] O'Casey was so offended by Yeats's remarks on his drama that he made the rejection letters public. And a year later, when the Abbey rejected his next play, *The Red Petticoat*, O'Casey wrote Robinson a letter that signified not only his personal outrage at the offence, but his knowledge that bureaucracy was now running the show: 'You are a rotten national theatre though, aren't you, in so far as concerns the encouraging of new talent? . . . God blast you all! When I am minister of education I'll have your subsidy cancelled!'[14]

On the Abbey main stage, the high ambition and freedom to experiment dreamed of in 1896 had been compromised by the responsibilities of a subsidized national theatre. However, the Abbey continued to take advantage of its position to create opportunities for more radical work, most importantly, opening the Peacock Stage, a small stage for experimental performance, in 1927. This space offered a platform for performances by students of the Abbey's new acting and dance schools, the Dublin Drama League, and other groups. For instance, it was the venue for a 1929 dance adaptation of Yeats's play, *The Only Jealousy of Emer* (1917). Retitled *Fighting the Waves*, the ballet was directed by Ninette de Valois, with music written for the piece by French composer Francis Poulenc. The Peacock Stage was the outlet for new possibilities in Dublin theatre in the late 1920s and, as we will see in the next chapter, it is from that outlet that a new generation of Irish theatre emerged.

4

New Voices of the 1930s and 1940s

The national theatre in Ireland sprang out of an indigenous cultural movement, nurtured and cultivated by Irish men and women with a range of backgrounds and ideologies. Once institutionalized through the Irish National Theatre Society, however, and given sponsorship by an official national government, the temper of the national theatre movement inevitably changed. Although the Abbey supported alternative dramaturgies by offering a stage space to groups like the amateur Dublin Drama League, and supporting the Abbey Schools of Acting and Ballet, Yeats's dream of a theatre inspired by the avant-garde aesthetics of the continent was receding in favour of a dramaturgy in the Abbey repertoire that served the more immediate needs of the new nation-state.

In the late 1920s, however, a new theatre company would offer Dublin the kinds of theatrical productions Yeats and Gregory had imagined years before. The Gate Theatre Dublin, founded by Micheál Mac Liammóir and Hilton Edwards, was the site for daring, experimental, cosmopolitan work in Ireland in the 1930s.[1] And while it owed a great debt to Yeats, it also carried the imprimatur of Beerbohm Tree, picking up the avant-garde thread professionally where the Abbey had let it drop. In its first decades, the Gate skyrocketed to international acclaim, and served as a springboard for playwrights, actors, and even other theatre companies. Still, as its leaders would agree, the Gate could not have achieved what it did without the existence of the Abbey to inspire its founders, to set a precedent for using the stage as a vehicle for national culture and, most importantly, to claim a kind of cultural responsibility as national theatre. Like a much older sibling, the Abbey had both an authority as national theatre and an accountability among the Irish people to hold up a particular ideal of national culture on its stage. Meanwhile, the Gate could play the role of the precocious younger sibling, free to experiment without the responsibilities and expectations placed on his older brother.[2]

This chapter examines the rise of new voices on the Irish stage in the 1930s and 1940s despite the encroaching conservatism of the Irish Free State. It begins with a discussion of the development of the Gate Theatre, followed by analysis of some distinctive playwrights who worked at the Abbey and other companies, and closes with a look at Irish theatre and its influence beyond Dublin. Among the diverse backgrounds and aesthetics of the artists and works discussed in this chapter, we see a common denominator of the stage being employed as a site to present experiences of dissent against the growing homogeneity of Irish life being promoted by the Fianna Fáil government. While much theatre of the period returned audiences to the iconic peasant cottage, some plays, like work by playwrights George Shiels and Teresa Deevy, entered that space with a difference, exposing the sexual repressions and social claustrophobia inherent for many in rural life. Yet other playwrights, like Mary Manning and Edward and Christina Longford, considered the upper-class Dublin drawing room with a style closer to Noel Coward than Lady Gregory. To explore the theatre of 1930s and 1940s Dublin and Belfast and its players, therefore, is to explore the presence of subcultures within the Irish Free State and Northern Ireland counter to the pastoral images promoted by their governments, and to see the foundations built for the international rise of Irish playwrights like Behan, Friel, Murphy, and Keane in the next generation.

Opening the Gate

The Gate Theatre was founded by Micheal Mac Liammóir and Hilton Edwards in 1928. In the ten years that followed, its founders introduced major Irish playwrights to the stage, worked with Irish and US actors, including Shelah Richards, Coralie Carmichael, Orson Welles and James Mason, and performed with their company internationally from Broadway to London to Cairo. Mac Liammóir wrote plays in Irish as well as English (a task Yeats could never do), and raised the bar for stage design and costume across the island. Edwards supported Mac Liammóir's talent with his own gifts in directing, lighting, and acting. He became notorious for the degree of discipline he demanded of the company for performance. What is surprising about these men's success in creating a second great Irish theatre company is that they accomplished their task with much praise and minimal controversy in ultramontane Catholic Dublin, despite being English and gay. While they did not advertise their 'true' nationality and sexuality – in fact, Mac

Liammóir constructed an autobiography for himself that had him born in Cork instead of London – they did not overtly deny or repress their difference either. They lived in the same home for decades. But their origins and status as 'outsiders' of the Irish status quo who chose Ireland as their personal and professional home ultimately served their theatre profoundly. Using the rubric of queer performance theory, one could argue, in fact, that Mac Liammóir's and Edwards's backgrounds 'queered' their theatre in a way that broke through the conservative aesthetics of most Irish theatre of the time to allow for a sensual and imaginative dramaturgy working simultaneously inside and outside Ireland's established dramaturgical frame.[3] The Gate performed Wilde's *Salome* and Yeats's *The Queen of the Great Clock Tower* in the 1930s with a finesse not yet seen on any Irish stage, for they captured the sensual tension of the works in a way that neither the Fay-influenced peasant realist nor the still-bodied 'art of staring into space' acting styles dominant across the island during this period could achieve.

Like his productions, Mac Liammóir's life was a beautiful invention. He was born in London to lower-middle-class parents, and named Alfred Willmore. He became a child actor – one of his first professional productions happened to be with another child actor at the time, Noel Coward – (Fitz-Simon 2002: 24) and at the age of eleven was hired by Sir Herbert Beerbohm Tree to play Macduff's son in *Macbeth*. From this production, he was cast as Michael Darling in Dion Boucicault Jr's incredibly popular production of J.M. Barrie's *Peter Pan*; and he performed the show in London and toured four months out of the year from 1911 to 1913 (Fitz-Simon 2002: 27). It was during these tours that Mac Liammóir would have seen Dublin for the first time. His childhood career also included the title role in *Oliver Twist* and a part in Tree's production of *Joseph and his Brethren*.

No child actor could have asked for better opportunities than MacLiammóir received in those days, working and touring with leading anglophone actors, such as Boucicault, Tree, and Mrs Patrick Campbell. It is also noteworthy that these experiences indirectly placed him within the sphere of Yeats, Shaw, Lady Gregory, and other great Irish theatre artists of the time, since the artists with whom he was working had close ties with the Irish stage; plus he had the support of his future brother-in-law, the English actor-manager Anew McMaster, who exposed him to a range of cultural events in London, including opportunities to see the Abbey players on tour.

When his voice broke, Mac Liammóir left the stage to pursue his interest in art, and enrolled in the Slade School, one of the most prestigious art schools in London at the time. But, at sixteen, he left the school to move to Ireland to live with Mary O'Keefe, a woman with whom he had developed a deep personal and spiritual friendship, and her mother; probably, Christopher Fitz-Simon suggests, to avoid being called into military service (41). Ireland was no exile for Mac Liammóir, however, whose interest in Irish culture had been burgeoning for some time. He was already learning Irish and signing his name with old Irish lettering while attending the Slade School. Despite a few contacts, Mac Liammóir only performed in a few theatrical and film productions in his first years in Ireland. Eventually, he joined McMaster and toured Ireland with his travelling theatre company. It was in Mcmaster's company, in 1927, that he met Hilton Edwards.

Like Mac Liammóir, Edwards was English. He was raised in London by his widowed mother, fought in the First World War, and more or less stumbled into acting in the early 1920s, performing bit parts and backstage work before his talent – especially his singing voice – caused him to stand out from the crowd. He worked steadily in Shakespearean comic roles at the Old Vic in London. When Edwards met Mac Liammóir on tour with Anew McMaster, however, he set his career path alongside him in Ireland. Edwards's gifts as a director, combined with his straightforward acting style, balanced out Mac Liammóir's more romantic inclinations on the stage, and they found a similar synergy in their personal lives. In 1928, they formed the Gate Theatre, named after Peter Godfrey's fringe theatre, the Gate Theatre, London, which had opened in 1925. Creating an amateur or semi-professional theatre company to produce avant-garde work in Dublin was not a new idea – the Dublin Drama League, the new Players, and the Jewish Dramatic Society, for example, had already established such companies – but no amateur group could boast the acting and design talent, and experience with work outside the realist vein that Mac Liammóir and Edwards possessed. Moreover, they were supported by extremely talented performers, including Coralie Carmichael, May Carey, and Fred Johnson.

Their first major production outside Anew McMaster's company was not a Gate production, but actually part of a very different project. They agreed to produce and star in Mac Liammóir's Irish language adaptation for the stage of the Diarmuid and Grannia myth, *Diarmuid agus Grainne* (1928), as the founding production for Galway's *An Taibhdheardhc* theatre, led by Liam O Briain. The production was well received, and Gate Theatre work in Dublin on the Abbey Theatre's Peacock Stage followed quickly on its heels.

The Gate's first production was *Peer Gynt*, was performed with a cast of forty-eight. Its abstract sets, including the use of black stairs akin to the design of Adolphe Appia, would become iconic on the Gate stage. This production was created with a shoestring budget on a stage 16 feet by 12 feet, before a house that sat only 102 persons. The other productions that season were an English translation of Mac Liammóir's *Diarmuid and Grainne*, and the first production in Ireland of Oscar Wilde's *Salome*, on a double bill with Evreinov's *Theatre of the Soul*. The production clearly did not fear Wilde's reputation nor the sexuality of *Salome*. Mac Liammóir recalled in his autobiography, *All For Hecuba*, 'in *Salome* we had a lovely set in black and silver and viperish green with the entire caste stripped almost naked . . . in a few elaborately painted head-dresses and loin-clothes'.[4] A waist-up photograph from the production shows a wild-eyed Coralie Carmichael, in the role of Salome, holding aloft the platter containing John the Baptist's head, and wearing only a sparkling sash around her breasts. Considering the furore *Salome* had created across Europe, and the accusations of immorality confronted by actresses taking on the role, this production does indeed prove that Dublin had an audience interested in challenging work and unafraid of seeing controversial performances onstage.[5] The Abbey had attempted similar kinds of scenography, and the screens for the theatre designed by Edward Gordon Craig still lurked in storage, but the sense of total *mise en scène* the Gate brought to the stage would inspire a general rise in interest and standards in the visual elements of the stage across Ireland. The Gate would make its true mark as an Irish theatre, however, when they debuted Dennis Johnston's expressionist play about post-revolutionary Ireland, *The Old Lady Says No!*

At the Abbey, but Not at the Abbey

The Peacock Theatre, the Abbey's experimental stage, was an ironic site for the debut of Johnston's play, because Johnston had been at work on the text since 1926 in hope of seeing it performed on the Abbey's main stage. Although trained as a barrister (he studied at Cambridge and Harvard), Johnston's heart belonged to the theatre, and he had been a denizen of the Dublin theatre scene throughout the 1920s. He acted and directed with several amateur groups, including the Dublin Drama League, Jewish Dramatic Society, and the New Players; and, in fact, was directing *King Lear* at the Abbey when his play was under consideration there. To please his family and maintain his professionalism as a barrister, however, his theatre work was accomplished under a stage name, E.W. Tocher. Gregory and Yeats took a great interest in Johnston, whom they hoped might take over as an Abbey manager when Lennox Robinson stepped down. Such attention would make any writer hopeful that his work would be looked on favourably by a theatre company. But the quality of his work was not apparent to the directors. Johnston had received some notes on the play from Yeats, who he felt did not understand the work, but he made Yeats's requested changes and resubmitted, only to have Yeats remain uninterested in the play. He recalled Yeats breaking the news to him while they walked together:

> We both seemed rather embarrassed as we walked a long way in silence. Finally he said 'I liked your play, but it has one or two faults. Firstly, the scenes I thought were too long.' He turned for a while and gazed at a coal boat in the Dalkey sound. 'Then,' he continued, 'there are too many scenes. If we put on this play we would annoy our audience and lose £50. We don't so much mind the £50, but we do not want to annoy our audience. So we're prepared to give you the £50 to put it on for yourself. (Adams 2002: 97)

Neither the play's ultimate success nor his future work with the Abbey could sweeten the bitter taste Yeats, Robinson, and Gregory's rejection left in his mouth. In his biography, Johnston recounts evidence of the directors' carelessness with his work, like a ring from a teacup being left on the first page; detailed quibbles about edits offered by Yeats; and even a recounting of a conversation he had with Lady Gregory as 'proof' that she did not read, or understand, the play (Johnston 1992: 60–2). So it is not surprising that, when he handed it to Edwards and Mac Liammóir, he had changed his original title, *Shadow Dance*, to a report to the world of Lady Gregory's rejection: *The Old Lady Says No!*

The Old Lady Says No! is a kind of dream play – an examination of Irish life in the late 1920s that deconstructs the central myths, figures, and texts that had been integral to the construction of early twentieth-century Irish cultural identity. The play is a brilliant pastiche of lines from melodrama, patriotic ballads, Irish classics, and street rhetoric. Like James Joyce's *Ulysses* and *Finnegans Wake* and, to a lesser extent, Sean O'Casey's *Plough and the Stars*, Johnston's play provokes its audience to engage with the cultural echoes of centuries of Irish writing and performance, and the way the legacy of language – from doggerel, to political speeches, to poetry – informs individual experience and perception of everyday Irish life.

The play begins as a clichéd melodrama about Robert Emmet, the hero of the Rebellion of 1803, and his love, Sarah Curran. The actor playing

Robert Emmet is called 'The Speaker' in the text, reminding the audience of the relationship between the actor onstage and the character being performed. Taking a page from Pirandello, Johnston gets the action of his drama started when an actor playing a British soldier meant to capture the Speaker accidentally hits him so hard that he passes out. The other actors onstage break character and call for a doctor (played by a plant in the audience) who goes on to the stage to offer aid. When the Speaker wakes up, however, the storyline shifts into the (unconscious) Speaker's dream world. In his dream state, the Speaker encounters such icons of Irish identity as Grattan's statue outside the gates of Trinity, parodies of artists and bureaucrats, a flower seller representing Cathleen ni Houlihan, and, finally, four shadows representing Ireland's great writers: Yeats, Shaw, Wilde, and Joyce.

The Old Lady Says No!'s rich and complicated text, with its floods of words, sounds, and imagery, ultimately celebrates Ireland's complex history and culture. But it also offers a sharp critique of the ways in which the Irish Free State replicated many of the prejudices and power structures in place before independence. By employing double casting, we see actors in part one with bit parts become very powerful characters or iconic figures in part two, the Speaker's dream. To comment on the power of nationalist iconography, the Speaker's love, Sarah Curran, in part one, becomes an old flower seller who evokes Cathleen ni Houlihan, the embodiment of the notion of Ireland as woman, in part two. To comment on military structures replicating themselves in neocolonial states, the British soldier in part one becomes, ironically, the General of the Irish Army in part two. And to remark on the rise of governmental bureaucracy, the stagehand of part one becomes the Minister of Arts and Crafts in part two.

Johnston does not pull punches in his critique of the manipulation of idealism and rhetoric in the face of moral complexity in 1920s Ireland through this play; but, ultimately, the drama ends in a hopeful mood for the future of the new nation. In the last speech of the play, the Speaker presents a poem of love for Dublin, the 'Strumpet city . . . Willful city of savage dreamers,/So old, so sick with memories!/ . . . But you, I know, will walk the streets of Paradise/Head high, and unashamed' (Johnston [1929] 1983a: 78). The Speaker then offers a benediction to his nation, as he pronounces, 'There now. Let my epitaph be written' (78). Before he was condemned to death, the historical figure Robert Emmet offered a speech from the dock, in which he proclaimed, 'When my country takes her place among the nations of the earth, then shall my character be vindicated, then may my epitaph be written.' The Speaker ending with these words points to the long-awaited establishment of an Irish state.

With no real plot, but a sophisticated intertextual design of literary and cultural quotes and allusions, *The Old Lady Says No!* is difficult for those unfamiliar with Irish cultural and literary life to follow, so it has rarely been performed outside Ireland. For many in its first audiences in Dublin, however, it was a radical departure from both the peasant realism dominant on the stage at the time and the more symbolic poetic drama more commonly adapted by the Irish avant-garde. And the marvellous acting and exciting use of lighting and movement by the theatre company on the Peacock's tiny stage offered the play its vitally important visual complement to Johnston's radical text. While a few found the drama 'blasphemous', *The Old Lady Says No!* was feted in Dublin, and established the Gate as a major force in the Dublin theatre scene. Within a year, the Gate was ready to move into its own theatre space, the Assembly room in the Rotunda at the top of O'Connell Street, less than a kilometre from the Abbey, where the theatre company is housed to this day.

Johnston's next play, *The Moon in the Yellow River* (1931), chose a still experimental, yet different, approach to discussing life in the Irish Free State. It was produced by the Abbey in 1931 and, although it received poor reviews in Ireland, it was performed internationally and ultimately gained a strong reputation. The New York Theatre Guild, one of the most respected avant-garde theatres in the world at the time, asked for the rights to the play in 1932 (Adams 2002: 117). This almost Shavian drama tells of a German engineer who has come to Ireland to build a power plant, only to have the plant destroyed by an Irish 'secret society' that the entire community knows about. In this talky play, we discover that even the Irish individuals whom the German engineer assumed would support the plant, including a fellow engineer, or government leaders, ultimately acquiesce to the anti-modern option of keeping industrial development out of the community. Despite lukewarm responses to his work from Irish audiences, Johnston wrote several more plays that were produced at either the Abbey or the Gate, and served on the board of directors at the Abbey, just as his wife, Abbey company member Shelah Richards, acted for both companies.

In fact, cross-pollination between the Abbey and the Gate grew throughout this period and, despite the typical fight for audience share, the theatres ultimately benefited artistically from each other. The Gate helped generate more theatrically sophisticated audiences and potential playwrights for the Abbey. Considering how cautious and narrow the Abbey's choices were becoming in the late 1920s (they passed on both Johnston's play and O'Casey's expressionist *The Silver Tassie* in 1928), Dublin theatre needed a site for excellent productions of top-level work; plus the Gate's brilliant costume, lighting, and set designs encouraged the Abbey to improve their own. The Abbey hired Tonya Mosiewicz in 1935.[6] At the same time, the Gate inherited many of its core ideals from the Abbey, especially from Yeats; and the legacy of the Abbey as a site for national and nationalist debate often sheltered the Gate from potential controversy. Since the Abbey was the subsidized, national theatre, the Gate was free of the kinds of ideological scrutiny from audiences, critics, and board members encountered at the Abbey, allowing them to take greater artistic risks. While the Abbey offered pictures of Irish peasant life, the Gate's repertoire, although peppered with new and classic Irish plays, also featured European expressionism, Russian realism, and workers' theatre from the United States. One of the most famous of these productions was the 1932 production of *Jud Süss*, featuring a teen-aged Orson Welles as the Duke. Welles had travelled to Dublin and, with neither letter of introduction nor any audition appointment of any kind, managed to gain an interview. After the strong success of this production, Welles maintained professional and personal relationships with Edwards and Mac Liammoir, and the trio continued to work together in both play productions and films in the United States, England, and Ireland.

The Gate Gets a Patron

While the Gate had, to some extent, shelter from political criticism of its representation of Irish nationalist ideologies, thanks to the Abbey, it also found its own benefactor in Edward, Lord Longford. He and his wife, Christine Pakenham, Lady Longford, became devotees of the Gate after seeing *Peer Gynt* at the Peacock in 1928. In 1930, when the company did not think they had money to continue their work in their new space at the Rotunda, Longford bought enough shares to keep the company afloat and place Longford on the board of directors, and he paid the bills of the young company for years. At first, his involvement coordinated well with Mac Liammoir's and Edwards's vision, although the founders grew occasionally annoyed by Lord Longford's tendency to hire talentless actors out of pity, even if he did pay their salaries. Over time, however, working closely on the board of the Gate inspired not only the Longfords' generosity, but also their inner playwrights.

In 1933, the Gate produced Lord Longford's play, *Yahoo*, a drama about Jonathan Swift, the man whom Longford called in his opening-night curtain speech, 'the father of modern Irish nationalism'.[7] W.B. Yeats's *The Words Upon the Windowpane* had considered Swift's legacy to Irish thought three years earlier. Like Yeats, Longford was interested in considering Swift's position as both insider and outsider in Irish national culture. Born and educated in Dublin, Swift moved to London where he became a literary and political celebrity, and a favourite of Queen Anne. With her death and the fall of the Tories from power, Swift returned to Dublin where he became Dean of St Patrick's Cathedral, and he held that post from 1724 until his death in 1742. Yeats and Longford, while not comparing themselves to Swift, probably felt an affinity with him, for Yeats was an Anglo-Irishman who dedicated his adult life to encouraging the national literary and theatre movements, and Longford, though an Eton and Cambridge-educated member of the aristocracy, learned the Irish language and supported the new government. Also, Swift was closely associated with a pre-Republican Irish patriotic ideology fostered by the Anglo-Irish in the eighteenth century – an ideology that would not have excluded Protestant aristocrats like Longford. Writing about Swift allowed Anglo-Irish like Yeats and Longford to consider the Irish patriot who sacrifices his position of imperial power for his national patriotism, but who is never completely accepted by his countrymen because of his ancestral position of imperial privilege.

In *Yahoo*, Longford portrays moments of conversation between Swift and such historical figures as Vanessa, Stella, and George Berkeley, that provide an overview of Swift's political and philosophical beliefs, and the many responses critical to his views and behaviours during his life. *Yahoo* also addresses how Swift's legacy had been ignored in the twentieth century, especially through the way his satire, *Gulliver's Travels*, was edited down from a sharp critique of Western civilization to a children's book. In the third Act, Lord Longford uses expressionist techniques to imagine both Swift's breakdown into insanity at the end of his life, and also his legacy to Irish national thought. Swift, played by Hilton Edwards, reacted onstage to both characters from his own time and from the twentieth century, as well as offstage voices reciting fragments of his own writings. As Swift grieves that Stella may be 'lost' to him, a chorus of voices recites the names of other individuals who are 'lost', 'Orrery, Delany, Hawkesworth, Sheridan, Johnson, Scott', and, moving forward to contemporary voices, ends with *'The Words upon the Window-pane*, by W.B. Yeats' (Longford [1933] 1936: 187). Also, as the chorus of voices sings lines from Swift's poetic auto-eulogy, 'Verses on the Death of Doctor Swift', a man dressed as a representative of the present time rises to protest the naming of a street in Dublin, Dean Swift Road, an actual event, saying that the street should 'be given some more national title, more suited to the traditions of a free people who have preserved in the darkest days the ideals of freedom, nationality, truth, and justice' (188). The curtain falls, however, as the voices get a last, triumphant word, singing that '. . . Love at length shall victor ride,/O'er tramped hate and prostrate pride' (191), intimating that Swift's sacrifices for his friends and for Ireland will ultimately triumph over the more scandalous aspects of his reputation, or the forgetfulness and expediency of history. The play had a healthy run at the Gate, and helped allay other losses accrued in the course of the season.

Women and Irish Theatre in the 1930s

While Lord Longford did enjoy success as a playwright, his wife, the English-born Christine Pakenham, Lady Longford, had the more productive writing career. Lady Longford began her foray into playwriting with translations and adaptations of Greek classics, the source of her research at Oxford before marrying Edward in 1925. In 1933, she chose a less lofty topic, adapting for the stage her novel of the same name, *Mr Jiggins of Jigginstown*, which was well received. The play tells of an eccentric Anglo-Irish landlord who must decide whether or not to leave his land and wealth to his selfish, expatriate descendants. While the play includes dialogues about Irish culture and class and religious divisions, reflecting Shaw's influence (in fact, the vegetarian Mr Jiggins appears to be modelled after Shaw), it also includes an element of screwball comedy similar to Longford's contemporary, the United States playwright George S. Kaufmann. Rather than leave his land to his Anglo-Irish descendants who see the land and its assets (ancient oak trees, thoroughbred horses) as moneymaking assets that should be exploited rather than preserved, Jiggins gives generous stipends to his servants, and the rest to the Department of Education of the Irish Free State to build a non-denominational school. John Cowell remarks that 'This play was based on a real-life oddity, Adolphus Cooke of Cookesborough, County Westmeath, who disappointed the expectations of his pretentious relatives by leaving his fortune to found a non-denominational school for boys. Cooke believed he would be reincarnated as a fox, and, sure enough, on the day of his funeral a fox was seen in his kitchen' (Cowell 1988: 94). Other important plays by Longford include her play adaptation of Jane Austen's *Pride and Prejudice*, which starred James Mason in its Gate Theatre debut in 1937, and her historical dramas of the 1940s, including her 1943 play, *Patrick Sarsfield*, written to mark the 250th anniversary of the Irish hero's death.

In 1936, the Longfords and Edwards and Mac Liammóir split into two organizations, the Gate Theatre and Longford Productions, sharing the theatre space and actors but less goodwill than before. Yet the arrangement did allow Mac Liammóir and Edwards the run of the theatre during the height of the Dublin theatre season, and freedom to tour the world in summer, travelling to such venues as the United States, England, Eastern Europe, and even Egypt. After Lord Longford's death in 1961, Christine, Lady Longford, returned the theatre entirely into the hands of Edwards and Mac Liammóir, and was appointed head of the theatre's board of directors.

Indeed, Mac Liammóir and Edwards were blessed with very talented collaborators, many of whom were women. They had not one but three leading women actors – Meriel Moore, Betty Sheridan, and Coralie Carmichael. And they also had an actor, playwright, and scholar in Mary Manning. Manning studied at the Abbey School of Acting under Sara Allgood in the 1920s, and acted at both the Abbey and the Gate. She became the founding editor of the Gate's quarterly journal, *Motley* (joining in the tradition of creating a journal to complement the theatre, started by Yeats with the Irish Literary Theatre), in 1929, and remained editor until she emigrated to the United States in 1935. It is remarkable that Manning edited a performing arts journal as impressive as *Motley* while still only in her early twenties. Its contributors included Frank O'Connor, Padraic Colum, Austin Clarke, and Francis Stuart, and it offered ample reviews, photographs, and illustrations of Gate theatre productions. Her 1931 drama (rev. 1933), *Youth's the Season – ?* a drawing room tragic-comedy in the vein of Noel Coward or Phillip Barry, became an early Gate Theatre hit. *Youth's the Season – ?* was one of the first plays to show Dublin's upper-class youth, and their quest for meaning amid their materialist lives fraught with family expectations. Robert Hogan remarked that Manning's 'incisive perception and satiric wit were beautifully evident in *Youth's the Season – ?* [sic] which still comes near to being the most sophisticated yet poignant study to come out of Dublin' (Hogan 1967a: 9). It also allowed Mac Liammoir and company to have a hand at a play of drawing-room sophistication with (upper-crust) Dublin accents. Manning wrote three more plays for the Gate before she emigrated to the USA, where she continued writing, with a focus on novels. Her adaptation of *Finnegans Wake*, *The Voice of Shem* (1955), was made into a film in 1966. She returned to Ireland and its theatre scene in the 1960s, and continued writing in England and Ireland until her death in 1999.

While Manning and Longford were breaking new ground at the Gate Theatre, another woman, Teresa Deevy (1894–1963) was busily becoming one of the most significant playwrights on the Abbey stage. Deevy was born into a large and prosperous Waterford family, and was encouraged from childhood by her mother to pursue her interest in writing. She went to university, but developed an illness that made her completely deaf. Still, she continued with her writing, and actually did not develop an interest in theatre until after she became deaf, and saw theatre in London while learning lip reading (Kearney 1997: 90–2). Throughout the 1920s, she was an active member of Cumann na mBan, and continued her writing. In 1930, *Reapers* was her first play to be accepted at the Abbey, and she moved with her sister Nell to Dublin where she lived and worked for several years before returning to Waterford. From 1930 to 1936, six of Deevy's plays premiered at the Abbey, and they were generally praised for their detailed look at character, and for creating a kind of Chekhovian sense of dialogue, with characters' language and behaviour thinly disguising a general sense of ennui or despair. Deevy's work received international recognition, and several of her plays were published in Ireland, England, and the United States. *Katie Roche*, her most famous drama, was published by Victor Gollancz in *Famous Plays of 1935–1936*, despite the fact that it had not yet been produced outside of Ireland.[8] In total, she wrote twenty-five plays, many of which were produced for radio or television.

Unlike the plays of the more worldly Manning or Lady Longford, which reflected the lives and interests of Dublin bohemian life, Deevy's dramas clearly fit into the peasant kitchen style of dramas dominant at the Abbey at the time. Yet, instead of focusing on male protagonists, Deevy's plays focused on and characterized the experience of rural Irish women and the choices – or lack thereof – they faced in Ireland during this period. Eileen Kearney remarks that 'In her brilliant portraits of romantic, high-strung, individualistic young women in rural Ireland, [Deevy] "catches them in flight at a moment in life when they put aside their youthful illusions and accept a greyer but more plausible adult reality"' (Callaghan, in Kearney 1997: 88). Deevy, who like her sisters never married, examined repeatedly in her plays the plight of women uncomfortable taking on the role of wife and mother extolled for them in the new nation; and, in doing so, she exposed the prejudices, hypocrisies, and even resentments that sometimes stemmed from the idealization and perpetuation of that ideal. For centuries in the European theatre tradition, comedy has ended in a marriage, representing the reconciliation of interpersonal conflict and the perpetuation of the societal status quo. Deevy, likewise, ends many of her plays in marriage, and even with her female protagonist excited by the prospect. Yet, from the audience's point of view, the events leading up to this end make the triumph of marriage at the end of the play appear, at least to some, a Pyrrhic victory.

This ironic take on marriage is poignantly clear in Deevy's one-act play, *The King of Spain's Daughter* (1935). The drama focuses on Annie Kinsella, a pretty twenty-year-old woman who is regularly beaten by her father, and is forced by him to choose between marrying a local man, Jim (who is also her father's co-worker and one of her boyfriends), and signing a contract to work in a local factory for five years. Jim wants to marry Annie, and has been saving money for four years to convince her to marry him. Annie, however, has a reputation for rebelling against the status quo: she is sexually involved with at least two men, including Jim, and has stated that she would rather go into service in London than take on marriage and motherhood. But, rather than grow bitter, she escapes through her romantic imagination. For instance, Annie is late with her father's dinner because she went into town to watch a wedding. She describes the wedding three times in very different, and always highly romantic terms, although we learn that the wedding was actually very sombre.

Characters like Annie in a play by Synge or Yeats are usually carried away by faeries, or escape their situation with the aid of another unlikely dreamer. But, in Deevy's plays, there is no *deus ex machina*. Annie agrees to marry Jim to avoid the factory, even though it means, to her regret, that Jim's two sisters will be thrown out of the house. But she represses the pragmatics of her choice by romanticizing the situation. At the close of the play, she only becomes excited about the match when she imagines that some day Jim may become jealous enough about her to cut her throat. Whether Annie is simply trying to make Jim a romantic hero, or in fact has developed a suicide wish, is up to interpretation; but, in either case, it is clear that Annie has transformed her personal despair into fantastic denial.

Deevy's play flirts with expressionism in its use of setting and props to show Annie's claustrophobic, abusive world. For instance, Deevy describes the setting as: *'An open space on a grassy road. At each side road barriers with notices "No Traffic" and "Road Closed"'* (Deevy 1935: 459). The barrier signs were put up by Peter and Jim as part of their work, but they also reflect the ways both men have cut off opportunities for Annie. Also, Jim offers Annie financial security by showing her his bankbook, which Annie throws on the ground, remarking, 'Oh, 'tis smudged and dirty! Why couldn't you keep it clean?' (464). Her first response to the book is that it reflects worldly things, instead of romance. Later, when she is trapped into the marriage, she will pick it up again and, looking at it, transform it from a symbol of middle-class tedium into a signal of latent passion.

Deevy also uses other characters to show the kinds of controls on women's behaviour in 1930s Ireland. Her father, who regularly abuses her, is pitied by others for having such a wilful child. He also has enough control over Annie to order her into a five-year contract with the factory, with marriage to Jim as her only escape. Jim's actions, likewise, reflect the double standard placed upon women. He threatens to tell the priest and Annie's father that she was 'at the crossroad last night . . . dancin' on the board, an' restin' in the ditch with your cheek agen mine and your body pressed to me' (464). The Dance Halls Act of 1935 had restricted public dancing, so Jim and Annie apparently attended a dance at the crossroads (an innocent version of a twenty-first-century rave), but the sexual double standard allows Jim to threaten to expose Annie's behaviour, knowing that he will be excused while she will be punished for it. Likewise, Peter catches the two of them in an embrace from which Jim refuses to release her, and Peter immediately assumes that Annie was 'leadin' [him] on' (464). Even the other female character in the play, Mrs Marks, perpetuates the sexist status quo. While disappointed by her own experience as a wife and mother, she chastises Annie for trying to break out of her role, sympathizing with the abusive Peter for having a wilful child, and even urging Jim not to marry Annie because she will be disobedient. And when Annie tells Marks that she dreads becoming a wife and mother, Marks replies, 'Fie on you then! Did you think you needn't suffer like the rest of the world?' (465). Is it any wonder Annie dreams of the King of Spain's daughter?

Deevy's best work, *Katie Roche* (1936), works along the same lines as her earlier one-act play. Again, we have a woman trapped in the assumptions of her culture, and the expectations and desires of those around her. Katie was born out of wedlock to a mother who died in childbirth, and so she bears the surname of the woman who took her in. At the start of the play, she is 'not quite twenty', and working as a maid in the home of Amelia Gregg, whose brother, Stanislaus, was in love with Roche's biological mother. Stanislaus proposes to Katie, although in his proposal it is unclear at first whether he is reminiscing over his love for Katie's mother, or actually offering his hand to his love's illegitimate daughter. Katie chooses the match over joining a convent or pursuing a relationship with a local boy, Michael Maguire; but in Act II it becomes clear that the marriage is a disappointment. Stanislaus calls Katie 'child' and corrects her grammar, while Katie grows frustrated by the lack of sexual intimacy in their union.

Katie's frustration leads her to flirt with her old boyfriend, Michael, with immediate repercussions. A wandering holy man, Reuben, whom Katie has known for years, witnesses her flirtation, reveals that he is in fact her biological father, then beats her with his walking stick. Michael reveals the flirtation to Stanislaus to avoid reprisal, telling him: '*(with a flash): She threw her arms around me. She held on to me tight. (Silence.) I wouldn't tell you at all, but my mother said it is better always to be on the safe side. (Silence.) I have nothing agen her. I don't wish her harm . . . All the same (with another flash) it wasn't a fair thing. And Reuben to come in, and find me like that*' (Deevy 1936: 668). Later, after Reuben learns that Katie's relationship with Michael has continued, he tells Stanislaus, 'She's not to be depended on. What she needs is humiliation; if she was thoroughly humbled she might begin to learn' (694). Katie's father, by not marrying her mother, has made Katie an illegitimate outsider. Michael, by flirting with Katie, has put her integrity as a wife in question. But, rather than accept their complicity in Katie's condition, they attack her for it.

The women in Katie's life, her sisters-in-law Amelia and Margaret, encourage Katie to take on female submissiveness, as Amelia has in spinsterhood, and Margaret has in a loveless marriage. Katie acquiesces to these women's advice when Stanislaus chooses, with Reuben's recommendation, to live abroad, where he can keep a closer eye on his child bride. Katie's despair at leaving all she knows is turned around when her sister-in-law Amelia urges her to 'be brave' (700), because now Katie has the 'something great to do' (701) she has been searching for all of her life – deny her own desires and devote her life to Stanislaus's happiness. At the beginning of the drama, Katie considered joining a convent in hopes of becoming a saint. At the close, she '*almost gaily*' (701) strides towards the life of a martyr, repressing her own needs for the sake of her husband.

Katie Roche was produced regularly by the Abbey in the 1930s, but fell out of the repertory later, to be revived at the Abbey in 1975, and then again in 1994 in an Abbey production directed by Judy Friel. Friel has described her frustration at directing the ending of this play, as it undermines any attempts to create a proto-feminist subtext to the drama.[9] Here, as in *The King of Spain's Daughter*, a lively woman must focus her imaginative energies on her role as wife, even though that imaginative leap forces her to deny personal and social realities. Deevy's plays expose and attack the dissonance between the ideal of domesticity thrust upon women in 1930s Ireland in exchange for the work and dreams they gave to the Irish Free State, and the reality of the post-revolutionary backlash for most Irish women to a self-perpetuating, misogynistic culture. And such a reading of the play was encouraged by the brilliant and energetic Ria Mooney and Eileen Crowe, the actors who played Annie and Katie, respectively, in their Abbey premieres. While Coralie Carmichael might dance as Salome for a few thousand members of the Dublin intelligentsia in 1930s Dublin, working-class country girls like Annie Kinsella and Katie Roche could legally kick their heels publicly only in carefully sanctioned dance halls. In the exposure of that reality lies the possibility of social critique and change. As Shaun Richards has remarked, 'The desire which Deevy's heroines display are not then so much extinct as dormant, each performance of her plays threatening their eruption in audiences who might choose to reject domesticity in favour of the Dionysian pleasures of the dance' (2003: x–xi).

Challenging the Church: Carroll and Clark

Two other notable playwrights addressing repression in the Irish state during this period were Paul Vincent Carroll and Austin Clarke. Both men were inspired to playwriting by experiences at the Abbey Theatre in the 1910s, only to have limited success getting their work staged there. Yet both men ended up developing international reputations despite their rejection at the national theatre. Carroll was born in County Louth in 1900, and lived there until moving to Dublin in 1914, where he 'entered training as a teacher, learned to drink a bottle of Guinness without spluttering and haunted the pit of the Abbey Theatre, to which I owe everything dramatic that I have' (qtd in Hogan 1967a: 63). After receiving his degree he moved to Scotland where he taught from 1921 to 1937 in the state schools (Hogan 1967a: 53), but his interest in Irish theatre continued, and he received his first Abbey main stage production in 1931. The play,

Things That Are Caesar's, won jointly with a drama by Teresa Deevy a new play prize competition at the Abbey. This drama strikes out against Carroll's views of hypocrisy and greed within the Catholic Church, as a priest convinces a young woman to obey her father and marry a rich man she does not love. After a year, the woman leaves the marriage and returns her wedding ring to the priest, for it was ultimately not a sign of the sacrament of marriage, but a token of trade. As she returns the ring, she remarks, '. . . it too belongs to Caesar' (53). Its 1932 production got a twenty-minute ovation on opening night. Kavanagh remarked that 'Carroll was the first writer to give the Abbey a play on an anticlerical theme which was handled with such skill that it could give no offense' (Kavanagh 1950: 164).

Carroll's finest play, *Shadow and Substance* (1937), also premiered at the Abbey, and was taken on tour to the United States, where it won the New York Drama Critics' Circle Awards for best foreign play of 1937–8. The Abbey rejected Carroll's next play, *The White Steed*, which was produced in New York by the Cort Theatre, and it won the New York Drama Critics' Circle Award for best foreign play of 1938–9. Carroll continued to write plays on Irish and Scottish themes through the 1940s and 1950s using several styles, but much of his oeuvre reconsiders but does not go beyond anti-clerical themes found in *Shadow and Substance*. D.E.S. Maxwell remarked that Carroll showed 'a rebellious, ambitious imagination that never wholly sought itself out' (1984: 137). Like the fiery Abbey Theatre that inspired him to write, Carroll's potential appears ultimately to have been circumscribed by his established success and his reluctance to offend his audiences or criticize too much the Church to which he belonged.

Austin Clarke was a poet, novelist and dramatist, who found inspiration in the verse dramas of W.B. Yeats, as well as other verse playwrights in Ireland and England during the 1930s. Clarke's verse plays turned to medieval Irish religious themes and mythology, and often included characters caught between obedience and desire. While a few of his dramas were staged at the Abbey, Clarke created new venues for poetic drama in Ireland, and founded the Dublin Verse Speaking Society in 1940. This company presented three seasons of verse plays (many by Clarke) on the Peacock Theatre stage from 1941–3, as well as broadcasting readings of dramatic poems on the rapidly developing Radio Eireann radio station until 1953. Clarke also founded the Lyric Theatre Company in 1944, which produced such verse dramas as T.S. Eliot's *Sweeney Agonistes* (1927), and the debuts of two of Yeats's last dramas, *The Death of Cuchulain*

(1939) and *The Herne's Egg* (1939). Yet, despite his influence as a poet, critic, and theatre administrator, his own career as a dramatist, like that of other verse dramatists in Ireland beyond Yeats, made a smaller impact.

George Shiels and the Rise of the Kitchen Comedy

While Deevy's dramas challenged Irish gender expectations, her contemporary, George Shiels, wrote kitchen comedies that, more often than not, used laughter to expose the hypocrisies of the new Irish middle class, and conflict between the old and new generations in Ireland. Shiels was born in Ireland but emigrated to Canada, where he worked as a labourer. He was crippled in a work accident, and returned to Northern Ireland, where he began writing plays. Like Deevy, Shiels's interest in drama and his writing style were informed by his disability. Deevy's dialogue includes broken sentences and uncomfortable pauses that sometimes feel Pinteresque. Both non-communication and non-verbal communication are eloquently demonstrated in his characters' speech and gestures. Shiels's dramas focus on gossip and intrigue that he claimed to have heard from visitors, since he was practically housebound. Shiels's first plays were written under the pseudonym George Morsheil, and were performed by the Ulster Literary Theatre in 1918 and 1919. His Abbey debut, two one-act plays entitled *Bedmates* (1921) and *Insurance Money* (1921), proved his ability to write easily producible drama that was eminently suitable for the Abbey players. But his dramas *Paul Twyning* (1922) and *Professor Tim* (1925) established his position as a master of the kitchen comedy – a title he would hold for two decades, writing twenty-seven plays in his career.

Shiels's talent for developing well-constructed comedies is apparent in one of his more critically acclaimed comedies, *The New Gossoon* (1930). Ultimately, the play offers an old comic plot about the tensions between youth and old age, and the struggles of courtship. *The New Gossoon*, however, ties these issues in with the tensions between tradition and modernity in the Irish Free State. The centre of the various love plots, Rabit Hamil, is, like Boucicault's Myles na cGopaleen, a poacher, infuriated that his twenty-year-old neighbour Luke Cary plans to ban Rabit from hunting on his property when he inherits the farm on his twenty-first birthday. This inspires Rabit to marry his daughter off to Luke, which will give him free reign to hunt Luke's land, and, with his daughter married, allow Rabit to marry a local servant girl.

Meanwhile, Luke has his own conflicts with his mother, Ellen, and his Uncle Peter, who disapprove of his motorbike, assumed womanizing, and plans to modernize and/or rent out the farm. When Luke calls his motorbike a hobby, Peter replies, 'Your six-pound hobby'll cost you a bit more before the Rabit Hamils and Mad Henleys have done with you. You've as many women dotted over the country as Brigham Young. If that's your notion of a hobby – or if it's your notion of Irish Freedom – then every man who fought and died for it was a fool and an enemy of his race' (Shiels [1930] 1936: 243). Luke replies, 'He was damned hard up for a cause that fought and died for this country. I'd as lief fight and die for Spike Island . . . Everything in this country is a mortal sin. It's a mortal sin to keep a greyhound, or a motor-bike; it's a mortal sin to go to a dance, or speak to a girl after sunset . . . I don't know how the population of this country was over eight million – at the time it was so holy, and no motorbikes' (243). Ultimately, the couples and conflicts are sorted out. Luke gets engaged to Sally, who immediately begins to transform Luke into a respectable citizen. When he asks for a kiss, she replies, 'I'll give you no kiss! I'm not marrying you to sit and kiss me . . . You're going to work' (265). She does, however, agree to ride on the motorbike. Luke's mother, Ellen, marries the farmhand, Ned, who has been working on the farm for half-wages for twenty years out of love for her, thanks to Sally teaching Ellen to be 'natural and honest' (267), instead of worrying about propriety. And Rabit loses the servant girl, Mag, but gains the rights to hunt on the Cary's land for life.

The New Gossoon is an enjoyable comedy, but historically it is interesting in the ways it simultaneously mocks and balances out the tension between tradition and modernity in Ireland during this period. Even the title toys with this theme, using an old, slang Irish term for a boy, a 'Gossoon', with the adjective linked to modernity, 'New'. Luke is a 'new old-fashioned lad', who shows the typical urges and idealisms of youth in Ireland (and the world) over centuries, but with the historical difference of growing up in a technically complex yet morally conservative nation that is both ancient, and younger than he. Ultimately, modern notions of materialism and sexual licence are overruled in favour of a hearty work ethic and the institution of marriage. But, at the same time, increased productivity through innovation on the farm, and a more frank and less class-based understanding of interpersonal relationships also win. While Shiels's kitchen comedies do possess a strong streak of irony and satire, they ultimately offered Abbey audiences an escapist reassurance that the Irish spirit could weather radical social and political change. Shiels was less concerned with articulating the costs of Ireland's transitions – or failures to transition – through colonialism to the neocolonial conditions of the Irish Free State and the six counties of Northern Ireland, than he was with telling a good story.

The New Gossoon is an actor's play; and the Abbey did indeed have fine actors in the 1930s, but their gift of comedy, along with the absence of Lady Gregory's guiding hand, and an increasingly bureaucratic board of directors, led the Abbey to slip into an interest in going after the easy laugh, and playing nearly everything like farce (Hogan 1967a: 5–8). Eventually, vehicles for the Abbey style, like Shiels's plays, began to elbow out other kinds of drama. Playwright Dorothy Macardle described the changes in this way:

> In order to change their programme every week the company resorted to frequent revivals at short intervals and to the revival of those plays which they could perform with most facility. Their range became restricted; their excursions from the cottage interior rarely led them farther than to a tene-ment room, a lodging-house bedroom or a 'parlour' in the 'suburban groove,' and the dramatists followed suit. For years we have seen plays which, quite obviously, have been written, not only for the Abbey Theatre, but for the Abbey players – for this actor's lift of an eyebrow and that actress's toss of the chin – and even for the Abbey property-room. I have heard the property man, in a tone of indignant protest, rebuking a new author who had made a demand considered exorbitant – 'a mug with a black pig on it' was the direction in the script. The author was categorically instructed as to what was and what was not in the property-room. 'So that another time you won't write ad-lib.' (Macardle 1934: 126–7)

Fortunately, this was not the attitude across the island, or even across Dublin. The Gate Theatre and Longford Productions continued to pursue innovative and challenging work, acted and staged beautifully, both in their own theatre and on tour across Ireland and the world. The amateur tradi-tion remained strong across Ireland, offering excellent productions of Irish plays in smaller communities. And, in Belfast in 1940, a group of amateur theatre companies gathered to form the Group Theatre (Bell 1972: 60–76).

The sheer number of individuals involved in the Group Theatre gave that company a deep pool of talent with which to work, and allowed them to perform a range of plays from the modern European tradition, from Henrik Ibsen, to Clifford Odets, to Terence Rattigan. But, as Sam Hanna Bell noted, 'the inner impulse and indeed the outer and public claim was for the Ulster play' (1972: 71). This meant that Northern Irish playwrights who had their work regularly performed at the Abbey, like George Shiels, St John Ervine, and Rutherford Mayne, were given new interpretations by the Group; and many critics felt that the plays gained added depth when performed for Northern audiences. David Kennedy said of Shiels's plays in the North, for example, that they 'have nowhere been better interpreted than in Belfast. It is not a matter of acting and production only – these are often better done in Dublin – but of that invisible cooperation between audience and stage: nuances of expression and character arousing over-tones of feeling, emotional harmonics, in the audience' (qtd in Bell 1972: 81). While some of this appears to be regionalist bravado, Kennedy's remarks also show that new performance strategies that reflected the aes-thetics, sensibilities, and concerns of local audiences, rather than aping the Abbey school, were becoming increasingly apparent. Indeed, from the 1940s, the Group Theatre enlivened classics that had grown sentimental and stale, provided a professional vehicle committed to producing new work, and, by touring Ireland as well as England, added a much needed counterpoint to what George Jean Nathan called the 'Erin Go Blah' (Nathan 1936: 24) on the Abbey stage. In the 1930s and 1940s the Irish stage may have yielded few 'universal' classics, but the new voices coming to terms with the new nation were deeply engaged in the task of moving Irish theatre from a nationalist dramaturgy designed to confront and destroy negative Irish stereotypes, to a national movement employing a range of writing and performance strategies that captured the voices and concerns of the many diverse voices in Northern Ireland and the new Irish Republic.

Part III

Rewriting Tradition, 1948–1980

Introduction to Part III

From the 1930s through the years of the Second World War (known as
'the emergency' in the Irish Free State), Fianna Fail maintained its policies
of isolationism internationally and conservatism internally. Yet the inevitable economic and demographic shifts across Europe following the war,
along with new policies and outbreaks of nationalist violence in Ireland,
led to radical socio-political change across the island. In 1948, the Fine Gael
Party finally overtook the Fianna Fail's sixteen-year monopoly over the
Irish government when John Costello became prime minister in 1948.
Under Fine Gael leadership in 1949, Ireland ratified the Republic of Ireland
Bill, removing the nation's last formal ties with the United Kingdom. The
UK responded with its own legislation that allowed Irish to live and work
in the UK without a passport or other legal formalities expected of foreign-
ers. This policy would have important implications with the steady rise of
Irish immigration into England in the 1950s. But the fate of the six counties
making up Northern Ireland remained a serious point of diplomatic con-
tention as well as sectarian violence. The Republic of Ireland continued to
assert its claim to the entire island, leading to vocal protests from the Protestant majority in the North. The UK responded to the Irish Republic's
assertion of rights with its own Ireland bill, in which it pledged not to give
up dominion over Northern Ireland without the consent of the Northern
Irish parliament. Thus, in the 1950s, the unionist, mostly Protestant majority and the nationalist, mostly Catholic minority in Northern Ireland grew
increasingly suspicious of one another. The Irish Republican Army began
a campaign of terrorist violence in 1956 in Northern Ireland, lasting until
the early 1960s, that served to increase the government's hard-line policies
against the Catholic minority.

Despite the resurgence of nationalist activity in Northern Ireland, many
of the people in the Republic of Ireland grew less engaged in the goal of
establishing a united island, even as their government asserted legislatively
its ultimate dominion over all thirty-two counties. The Republic was
experiencing economic stagnation, and emigration rates were very high

throughout the decade, with many young persons finding work in England. Within the nation itself, rural populations decreased while city populations were on the rise (Brown 2004: 200–2). Thus, even though rural Ireland was becoming more and more sparsely populated, Dublin maintained its dynamism, and boasted a crowd of intellectuals and university students who enlivened the city, with a Bohemian sensibility and an interest in both local artistic developments and European trends.

Throughout the 1950s, Fine Gael and Fianna Fail traded power from election to election in the Republic. In 1959, Ireland moved in a very new direction. Sean Lemass took control over Eamon de Valera's Fianna Fail Party, and carried forth an aggressive economic policy that moved the country away from protectionism and towards industrialization. One of his major successes, the formation of Aer Lingus, Ireland's national airline, reflects how Lemass welcomed opportunities for opening Ireland to foreign engagement and economic investment, a very different strategy from that which had been followed in earlier decades. In the nation's first decades, it held on to isolationism and protectionism; now, it touted its geographical position, its natural resources, and even its comparatively inexpensive, educated professional class, as an asset to be exploited on the international market. Lemass's Programme of Economic Expansion (1958–63) actually surpassed its 2 per cent goal, accruing a 4 per cent growth rate for the Irish economy during that time (Brown 2004: 203). Lemass's philosophy that 'a rising tide lifts all boats', however, left some Irish concerned that Ireland's nationalist ideals and cultural autonomy were being sold to the highest bidder.

These shifts in priorities naturally affected notions of cultural identity and its propagation within Ireland. The nation was built on an idealized image of its culture as ancient and racy, of the soil. Industrialization, emigration, families moving from extended family networks to nuclear families in the cities, and the influence of English and European news and arts through television and radio broadcasts rapidly shifted the cultural experiences and goals of many Irish towards modernization over tradition. Irish language lessons remained mandatory in the schools, but fewer people were speaking it in everyday life. Investment in technical schools prepared the younger generation for jobs in industry. And the consummation of Irish collaboration with post-war Europe's economic and social agendas was its incorporation into the European Community in 1973. The image of the idealized Irish peasant within the nationalist movement at the start of the century was replaced with cynical expressions of the personal hardships and oppressions fostered in Irish rural life. Patrick Kavanagh's poem,

'The Great Hunger', did not mourn the famine as its title implied, but addressed the sexual frustrations concomitant with familism in rural Ireland. Irish art no longer attempted to mytho-poeticize an idealistic Irish past, but instead to seek out the directions in which the nation was going.

As the Republic continued to concentrate on economic development, Northern Ireland was compelled to focus on the outbreak of sectarian paramilitary violence that would haunt the region for the rest of the decade. The Troubles, as the period would come to be called, were stirred up by violent government response to peaceful civil rights demonstrations in Northern Ireland in the late 1960s, most notably in Derry in 1968. In 1969 British troops were sent in to Northern Ireland to keep the peace. What was supposed to be a brief mission turned into a thirty-eight-year occupation by the British army. Increasing violence among the British army, the Royal Ulster Constabulary, and organizations such as the Irish Republican Army and the unionist Ulster Volunteer Force led the government to eye all nationalist demonstrations or acts of civil disobedience with great suspicion.

This atmosphere certainly contributed to Bloody Sunday, when British troops opened fire on a group of demonstrators in the Catholic Bogside neighbourhood of Derry in 1972. Thirteen people were killed and dozens injured. None of those killed were carrying weapons and a few were shot in the back, yet the Widgery Tribunal investigating the cases shortly after the event absolved the British soldiers of any wrongdoing. This tragic event, and the violence that ensued, led to the dissolution of Stormont, Northern Ireland's parliament, and the suspension of many civil rights, including habeas corpus, for Northern Irish citizens suspected of involvement in terrorist activities. Paramilitary organizations like the Irish Republican Army and the unionist Ulster Volunteer Force began violent campaigns against one another. Terrorist attacks occurred throughout Northern Ireland and the United Kingdom.

The British government responded to paramilitary campaigns by criminalizing those involved, and in several cases arrested and convicted individuals who were later discovered to be innocent of terrorist crimes. In 1976, when the British government denied IRA members in British prisons prisoner-of-war status, IRA prisoners began a series of civil protests that culminated in the hunger strike of 1981. During that hunger strike, ten men died, including Bobby Sands, a leader of the protest, who was elected to parliament while on strike. One hundred thousand persons attended his funeral.

Citizens of the Republic of Ireland in the 1970s had mixed opinions about the Troubles and the appropriate personal and governmental response to it. Most were sympathetic with the Irish nationalists in Northern Ireland, but the uses of terrorism and other forms of violence raised questions. In addition, a growing 'revisionist' view of the history of twentieth-century Ireland that questioned the necessity of the war for independence and posited that Northern Ireland might indeed need to remain outside the jurisdiction of the Republic led to heated debates on both sides of the border. But it was those debates, those questionings of Ireland's past and imaginings of its possible future, that inspired new ideas in Irish theatre, as playwrights and players sought to break out of the traditional aesthetic frames and challenge the suppositions of the dramas of previous decades, or returned to those forms in ways that gave them new meanings in the light of current events.

This section looks at the 1950s as the start of a new generation of Irish creating a new wave of Irish theatre, influenced by the economic and demographic shifts in the nation, rising interest in and anxiety about modernization in the Republic, and violent unrest in Northern Ireland. As the isolationism of the 1940s gave way to moves towards globalization in the Republic, and identity politics grew increasingly urgent and violent in Northern Ireland, Irish theatre on both sides of the border maintained and developed its decades-long tradition of using the stage as a laboratory for investigating cultural crisis and imagining new solutions. In the early decades of the twentieth century, proponents of the Irish dramatic movement argued whether politics or art should be the concern of Irish drama. By the late 1970s, on both sides of the border, theatre was expected to offer both an intelligent critique of Irish culture, and an artistically profound experience. It is remarkable how many productions would succeed in attaining that goal.

5

Irish Theatre in the 1950s

The 1950s was a dynamic decade for European theatre. England's Angry Young Men, Jerzy Grotowsky's revolutionary experiments in Poland, and the Berliner Ensemble's work in East Germany, all served to revive performance in countries exhausted by war and needing new models for exploring through performance a post-war and even a post-modern world. Echoes of those theatrical revolutions made it to Ireland, but Irish players wanting to respond to these calls for radical artistic change often found that the insularity of the Irish theatre world, and of Irish ideology in the 1950s, made innovation artistically and politically difficult. This dilemma was especially the case at the Abbey Theatre. As noted at the end of chapter 4, an energy and earnestness about theatre as a vehicle for representing ideas about Ireland and Irishness persisted among amateur theatre groups throughout the 1930s and 1940s, but performances at the Abbey Theatre had grown increasingly stale. By 1941, Yeats and Lady Gregory had both died, although their managerial protégé Lennox Robinson remained at the theatre, and Ernest Blythe, an Irish politician, had become the managing director of the company. Blythe's appointment was in some ways an appeasing gesture on the Abbey's part towards the Fianna Fail government, which was suspicious of the Abbey Theatre's ability to embrace and reflect their ideological sympathies. It is certainly telling that Robinson, the Anglo-Irish Abbey veteran, was overlooked for the post in favour of the Fianna Fail leader and Civil War veteran. Blythe's directorship seemed to ensure a focus on Irish language theatre at the Abbey, as well as support for plays that reflected the values of rural Catholic Ireland, as interpreted by Fianna Fail.[1] But Blythe was not a playwright or theatre lover turned theatre manager, as the Abbey's previous directors had almost all been. Ultimately, he was a bureaucrat, and he made decisions based not on aesthetics, but on economics and ideology.

Blythe was an active nationalist from his youth who had served heroically in the war for independence and Civil War, and served as a member of the Dail and in several Cabinet positions, including Minister of Trade and Commerce, in the 1920s and 1930s. As theatre manager, he chose plays based upon their financial benefits and, most famously, was thought to choose actors based on their pronunciation and skill in the Irish language rather than their acting talent. It is urban legend, however, that he only hired fluent Irish speakers (Mac Anna 2001: 171). Blythe did hire Tomas Mac Anna to be the first to hold a new position of Gaelic producer in 1947. Mac Anna, like many Irish theatre practitioners going back to Hilton Edwards and Michael Mac Liammóir, was inspired to pursue a life in the theatre by seeing Anew MacMaster's company perform in his hometown of Dundalk (179) and he soon became involved with the amateur Dundalk Little Theatre. After working at the Abbey as a volunteer for several years, Blythe gave him the position, as long as, MacAnna recalled, 'I was willing to learn and not regard myself as a sort of Gaelic-speaking Orson Welles, sent by Yeats or Gregory or the rest of them . . . to save the Abbey from its long-expected demise' (Mac Anna 1988: 168). Blythe's remark reflects the kind of siege mentality to which he had succumbed, living in the shadow of theatrical genius and historical nostalgia while trying to push a Fianna Fail agenda in the theatre.[2] Mac Anna learned his trade well as Gaelic Producer at the Abbey, producing one-act plays in Irish, and translations of Jalabert, Molière, and Chekhov in a range of styles (Mac Anna 1988: 170). To increase his range even further, Mac Anna was also responsible for the annual Irish language Christmas pantomime. Mac Anna remembers the pantos fondly, noting that at the time the Abbey 'was a young company and they could dance and they could sing and it was a break for them from doing the ordinary plays where farmers were ruined in the third Act and all that sort of thing' (Mac Anna 1988: 279). And, if the Irish language were indeed to be a dynamic part of Irish culture, there needed to be room for camp as well as high art and classic myth, although whether Gaelic low-brow belonged on the national theatre stage is up for debate. Peter Kavanagh, however, reported in horror the sight of the 1945 panto, which included 'a "leg show", and its highest point of distinction was the excellent translation of the popular hit 'I Got a Gal in Kalamazoo' (Kavanagh 1950: 183).

In an uncharacteristic bow towards the Abbey tradition, and to skill over ideology, the theatre did hire Ria Mooney as artistic director in 1948. Mooney had two decades of experience and an international reputation, after working as a star performer at the Abbey, Gate, and Gaiety theatres in Dublin, as well as performing in London and on Broadway.

Mooney quickly grew frustrated by the clumsiness of the actors and the limited artistic freedom afforded her by Blythe. She did manage to hire new talent in acting and design, produced good productions of Abbey classics despite the limited rehearsal time afforded productions as a cost-cutting measure, and even dealt with the controversy surrounding Seamus Byrne's *Design for a Headstone*, a play dealing with a Republican hunger strike in an Irish prison, in 1950. But this Abbey-trained actor, with a sterling reputation as a performer and director of Irish classics from peasant dramas to verse plays, struggled against uninspired new actors who were perhaps hesitant to accept the authority of a woman manager, unbendable veteran actors who did not want to accept the authority of anyone, and a policy in lockstep with Fianna Fail ideology. 'I wanted the public to have colour and excitement in their theatre – the kind of theatre I had known outside the Abbey,' Mooney wrote in her autobiography,

> except that now I wanted the colour to flow from the work of Irish play-wrights . . . I did not have to wait long before I realized that however much I might strive to implement my theories, which were viewed as being 'grandiose,' my engagement in the theatre was looked upon as being a 'holding' position until such time as Irish-speaking Directors could take over. I was told that the nation was at war with the English language. (qtd. in Hunt 1979: 174)

Indeed, the war between Mooney and Blythe reflects a larger cultural war at the time between traditional nationalist ideals that upheld rural life, Catholicism, and the Irish language tradition as an anti-imperial response to English domination, and a more urban and modern Irish cultural identity. The latter found the image of the Irish-speaking rural man or woman less relevant in a generation where the majority of Irish lived in cities, and the Irish countryside had become increasingly depopulated by economic depression, emigration, and shifts in employment towards industry. Mooney wanted a theatre built upon Ireland's rich theatrical legacy that included a majority of Anglo-Irish writers while also welcoming innovations and voices with diverse points of view. Blythe and his supporters wanted the National Theatre to serve as an educational tool, promoting an ideology in decline and ultimately of limited interest to the Dubliners who would patronize the Abbey, or to other major European theatre companies with which the Abbey had once claimed parity. This ideological tug-of-war would last beyond Mooney's tenure at the theatre, right up to Blythe's retirement in 1967.

The Abbey Theatre's history in the 1950s begins, famously, with a fire. On Wednesday 18 July 1951, 'at about 1 a.m.', a fire began on an upper floor of the Abbey Theatre and, within minutes, the building was engulfed in flames. The company lost all of its scenery (including the screens Gordon Craig had designed for Yeats years before), most of its costumes, and most of its scripts and other archives (Hunt 1979: 175). 'The Old Lady had set fire to herself,' Hugh Hunt remarked (175), as if the fire was a ritualistic self-immolation of the physical remnants of the nationalist experiment that had brought together some of Ireland's greatest artists and activists in the early twentieth century, occurring in response to the artistic and ideological decay that had overtaken the work performed within the building. But the spirit of 'The Old Lady', be she Cathleen ni Houlihan or Lady Gregory, had already moved beyond the old Mechanics Institute on Abbey Street into theatres and community halls throughout Ireland and England, and echoes of its work could be found in Edinburgh, London, New York, and Hollywood. And perhaps it set a fire in the hearts of the members of the Abbey. Ria Mooney initially suggested at a meeting the morning after the blaze that the theatre be shut down until repairs were completed or a new venue found. Legend has it that the Abbey's head carpenter, Seaghan Barlow, offered a different opinion: 'The Abbey Theatre has never closed its doors except during Easter Week 1916. We must keep faith with the public. Even if we are to recite it on an otherwise empty stage tonight, we must give a performance!' (McGlone 2002: 116). That night, Mooney led her novice cast through the scheduled play, *The Plough and the Stars*, on the much smaller Peacock stage before an emotional full house. 'After the final curtain, a relative of Lady Gregory's appeared like a specter out of the playhouse past with "a magnum of champagne to drink to the memory of those who had gone"' (McGlone 2002: 117). A few months later, the National Theatre Society settled into a temporary home at the Queen's Theatre, a Victorian theatre famous as the home of Irish melodrama in the 1890s, until the state completed building them a new theatre. The new Abbey was supposed to be built in two years. It took fifteen.

Contemporaries of the period saw the razing of the Abbey Theatre building as a signal of the death of a national institution. It was easy to idealize the days when one would see artists of the calibre of Yeats and Gregory in the audience, or be part of the controversies surrounding productions like *The Playboy of the Western World*. And it was true that the National Theatre Society in those early years, despite its dry spells, quarrels with different nationalist communities, and often half-empty houses, was instrumental in developing a drama and performance aesthetic that contributed to Ireland's notion of itself in an era of revolution, and influenced theatre practice around the world. But in 1950, the Republic of Ireland and Northern Ireland faced new, very different, political and cultural challenges. The Irish theatre, like any theatre movement engaged in its community, needed to respond in new ways. With the need for change in mind, we might even read the Abbey fire as not only a marker of the end of an era for the National Theatre, but as the start of a new and important period in Irish theatre history. In his essay 'Irish Theatre: The State of the Art', Fintan O'Toole termed this period the 'second wave' in Irish theatre, as playwrights and companies began to critique the national, cultural, and even theatre histories that informed plays of the previous era (2002). Just as the Republic of Ireland was looking towards the future of the Irish nation, so playwrights and performers sought out plays and performance practices that would address the new realities and challenges confronted by the nation. This second wave, like the first wave of Irish theatre, eventually carried its aesthetic all the way to the shores of England, the European continent, and North America. But it also learnt from the aesthetics of those theatres, and brought new dramaturgical strategies back to Ireland.

This chapter explores some of the ways Irish theatre addressed the major cultural shifts that occurred from the 1950s to the 1970s in both the newly formed Republic of Ireland and Northern Ireland. It will examine how some of the most pressing issues of the period – emigration, urbanization, and the Troubles – were addressed through theatre. It will also discuss how the rise of new theatres like the Pike, and of producers like Phyllis Ryan and Mary O'Malley, dealt with local concerns or avant-garde work that the Abbey or other major theatre companies would not or could not take on. This chapter will also look at particular flash points and controversies surrounding Irish theatre during this period, and how these reflected Ireland's anxiety about theatre as a site for challenging cultural and political ideology. The Republic and Northern Ireland underwent tremendous social change between 1948 and the 1980s, and its theatres changed with them.

Performing the Irish Landscape

The most dominant cultural image of the Irish west from the 1950s is not from Irish theatre, but from Irish-American film. In 1952, John Ford released his labour of love, *The Quiet Man*, starring Irish-born and

Irish-speaking Maureen O'Hara, Abbey legend Barry Fitzgerald, and one of Ford's favourite US actors, John Wayne. Filmed in the actual Irish west, *The Quiet Man* turned Maurice Walsh's 1933 short story into a rollicking melodrama about an Irish emigrant returned home. In the film, Sean Thornton (played by Wayne) returns to Ireland haunted by the ghosts of his harrowing experiences in Philadelphia, Pennsylvania, working in the steel mills, then becoming a prizefighting boxer and killing a man in the ring. Thornton's return to his homeland is a return to a pre-modern, idyllic Ireland, where the Irish language is still used, and the Catholic priest keeps the community in line. Thornton buys his family home and offers a dowry for Mary Kate Danaher, a beautiful local played as a stereotypical 'wild Irish girl'. Danaher desires to bring her inheritance with her into her new home, but her brother will not release it, and Thornton grows angry that she insists upon it, seeing it as a sign of crass materialism and an attack on his ability to support her, rather than a principled claim to what her mother had left her. At the end of the film, however, Danaher, despite (comically portrayed) public humiliation from her husband, takes the hard-won money and throws it into a fire, thus sealing her commitment to – and material dependence upon – her husband.

Ford's film remains a Hollywood classic, and won Academy Awards for both best director and best cinematography. In fact, tour coaches in County Mayo to this day regularly pause at sites that appear in the film, and one can even visit a reproduction of Thornton's white thatched cottage in the film. But *The Quiet Man's* idyllic image of Ireland as a pre-modern utopia – a real world Brigadoon to which American émigrés could return to a simpler life – was a far cry from the actual experience of the Irish west in the 1950s, where emigration was emptying out the countryside, and small farms were decaying or disappearing. And, while Ford's film looks back at an Ireland that nostalgically echoes the plays of Boucicault (see Gibbons 1996; Cullingford 2002), Irish theatre in the 1950s conjured up images of rural Irish life that are more in line with dark humour against the lifeless landscapes of plays by Samuel Beckett.

Beckett's Landscapes of Irish Memory

While some consider Beckett an international rather than a national writer and thus peripheral to the Irish canon, Beckett's influence on Irish theatre (and Irish theatre's influence on him), as well as his participation in Irish theatre from abroad, make it impossible not to include him in a study of modern Irish drama. As Ireland grew increasingly conservative after the Civil War, isolating itself from European affairs and setting out strict codes of censorship, many Irish writers chose to work outside the country. In 1931, Daniel Corkery listed thirty-six non-resident Irish writers who were continuing to impact Irish letters (Ward 2002: 238). Among them is Samuel Beckett. As a young man, Beckett made Paris his home, but he never gave up his Irish passport. Indeed, even in his francophone drama, Beckett remained in close touch with his Irish dramatic heritage, was engaged in the Irish theatre (he was one of the first members of the Aosdana), and inspired new kinds of Irish theatre work. In fact, Beckett provided mid-twentieth-century Irish theatre with what John Harrington calls a 'countertradition: an alternative vision which is not simply a departure from Irish traditions and practices but a departure fully formed by its dissent from the prevailing aesthetic' (2004: 168). Conversely, Katherine Worth has noted Irish theatre's influence on Beckett's work, and the ways he translated images, scenarios, and motifs from Irish playwrights – especially Yeats and O'Casey – for his own plays: 'The plays themselves tell us of his allegiance. It is easy to hear behind Hamm's stories or Winnie's romancing the tale-telling of the Douls, behind the knockabout turn of Hamm and Clov, O'Casey's sardonic, and farcical double-acts – the blind and paralysed pair in *The Silver Tassie*, the neatly afflicted Chair Attendants in *Within the Gates* – as behind them those other blind and lame beggars of *The Cat and the Moon* (Worth 1986: 242). Likewise, the geography of Ireland – from the lonely and barren burren in the west of Ireland, to the Eastern Ireland port town of Dun Laoghaire – is reincarnated in Beckett's drama into a world of metaphoric landscapes.

Beckett was born to an Anglo-Irish family in Foxrock, a Dublin suburb, in 1906. He studied Modern Languages at Trinity College Dublin, and earned the Gold Medal, the highest award for scholarship. During his Dublin days, Beckett regularly visited the Abbey Theatre. In 1928 he became a lecturer at l'Ecole Normale Superieure in Paris, and met James Joyce who, by that time, had already established an international reputation for his writings about Ireland from his position of self-imposed artistic exile on the continent. The two developed an intense professional relationship, with Beckett employed as Joyce's assistant during the period he was at work on *Finnegans Wake*. The relationship ended abruptly in 1930; but, while Joyce's influence is reflected in works like Beckett's novel *Murphy* (1938), the end of their collaboration enabled Beckett to find his own voice (Junker 1995: 18–19). Throughout the 1930s, Beckett belonged to very different communities, writing in French and English, and borrowing from French and Irish literary traditions, but still working mostly with prose rather than drama. During the First World War he fought in the French Resistance, and, in the years after, worked for the Irish Red Cross in St- Lô, Normandy, and France.

In 1953, one of Beckett's first plays, *Waiting for Godot*, was performed in Paris at Theatre de Babylone, a small, avant-garde theatre space in Mont-parnasse. The two-act drama observes two days in the lives of two tramps, waiting beside a tree on the side of the road for a man named Godot. They fill their time with talk; and, in each Act, are visited by a man named Pozzo and his servant Lucky, passing by Vladimir and Estragon on their way to some other destination. And at the end of each day a small boy arrives and tells the men that Godot will not come on that day. The strangeness of the drama – Vivien Mercier called *Waiting for Godot* 'a play in which nothing happens, twice' (Mercier 1956, qtd in Morash 2002: 207) – meant that it took several years to find a willing producer, even in the heady avant-garde atmosphere of late-1940s French theatre. When it was finally staged, the play exploded in notoriety and popularity, and was performed in an English translation by the author two and a half years later. That first anglophone production, surprisingly, was not in London, but in Dublin, in the forty-five-seat Pike Theatre, a small space run by the young theatre directors Alan Simpson and Carolyn Swift. It appeared, in a slightly bowdlerized form thanks to the Lord Chamberlain's control, in London earlier in that year, and, after a disastrous first North American run in Florida, established itself as a watershed work of theatre, and Beckett as a leading voice in what Martin Esslin would term 'the theatre of the absurd', with its Broadway debut in 1956.

Waiting for Godot remains one of the most influential plays of the twentieth century. And it is also a drama that makes visible – especially when performed by Irish actors – the influence of Beckett's Irish experiences and sense of Irish identity on his work. In *Beckett: The Irish Dimension*, Mary Junker carefully outlines specific references to Irish geography, language, and culture in five Beckett plays, including *Waiting for Godot*. For instance, she recognizes that the 'skull in Connemara' in Lucky's speech may refer not just to the region in the west of Ireland, but also to the Turoe Stone, 'an anthropomorphic image of pagan worship, dating from around 279 BC' (1995: 49). She also identifies Irish language words like '*bladar* – flattery or coaxing; *blathering* – talking, pleasantry; *dudeen* – a small clay pipe' (54) in the play, as well as Hiberno-English turns of phrase in the English language version of the work.[3]

But the play is also strikingly evocative of Irish history in its portrayal of exile and absence. Joseph Roach, for instance, finds in the echoes and silences in the dialogue of the play, along with the setting itself, the ghostly history of the Irish famine. He also sees remarks on famine in *Waiting for Godot* in the scarcity of food available in the play, and the fleeting, mobile presence of Pozzo (representing the absentee landlord) and his servant, Lucky.[4] But Beckett does not turn his drama into a straightforward analogy of the famine and its legacy: rather he simultaneously evokes that moment while placing it in a landscape on which other famines, other displacements, other ruptures in culture and history can be considered. 'History in Beckett's play,' Roach remarks, 'like so much else in the work of this most physical of playwrights, is made palpable, present to the senses even as absences – a silence, a stillness, an unbroken horizon. His art mimes the "violence of the unutterable" in a place – at once remembered and prophesied – where the bounty of the earth is bestowed on the profusion of its graves' (2002: 92).

Beckett would continue to be one of the leading avant-garde playwrights in the world until his death in 1989. His legacy of dramas in English, French, and without spoken words, continues to challenge performers and audiences around the world, and his work is a subject of international academic study. And, while it is true that Beckett's work transcends easy codification as belonging to one aesthetic school or national project, it is also true that his theatre was deeply informed by his personal and theatrical experiences in Ireland. The landscapes and legacies of Irish history haunt many of Beckett's plays, just as his plays haunt much Irish playwriting that has occurred since the mid-twentieth century. In the Derry cemetery of McGuinness's *Carthaginians* (1988), in the gendered no place of Marina Carr's *Woman and Scarecrow* (2007), Beckett's ghostly landscapes and evocative archetypes continue to trace an Irish counter-tradition for remembering Ireland's history on and off the theatrical stage.

Molloy's Mid-Century West

At the same time that Beckett's absurdist dramas were receiving attention across Europe and North America, M.J. Molloy was creating similarly archetypical dramas addressing the crisis of emigration on Irish rural life. Like George Fitzmaurice's fantastic realist plays in the 1930s, Molloy's dramas are inhabited by characters desperately trying to making their life experience meaningful in the face of the only life they know crumbling around them. Molloy was studying for the priesthood when a crippling bone disease forced him to leave that calling and, remembering his fondness for the productions of the Abbey Theatre, he turned to playwriting, and had his first Abbey production in 1943. And, while his dramas seem on the surface to belong to the realist tradition of the 1920s and 1930s, they also possess a political acumen that addresses Ireland's mid-century political crossroads. For Molloy, the decay of wealth, environment, and population in the Irish west signalled a failure on the part of the Irish government, and his plays can be read as an urgent call for sustainable development of that region. A year after Ford's nostalgic romp through a robust Irish west, Molloy staged a western community of old men and women huddling in the shadow of a decaying big house, the house itself symbolic of another dying Irish cultural tradition. The play, *The Wood of the Whispering* (1953), shows rural Ireland as 'a place of failure, thinned by emigration in a sort of reverse eugenics so that only the mad and impotent remained' (Morash 2002: 212).

The play opens on a setting that is grim indeed. Sanbatch Daly, a decrepit old man who has never married, finds himself squatting on the land outside the recently sold big house of the d'Arcy family, the former Anglo-Irish landlords of the region. The d'Arcy legacy literally haunts the region in the ghost of a woman raped by a d'Arcy landlord who claimed the droit de signeur a century before, even though the last of the d'Arcys, a scholar at Oxford, has lost the family fortune to alcoholism (Molloy 1998: 118) and sold off most of the estate. Sadie Tubridy, an agoraphobe who does not speak, lives nearby, brokenhearted that during her childbearing years no one in the village could afford to marry her. Other characters in the play are similarly broken in spirit or body, like Paddy King, a bachelor farmer in his seventies who '*had been a fine looking man probably, but now he is doting and imagines that he is still as young as he feels . . . [H]e has no doubt that he is the lady-killer of this country-side*' (125). Fortunately, there is enough youth in characters like Kitty, the only young person left in the county, Con, a man helping harvest the d'Arcy woods for industry, and Sheila Lanigan, who has returned briefly from England to help her father, to offer the community a glimmer of a future.

Despite the ruin and despair surrounding the characters, Sanbatch's tenacity manages to infect a life spirit into the dying community. In fact, Sanbatch even hints at earlier roguish characters like Boucicault's Myles na cGopaleen in *The Colleen Bawn*, or George Shiels's Rabit in *The New Gossoon*. By the end of the play, Sanbatch manages to arrange three marriages of couples who will remain in the community. Sheila will marry

Mark, the only young farmer still living there, and another couple – Con and his fiancée Kitty – will 'adopt' Sanbatch and help restore his farm. The third couple, Hotha Flynn and Sadie Tubridy, will not populate the community with children, as Sanbatch hopes the other pairings will, but instead will guarantee that Hotha and Sadie will not be alone in their old age.

Sanbatch's old-fashioned matchmaking creates a glimmer of hope for the future of his community which, like the house and forest surrounding it, has been abandoned or sold off by shifting economic and social circumstances. Sanbatch's comic success, with his refusal to give up on his rural community even when his own home has literally fallen in on him, serve as admonishment against what Molloy saw as a neocolonial governmental response to rural depopulation in the Republic of Ireland. In his 1961 preface to the play, Molloy bemoaned what he saw as neocolonial policies in Ireland that made the nation ripe for exploitation by larger powers, and that were made worse by the shrinking population. While the newly established nation of Israel grew in population and power, Molloy argued, Irish communities were disappearing with painful individual and national results, although Ireland's 'suburban depopulation enthusiasts' (112) were unaware of the problem. Molloy, however, makes the rift between the increasingly lonesome west and urban Ireland painfully clear when he describes how well the play was understood and performed by two amateur theatre companies from 'two tiny rural villages: Inchovea in County Clare and Killeedy in County Limerick, which between them won half a dozen drama festivals with it – before their dramatic societies were shattered by emigration' (112). Molloy's Irish west did not indulge in nostalgia for an idealized peasant life that never existed, but bemoaned the loss of real Irish communities to poor planning, and foresaw that such dissolutions meant not just the rise of 'eccentric old bachelors' (112) on the rural landscape, but also the weakening of Ireland's autonomy in cold war Europe. Molloy argued that:

> For forty years our slave-born economic and financial experts have continued to assure our slave-born political leaders that depopulation is all for the best; that big cattle ranches and big grain ranches are more economic than small farms. But neither cattle nor combine harvesters have ever fought for their country as small farmers have been known to do. (Molloy 1998: 111)

The dark, or even macabre, nature of Molloy's plays, with their strong sense of history, led many of his contemporaries to see him as a new J.M. Synge. Yet reviews of Molloy's work complained of a dissonance between the seriousness of his subjects and the comic acting and lively laughter of their performances at the Abbey (McGlone 2002: 102, 132). Molloy employed century-old tropes from both folk traditions and Victorian melodrama, to create his dark and deeply political, but also absurdly funny plays. Under Ria Mooney's hand, the Abbey performed the drama as both an exposure of the crumbling ways of life in rural Ireland, and a celebration of the spirit holding on to the possibility of survival or transformation. It is difficult, over half a century after those reviews were written, to determine whether the critics missed the deep irony in performance, or whether they were reacting to a still-weak theatre company going for easy laughs; but the critical reaction to *The Wood of the Whispering* does reveal that something new was happening in Irish dramatic writing – a complex and energetic style was emerging in 1950s Ireland in response to the disappointments and uncertainties of a rapidly changing nation, and the unfulfilled promises of the revolution forty years before.

This new kind of rural play may not have done well with Dublin critics, but it was hugely popular among amateur theatre companies. Indeed, the roots of Ireland's second wave lay not in the artistically divided and frustrated Abbey, but the lively amateur theatre movement across the island, with very different rules of aesthetics and spectatorship. As early as the mid-1940s, Christopher Morash notes, drama festivals bestowed honour on amateur companies according to strict rules 'by adjudicators from the professional theatre', and that there were 'a network of such festivals throughout the country, cutting across the Border and opening up parts of the country ignored by the traditional theatre geography' (2002: 211). This energy would be absorbed into national cultural events like the An Tostal festival in 1953, the All-Ireland Drama Festival in 1953 (210–11) and, ultimately, the Dublin Drama Festival in 1957. Despite the strict structures imposed on performances in the festivals, their audiences were far more aggressive in their responses to the work than the bourgeois audiences at the Abbey and the Gate. Molloy noted that 'The rural Irish audience is an Elizabethan audience. They're very rough – they come out for a night's fun, and if they don't get it from the stage they'll make it for themselves in the auditorium. That's why the first question asked after a production in my part of the country is "Did ye get good silence?" or "Did they give ye a hearing"?' (*Irish Times* 10 September 1955). Gus Smith and Des Hickey even report on the regular betting on the plays in these theatre contests (1992: 65). While these audiences may have been rowdy, they were also intelligent, informed theatregoers whose impact on Irish theatre mid-century was profound. And, despite the poor conditions in which the plays were often produced, they gave new playwrights the opportunity to develop their work through production; and the royalty cheques from these groups allowed playwrights like George Shiels and T.C. Murray to continue to live and work as playwrights full time in Ireland (Morash 2002: 195). It was out of this rich movement that John B. Keane emerged in the late 1950s, to become a major force in Irish dramaturgy for the rest of the century.

Freedom to Experiment: The Pike Theatre

Along with the rich tradition of amateur theatres in the small villages and towns of Ireland, new theatres with radical agendas emerged in both the Republic and Northern Ireland throughout the 1950s. The most famous and influential of these in the 1950s was the Pike Theatre. The Pike was founded in 1953 by Alan Simpson and Carolyn Swift, partners in life and onstage who, like Hilton Edwards and Michael Mac Liammóir three decades before, learned much of their craft by touring with Anew McMaster's company.[5] Simpson and Swift rented a very small space near Trinity College that could seat around forty-five or fifty audience members. The quality of their productions, and their controversial choices, made this tiny space the site of some of the most important – and most controversial – productions in Ireland in the 1950s.

The Pike's first major gift to the Irish stage was its cultivation of a new playwright, Brendan Behan, whose radical look at urban, working-class Ireland disrupted the Irish genre in a way that had not occurred since Sean O'Casey. While other Irish playwrights were continuing to explore realism, Behan looked back to melodrama and the music hall – not a surprising choice considering his family's close connection to Ireland's popular theatre tradition. Behan's uncle, P.J. Bourke, managed the Queen's Royal Theatre, the 'house of Irish melodrama', in the early twentieth century. Another uncle, Peadar Kearney, was a stage manager at the Abbey and the author of the Irish National Anthem, 'Soldier's Song'. The family's nationalist politics did not present themselves merely through art, however; and the Behans' strong Republican leanings led Brendan to become very active in the IRA from an early age. At sixteen, Behan was sent to reform school for involvement in a bombing in Coventry, and in 1942 he was arrested for attempted murder and spent several years at Mountjoy Prison and at Curragh Military Camp. He was released as part of a general amnesty in

1946, but was imprisoned in Manchester a year later for attempting to help an IRA prisoner escape.

It was in prison that Behan began to write, and when the Abbey rejected his play about prison life, *The Quare Fellow*, he offered it to the Pike. The Pike's directors readily accepted it, and produced it in 1954. Originally written in Irish and titled *The Twisting of Another Rope*, after Douglas Hyde's 1899 play, *The Twisting of the Rope* (*Casadh an tSugain*), Behan's first produced play traces the twenty-four hours before the execution of a prisoner in an Irish jail. In the course of the play, we get to know a range of prisoners and their guards, learn a little of their stories, and see how fiercely the prisoners struggle to maintain a sense of self, purpose, community, and dignity within the rigid structure of prison life. The prison itself can easily be read as a metaphor for human experience, with its inhabitants representing humanity's general search for existential meaning – indeed, the play resonates with dramaturgical strategies used by Beckett during the same period. Yet the drama also draws from Behan's own prison experiences, and hints at the ways individuals in the prison have fallen through the social fabric.

Although the men are in an Irish prison, it appears to have been built by the British; and the drama hints that, although the flag over the prison has changed, the class and social systems have not. As an old prisoner puts it, 'the Free State didn't change anything more [in the prison] than the badge on the warders' caps' (Behan 1978: 59). At the start of the play, we hear a prisoner singing about prison life, but we see no prisoners. What we do see are the locked doors to the prisoners' cells and a sign on which 'is printed in large block shaded Victorian lettering the word "Silence"' (39). Thus, from the rising of the curtain, the play juxtaposes a pre-revolutionary social order and the attempts of individuals trapped in this order – inmates as well as others – to resist it. Prisoner C, 'the boy from the island' who speaks Irish and English with a Kerry accent, is befriended by an Irish-speaking warden. When two older prisoners receive a massage on their rheumatic legs, they sneak drinks out of the bottle of liniment when the doctor's back is turned. Two younger prisoners sneak peeks at the girls hanging laundry in the women's prison nearby. The main business for the prisoners during the play, however, is talk of 'the quare fellow', or the man condemned to die, and the bits and pieces of his story that we learn in the course of the play lead us to feel for his plight. The desire for life and expression, however, is felt most viscerally in the play at the moment of the Quare Fellow's death. As the hour of the hanging strikes we see '*The WARDERS cross themselves and put on their caps'* while *'From the PRISONERS comes a ferocious howling'* (121). Throughout the play, we do not see the condemned man, but we hear secondhand of his desire for sound, even as the warders try to cut him off from signs of the other prisoners. He even makes a request through one of the more sympathetic warders for a young prisoner to sing a hymn at midnight for him. The howling from the prisoners at the moment of his death, therefore, is not a sign of disrespect but a keening, and a refusal to accept quietly the quare fellow's death at the hands of the state.

The Quare Fellow was a tremendous success at the Pike, and its critical celebration led to productions at both the Abbey Theatre and Joan Little-wood's Theatre Workshop at the Theatre Royal, Stratford East, in 1956. A year later, Jose Quintero directed the play at Circle-in-the-Square in New York (Hawkins 1997: 25). Behan's drama about IRA activity in mid-twentieth-century Ireland, *An Gial* (*The Hostage*), was performed in Irish by Gael Linn at Damer Hall, Dublin, in June of 1958 (Hawkins 1997: 26), and a translated and adapted production in English opened in London (again directed by Littlewood) in October of that year. Thus, within four years of his first theatrical production, Behan was internationally famous and, thanks to some charismatic (i.e., drunk and subversive) appearances on television and radio in England and the United States, he had attained a celebrity abroad beyond his plays. Critics of Behan's international celeb-rity remark that outside Ireland he became a kind of stage Irishman, while others saw his fame as a sign of the media's ability to dissolve borders between Ireland and its diaspora communities in the United States. There was also, as Alan Simpson noted, suspicion that Littlewood's Theatre Workshop had co-opted Behan's work for their own artistic ends, espe-cially *The Hostage*, which went straight from an Irish language production in Dublin to an English language production directed by Littlewood. Littlewood's collaborative style, linking high and low aesthetics, and use of Brechtian dramaturgical elements were very much in keeping with Behan's own politics and aesthetics, however. They were also at the vanguard of a new, radical movement in contemporary anglophone theatre that sought to radicalize the stage politically and artistically to address the crises of the post-war world. Despite questions of the autho-rial integrity of Behan's plays, in the long run, Behan's collaboration with Irish and English directors and international exposure made his plays part of an international movement to radicalize anglophone theatre, and his dramas, in turn, helped to radicalize the dramaturgical strategies on the Irish stage.

The Pike's other great theatrical coup of the 1950s was its first production of Samuel Beckett's *Waiting for Godot*, in 1955 – a production that
reflects the Pike's openness to new work, and its audiences' hunger for it,
and also radical playwrights' willingness to trust Simpson, Swift, and their
actors with their work.[6] The Irish government, however, was less comfortable with the Pike's sense of freedom, and exercised its authority over it
in 1957, when it shut down the theatre and arrested Simpson on an obscen-
ity charge over its production of Tennessee Williams's *The Rose Tattoo*. The
Pike decided to produce the play as its contribution to the first Dublin
Theatre Festival, an event organized by Brendan Smith and sponsored by
Bord Failte (the Irish tourist board) to stretch the tourist season and
promote Ireland's cultural capital (Morash 2002: 210). The Pike, heady on
its commercial and critical success over the previous years, reserved rental
of the Gate Theatre space for after the festival, planning to increase its
receipts by performing the play there. What the Pike did not anticipate was
that they would be scapegoated by still-dominant conservative forces
within Ireland that would shut the play down because of the suggestion
of a wrapped condom appearing onstage. At one point in *The Rose Tattoo*,
a condom falls out of a character's pocket, and he kicks it under a piece
of furniture. A female character sees it and, infuriated by its owner's pre-
sumption, throws him out of the house. Unable to procure an actual
condom, since such contraceptives were illegal in Ireland at the time, the
actors in the Pike production used a square of paper. The representation
of the illegal object, however, was enough for a group of plain-clothes
operatives to stop the production and arrest Simpson. Ireland had certainly
had its share of controversy over the morality of theatre productions. But,
for the first time, a major theatre production was being censored by the
state, under the encouragement of the Church. Although the case was
ultimately thrown out of court, its emotional and economic costs were
high for the Pike. The event certainly contributed to the Pike's eventual
closing and the dissolution of Simpson and Swift's marriage (Whelan
2002: 16).

In 1958, the Church flexed its political and cultural muscle at the An
Tostal Festival, when Archbishop John McQuaid refused to allow a Votive
Mass to be said for the festival in protest at the organizers' inclusion of
Sean O'Casey's *The Drums of Father Ned*[7] and *Bloomsday*, a dramatization
of Joyce's *Ulysses* by Allan McClelland, among the events. Beckett, infuriated, withdrew his own play from the festival in support of free speech,
and both Beckett and O'Casey refused to allow their work to be performed
in Ireland for years afterwards.[8] Indeed, events like the *Rose Tattoo* contro-

versy and McQuaid's stand at the An Tostal reflected the growing tensions among the rise in new and radical voices in Irish arts, the desire among the Irish government to capitalize on the economic and social profitability of this artistic innovation through tourism, and political anxiety about the effect of this new theatre movement on the conservative Catholic moral and cultural values on which the Irish Republic had been built. While it is true that the Republic of Ireland would not go after a theatre production with the same vociferousness again, and that *The Rose Tattoo* went on to have a highly well-received production that thrust Anna Manahan into stardom once the case had been thrown out of court, one can only guess at the kind of chilling effect the controversies of 1957 and 1958 had on future Irish theatre. Theatre in the Republic in the 1960s would continue to explore the changing states of Irishness in the changing Irish state, but in a fashion that took on the dramatic tropes of the previous generation, with a new sensibility that questioned assumptions about both Irish dramatic aesthetics, and Irish identity and history generally.

6

Irish Theatre's Second Wave

From the late 1950s, the hunger for performance generated by the amateur theatre groups in Ireland, along with innovations by professional groups at home and abroad like the Pike Theatre and Joan Littlewood's Theatre Workshop, vivified Irish theatre. A deep pool of talent among actors and producers, and knowledgeable and enthusiastic audiences, enticed writers to try their hand at writing for the stage. Out of this energetic milieu emerged a group of playwrights who would help transform the aesthetics of Irish realism. These playwrights, including J.B. Keane, Brian Friel, Tom Kilroy, Tom Murphy, and Hugh Leonard, established what Fintan O'Toole termed a 'second wave' in Irish theatre. There is no shortage of writings on these dramatists. This chapter, therefore, does not attempt to overview their long, influential, and prolific careers but, rather, to situate their origin in the context of other cultural and political movements and events of the time, thus pointing to their influence in future decades and on later playwrights.

Fighting for the Land: J.B. Keane

Born in Kerry in 1928, and raised by a father who was a national schoolteacher in Listowel (Kealy 1993: 20), Keane was exposed to litera-ture and oral storytelling from a very early age. He lived in Northamp-ton, England, briefly in the 1940s, working 'a variety of jobs, including two years as furnace operator at British Timken' (Kealy 1993: 19). He returned to Ireland, became a publican in 1955, and continued his dual career as pub owner and nationally prominent writer of plays and novels until his death. Keane's first plays were rejected by the Abbey Theatre, but won awards on the amateur theatre circuit, and were ulti-mately picked up by the Southern Theatre from Cork, a company founded by James N. Healy (founder of the Dublin Theatre Festival), Frank Sanquest, and Dan Donovan, and by Phyllis Ryan's Gemini Pro-ductions. These groups created the first productions of almost all of

Keane's plays, even after the Abbey began including Keane in their repertory.

Keane's dramas beautifully portray the tragic impact of emigration and modernization on a rural culture whose very identity is inextricably linked to the legacy of fighting for, nurturing, and protecting their land. In his 1965 play, *The Field*, for example, Bull McCabe, a fierce and violent man hardened by struggle, seeks to buy a field that will connect his land to the river, allowing him access to water for his farm. For years, he has had rights to this field, which he has significantly improved; and, now that this field is being sold by its recently widowed owner, he believes he has the right to purchase it. Since he is a leader of the community with strong familial and business ties, his neighbours are too intimidated by him to bid against him for the property. But before the land goes to auction, a stranger arrives who wants to purchase the land to build a cement factory – a move that will not only ruin Bull's farm but also damage the surrounding lands. Attempting to intimidate the stranger away from buying the field, Bull inadvertently kills him. While there are signs that Bull does feel guilty for his actions (he pays the widow more than he originally planned for the field, but less than half what the stranger was willing to pay), he refuses to admit his guilt and intimidates those closest to him to affirm his alibi. At the close of the play, the police sergeant and the priest try one last time to convince Bull to confess to the crime they all know he committed, but he does not submit, thinking that his actions were justified by his right to own the field.

> There's two laws. There's a law for them that's priests and doctors and lawmen. But there's no law for us . . . When you'll be gone, Father, to be a Canon somewhere and the Sergeant gets a wallet of notes and is going to be a Superintendant, [my son's] Tadhg's children will be milking cows and keeping donkeys away from our ditches. That's what we have to think about and if there's no grass, that's the end of me and mine. (Keane [1965] 1994a: 166)

Bull is a murderer who has short-changed a widow, but he has also managed to save the field and his community from the negative environmental impact of the cement plant. Yet although he has won this battle, it is clear that he is merely holding off his inevitable displacement with the encroachment of modernity into his community.

In the play *Big Maggie* (1969), it is an overpowering matriarch who defies convention and law to maintain her hold on the family land. On the death of her abusive husband, Maggie Polpin holds tightly on to the reigns of her household, possibly even hiding her husband's will so that she can maintain control of the property. Her bitterness over the cruelty of her violent, loveless, and almost sexless marriage makes her overly controlling of her children and their own desires for career and marriage. She threatens to disown a son who wants to marry a girl with no dowry, and she ruins a daughter's marital plans by seducing her daughter's fiancé. Although Big Maggie claims to do these things to protect her children, it is clear that her actions stem from her resentment towards her own failed marriage, and towards anyone – including her own children – who has a chance of the fulfilment in their youth she never gained. At the end of the play, Maggie offers a deeply revealing monologue that describes her sexual frustration and anger, directed not just towards her husband but also to the Church that alienated her from her own sexuality.

> Do you know my husband never saw me naked? He never saw me white and shiny and shivering without one blemish on me from head to heel. I must have seemed as frigid and cold to him as a frozen lake. How could I thaw with my upbringing and my faith, my holy, holy faith. . . . Oh I curse the stifling, smothering breath of the religion that withered my loving and my living and my womanhood . . .' Tis a wonder that I didn't surrender entirely to insanity in a country where it was a mortal sin to even think about another man . . . I'm too long a prisoner but I'll savour what I can, while I can and let the last hour be the sorest. (Keane [1969] 1994b: 234–5)

Keane was a master at capturing the tragic toll of holding on to the land and tradition in a changing world; and, as *Big Maggie* attests, he was also one of the most sensitive playwrights of his generation to the plight of rural Irish women. Catholicism celebrated motherhood while at the same time condemning sexuality outside procreation among married couples. Likewise, Irish national ideology after the war made the role of wife and mother a kind of patriotic duty. But the legacy of familism and unhappy marriages often led to resentment among women in Ireland, who wittingly or unwittingly enforced the same, strict status quo on other women. After all, these were the decades when the Madeleine Laundries across Ireland held Irish women in servitude to the Church for their lives as penance for such social offences as getting pregnant out of wedlock, or even for appearing too rebellious. Teresa Deevy's work in the 1930s, as we saw in chapter 3, illustrated the painful enculturation of female free spirits or young brides to obey cultural dictates as well as the consequences of the slightest sexual disobedience. Likewise, Keane's plays captured with equal compassion both the sentimental tragedy of the young woman torn between love and duty, like the eponymous character in his 1959 play, *Sive*, and the more poignant tragedy of the older woman mourning her limited life choices, like Sive's aunt, or Big Maggie. Big Maggie's sexual frankness in middle age makes her a radical character even today, not only in Irish theatre but in Western theatre generally. It has also become a coveted role for Irish actresses, and has been played by such leading lights of the Irish stage as Anna Manahan (for whom it was created) and Brenda Fricker.[1] Phyllis Ryan remarked of the drama that its expression of intergenerational conflict, cultural change, and sexual mores struck an unprecedented note with audiences across Northern Ireland and the Republic. Ryan noted:

> No play I can remember in a life spent in theatre made such a powerful impact on the Irish playgoer. In terms of business, any previous records were broken all over the country. In terms of emotive response from audiences, it seemed they could not get enough of his play, and large numbers of people from every walk of life went four or five times to see it. There was, it appeared, a Maggie Polpin in every household. (Qtd in Smith and Hickey 1992: 166)

Irish audiences were ready for Keane, even if the Abbey would not, or could not, take a chance on the Kerry publican. Thanks to the amateur theatre movement, however, and entrepreneurs like Ryan, revisions of the Irish theatre tradition danced in time to the longings and needs of audiences from the Olympia Theatre or the Cork Opera House, to a rural community hall basement.

Murphy and Friel's Historical Remembering

Perhaps the most strident commentator on mid-twentieth-century Ireland found among the second wave is Tom Murphy. Born in Tuam, County Galway, in 1935, Murphy, like J.B. Keane, received his early theatrical training by working with amateur theatre groups, in his case the Tuam Little Theatre Guild (Lanters 1997: 231) in the 1950s. In 1959 he 'won the manuscript prize at the All-Ireland Amateur Drama Competition' (231), but Ernest Blythe rejected his work for the Abbey, crtiticizing it heavily. Murphy then decided to move with his family to London to write for radio and television. While in London, he received a first professional production of his play *A Whistle in the Dark* with Joan Littlewood's Theatre Workshop. In this drama, Michael Carney, an Irish emigrant from rural Mayo living in urban England, and his wife, Betty, have their home and ultimately their lives taken over by other emigrating family members. By the end of the play, both Michael and Betty have moved out, leaving the house in the anarchic and angry hands of Michael's brothers and father. The plot and staging reflects the menacing theatre aesthetics of Harold Pinter's *The*

Caretaker or *The Homecoming*,[2] in which strong personalities use intimidation, as well as verbal, emotional, and physical violence to overpower other figures. Anthony Roche considers the Carney brothers' behaviour to reflect the anti-imperialist frustration of these economic exiles, who are in conflict 'between themselves and internalised figures of authority, whom they resent and admire, simultaneously want to do down and impress. In terms of the play's setting, there is the ambivalence of the Irish characters of living in England and earning money there while still trying to maintain a distinct cultural identity, of seeking to impress those around you in ways that only confirm their worst stereotypes' (1995: 140). Such an unflinching look at the violence and vulnerability felt by many of Ireland's millions of emigrants in the 1950s was pointedly counter to the images of Irish life still promoted in most Irish plays: the very idea of setting an Irish play beyond Ireland's geographic boundaries was radical in 1961, and would remain so for several decades to come. Thus, it is not surprising that, when Ernest Blythe saw a production of the drama at the Olympia Theatre, Dublin, in March 1962 he said, 'I never saw such rubbish in my life' (Roche 1995: 132).

Although several of his radio plays were produced in Ireland in the early 1960s, Murphy's work did not become a regular sight on the Dublin stage until the late 1960s. Even then, the critical assessments of his plays were quite uneven, for his loose plot structures, violent plots, and rough characters made some bridle that they were offering too negative a portrayal of Irish personality.[3] However, when Murphy struck the correct note with his Irish audiences, it resonated to the core of their national experience. Such a response emerged at the Peacock Theatre in 1968, when the Abbey, now under the direction of Tomas Mac Anna after Blythe's retirement, produced Murphy's play of one of Ireland's greatest historical traumas, *Famine*.

Inspired by Cecil Woodham Smith's important historical work, *The Great Hunger*, and informed by extensive research of both the Irish famine and the experience of famine in other cultures, Murphy's play captures in twelve episodes the tragically grotesque physical and social effects of the potato blight on the Irish landscape and the Irish psyche. The famine, Murphy has written, is not the only cause of what he calls 'the moodiness of Irish personality', but it also 'is a racial memory, it provides a debilitating history and that it has left its mark [on contemporary Ireland and Irish] I have no doubt' (Murphy 1992: xi). Thus, Murphy posits that the play is ultimately not just about the victims of famine in 1846, but 'the moody self and my times' (xi). In Brechtian fashion, Murphy's episodic narrative creates a cognitive distance in the drama that allows us to grieve the horrors of the famine while simultaneously engaging with the famine's continuing social legacy. In the course of the play, different characters starve, acquiesce to imperialist authorities, resist starvation through violence, and emigrate. And each kind of act in the face of famine is seen by Murphy as shaping the future of Irish history. Malachy, for example, a character who violently resists imperial power and its absurd policies in the face of the national disaster, disappears in the play, but what has actually happened to him remains a mystery.[4] For Murphy, this amorphous subject position makes Malachy:

> the violent *consequence* of famine. (As the play's different levels began to find the overall balance, I saw Malachy as a foretaste of the atrocities that were to follow in the Land Wars; I saw him, also, as a precursor in a direct line that led to Michael Collins, the great, decisive, guerilla leader who came seventy-or-so years later.) And, of course, Malachy is the personification of a revenge-theme taken up by other characters. Or, he has gone to America where, like other Irish emigrants, he becomes a gangster and fathers gangsters, like machine-gun Kelly or Legs Diamond – Capone-like. Whichever, he is a violent part of the future. (Murphy 1992: xvii)

But these violent characters are clearly shaped by the trauma of institutional violence, demonstrated powerfully through visual and verbal elements of the play. From the first episode, the panic among the farmers that the crops will fail for the second year is palpable. The farmers' elation and excitement at finding their power to intimidate and conquer through violence after they overturn a corn cart is predicated by the carter's inability to grasp why the farmers would sell their oats when they had nothing to eat, not realizing that they sold their oats to afford their rents. The absurdity of capitalist bureaucracy that blinds even witnesses of the famine to the truth of the situation is overturned, like the cart, by a more primitive and straightforward example of survival of the fittest. The violent act of stealing the oats, however, pales when compared to the social violence of exporting food while those who raised it starve to death. Likewise, in one of the most chilling scenes in the play, a young couple woo under the moonlight (the young man, Liam, gives the young woman, Maeve, an apple and some nuts that he has hidden away), unaware until the moon shines full through the clouds that the corpse of a mother and child and the dying father lie only a few feet from them. As the young couple take the first steps towards sexual union, highlighted with such imagery as the woman eating an apple in a natural setting like Eve in the garden of Eden, the ultimate inability of the land to support any children who might emerge from their relationship is made horrifyingly clear in the dead mother and child lying at the lovers' feet. Procreation is corrupted and cut off by the unnaturally devastating effect on the population due to one crop's failure.

Notably, Murphy carries the tragedy of the famine across the diaspora, seeing 'the future' of Ireland as one that encompasses not only the island's geographic borders, but also the centres of industry across Europe, Australia, and America, where the Irish experience influences the cultures of both their home country and the new lands they have made their homes,[5] economically, socially, and mythically. Indeed, *Famine* quickly became regarded as a major and influential Irish work, but just as the play's plot and aesthetic strategies address the Irish diaspora, so did they address and contribute to the avant-garde innovations that had radicalized the English stage since the 1950s. Like Sean O'Casey, Murphy wrote of the national struggle as an economic struggle, and he saw the legacy of Irish abjection informing the Irish psyche and Irish behaviour in communities throughout the world. As Ireland grappled with economic crisis, rapid modernization, and a rural population emptying into cities at home and abroad, characters like the Carney brothers or Malachy expressed the desire among many emigrants to resist the colonial stereotype and the sense of imperial abjection or superiority that they confronted away from home. In later Murphy plays, like *The Gigli Concert* (1983), this desire to outrun history translates into a desire for a kind of spiritual transcendence, but at the core of Murphy's works lies a sense of personal pain created from an internalized, historically grounded sense of loss. The dramaturgical strategies he uses to take us to that core were influenced by both the aesthetics of the Irish stage of previous generations, and Brechtian-influenced dramaturgies examining the intersections of history and class across 1950s Europe.

Murphy's contemporary, Brian Friel, also helped reshape the look of Irish theatre thanks to exposure to theatre practice abroad. Born in Omagh, County Tyrone, in 1929, Friel lived and studied in Derry and Maynooth before becoming a teacher and writer. His experiences as a Catholic living on both sides of the border of Northern Ireland and the Republic informed his sense of identity and the ways he would address the Irish question in his critical writings as well as his plays. By 1960, he had gained enough success to retire from teaching and write full time (Farquharson), but he still considered himself an underdeveloped playwright. To build his skills, he received permission in 1964 to observe the rehearsal and production practices at the Guthrie Theatre in Minneapolis, Minnesota, USA, as part of a dramaturgy programme there. The Guthrie Theatre was founded the year before by Tyrone Guthrie, an internationally famous actor who was born in England to Irish parents, and maintained intimate ties to Ireland throughout his life. In 1960, Guthrie, in collaboration with other actors, private and government grants, and the city of Minneapolis, decided to create a regional repertory company to cultivate excellent and innovative productions outside the growing commercial pressures of Broadway. Friel returned to Ireland from Minnesota with a new sense of dramaturgy, and a new play, *Philadelphia Here I Come!* The Gate Theatre's Hilton Edwards agreed to direct the drama, and provided the lighting and the design for its first production as part of the 1964 Dublin Theatre Festival. The play was a tremendous success and, just as Murphy's *Famine* would a few years later, pushed the aesthetic of the mainstream Irish stage beyond the realist settings and situations on which it continued to rely, despite Beckett and Behan's success with much more radical forms.

Philadelphia, Here I Come! is not a complete break from Irish scenographic tradition, however. In fact, a kitchen is indeed a major element of the design of the play. But even more prominent in the play's design was the bedroom of the twenty-five-year-old protagonist of the drama, Gar. A third, less specific, space is present on the stage for 'flashbacks' of experiences in Gar's life, or scenes like his trip to a pub with friends. Gar, or Gareth O'Donnell, is the son of a County Councillor and shop owner, who lives with his father and the family housekeeper, but whose mother died of medical complications a few days after he was born. The play is set on the eve of his emigration to Philadelphia, where he will stay with his mother's sister – a woman who wants to 'adopt' Gar since she had no children of her own – and work in a job at a hotel that his aunt has arranged for him.

Friel exposes the sense of rupture experienced by the individual moving from homeland to diaspora by literally splitting his character in two. Gar is played by two actors – 'Public Gar' and 'Private Gar'. In the stage direction, Friel explains that *'PUBLIC GAR is the Gar the people see, talk to, talk about. PRIVATE GAR is the unseen man, the man within, the conscience, the alter ego, the secret thoughts, the id'* (Friel 1984a: 27). Private Gar, being an alter ego, is seen by no one on stage and only heard by Public Gar, who engages with Private Gar throughout the play. In Gar's bedroom, his two selves engage freely in conversation: in other spaces, their interactions are more subtle. These halves consider such matters as the future that awaits him, his difficult relationship with his father, and his heartbreaking love for a local woman, whose father, an Irish senator, refused to allow them to marry (his emigration, in fact is occurring on the heels of his love's marriage to a more 'appropriate' man for a senator's daughter).

At first Gar seems elated about the change – he sings 'Philadelphia, Here I Come' to the tune of the vaudeville song made famous by Al Jolson in the 1920s, 'California Here I Come'.[6] But his eager resolve wears thin during the course of the play. As he comes closer to leaving all that he knows and loves, he grows frustrated that no one seems to acknowledge that this is his last evening in the community, as if he has already left. In the last scene of the play, Gar returns from his night on the town, and watches the housekeeper, a mother figure for him for years, head off to bed. Private Gar says: 'Watch her carefully, every movement, every gesture, every little peculiarity: keep the camera whirring; for this is a film you'll run over and over again – Madge Going to Bed On My Last Night At Home . . . Madge . . . (PUBLIC and PRIVATE go into bedroom.) God, Boy, why do you have to leave? Why? Why?' Public Gar responds, 'I don't know. I-I-I don't know' (Friel 1984a: 99).

While *Philadelphia, Here I Come!* is more sentimental in its characterizations and less urgent in its politics than Murphy's work, it captures beautifully the imaginative world of its protagonist, and mourns the societal limits in his community that make emigration necessary for him to achieve a maturity and independence that he has been unable to attain living in his father's house as his shop assistant. But the cost of this personal fulfilment is societal dislocation. Seamus Deane remarks that:

> The central figures in [*Philadelphia* and other early Friel plays] find themselves torn by the necessity of abandoning the Ireland which they love, even though, or perhaps because, they realize that they must bow to this necessity for the sake of their own integrity as individuals rather than as a consequence of economic or political pressures. Although the different kinds of pressure forcing them to leave their homeland are interconnected, their ultimate perception is that fidelity to the native place is a legal form of nostalgia, an emotion which must be overcome if they are, quite simply, to grow up. ('Introduction', 1984: 13)

In light of Deane's critique, Friel's play could be read as both a statement about emigration and exile in mid-twentieth-century Ireland, and as an example of the universal trope of the *Bildungsroman*, focusing on Gar's escaping Ballybeg's stultifying provinciality, cultivated by decades of conservative social policies for 'a more metropolitan, if shallower' world (Deane 1984: 13).[7] It is not just Gar, however, who is trapped in this dilemma, but also Friel's audience themselves who, like Gar, are torn between their desire for the nostalgia of Ballybeg, the imaginary

Donegal town Friel invented for this drama and would continue to use as a setting in later plays, and the need for representations of Irish community more in keeping with Ireland's changing demographics. Friel's play simultaneously entertains our longing for a sentimental and nostalgic look at a small Irish town, and reveals the cultural oppressions that underlie that romanticized image, as well as the historical events that break that image apart.

Theatre and the Troubles

Four years after Friel's expression of small-town life in Donegal appeared at the Dublin Theatre Festival, a much more urgent and violent drama was unfolding on the streets of Derry and Belfast. Civil rights demonstrations by Northern Irish Catholics led to violent exchanges between demonstrators and police. By 1969, British troops had entered Northern Ireland as peacekeepers, but soon found themselves in the eyes of many in the position of an occupying army. The situation quickly exploded into accelerated activity by Republican and Unionist organizations, like the Irish Republican Army and the Ulster Defence Association. In Belfast in 1971, for example, the city saw '73 pubs destroyed with 4 clubs and 185 shops put out of business' (Byrne 2001: 8). While this severely affected theatregoing in Belfast and other major cities, smaller communities continued to produce plays (Byrne 2001). While initially some officials expected the theatres to provide escapist fare during such troubled times, in fact the theatre in Northern Ireland responded immediately to the activities in its streets by producing classic plays dealing with political violence, from Sean O'Casey to Buchner's nineteenth-century play, *Danton's Death*. The urgency of the violent crisis in Northern Ireland inspired playwrights like Stewart Parker, John Boyd, Patricia O'Connor, and playwright/community theatre producer Martin Lynch, as well as actors like Stephen Rea, Liam Neeson, and Marie Jones to produce theatre deeply engaged in addressing the crisis.[8] As David Grant remarks, 'One of the great ironies of the last thirty years is that the political turmoil which is usually seen as having rung the death knell of local theatre [in Northern Ireland] may, in fact, have been its salvation' (2001: 29).

The leading theatre in Belfast during the 1970s was one of its most artistically distinguished – the Lyric Players Theatre.[9] Thanks in part to a government subsidy, the Lyric continued to produce theatre in Belfast city despite threats of violence and smaller attendance numbers. Mary O'Malley and her husband, Padraic, founded the Lyric Players in the 1950s to produce poetic drama – their first performances included Yeats's dance play *At the Hawk's Well* and *The Dreaming of the Bones* (Bell 1971: 84–5) – as well as international fare. Also, in the spirit of the Abbey and the Gate theatres, O'Malley began publishing a companion journal of writing and criticism, *Threshhold*. The journal included contributions by pillars of the Irish literary renaissance, like Padraic Colum and Desmond Ryan, as well as newer voices, like John Montague, Tomas Kinsella, Mary Beckett, and Seamus Deane. By the 1960s, the Lyric Players had established a reputation as the predominant interpreter of Yeats's drama (Bell 1971: 85). They also produced plays by Sean O'Casey, and Mary Manning's *The Voice of Shem*, a drama based loosely on *Finnegans Wake* (Bell 1971: 85–6). In 1968 the company moved into a new performance space and, in 1971, they were one of two companies to receive funding from the Arts Council (Byrne 2001: 11).[10] The Lyric responded to its new venue and new funding with a wider artistic mission to address the political crisis in the community around the theatre, opening a school of drama and beginning to work with theatre for youth.

In 1971, the Lyric produced John Boyd's drama about sectarian violence, *The Flats*, which would become touted as the first Troubles play. The drama follows a Catholic family living in government housing in 1969, shortly after the arrival of the British army, who get embroiled in civic unrest. *The Flats* is often critiqued for being too sentimental in its portrayal of political violence, and for not offering ideas about a solution (Bell, Grant). In fact, some critics see Boyd's play as an example of what came to be called the 'Troubles play' – a drama that focused on the impact of the war on a small group of individuals, that did not ultimately look at systemic causes for the violence or posit strategies for change. However, *The Flats* did break new ground by representing contemporary events through performance, and by looking at Northern Irish violence as a class and gender issue rather than simply a matter of religion. In 1975, Patrick Galvin's *We Do It For Love* provided a satiric look at Belfast violence. David Grant notes that, 'Outsiders were aghast at the uproarious response to jokes aimed directly at the violence. But in 1975, what suspect devices throughout the city were doing too literally, in a packed Lyric Theatre the laughter – figuratively – lifted the roof' (2001: 32). These Lyric productions broke ground for new Northern Irish voices, such as Stewart Parker and Martin Lynch, to take the stage in future years.

Theatre in the Irish Republic, likewise, developed a body of work about the Troubles, but the Abbey's first attempt at such a drama, a satirical review entitled *A State of Chassis*, penned by Jon D. Stewart, Eugene Waters, and Abbey director Tomas Mac Anna on the Peacock Stage, led to a minor riot. Once again, the Abbey misjudged the tone of its audience by choosing satire to describe a struggle over which its audience would be particularly sensitive.

On the opening night, a number of Northern Irish politicians were in the audience, including a group led by Eamonn McCann, chairman of the Derry Labour Party, who broke up the performance just before the inter-mission by taking the stage, announcing their objections to the play and handing out leaflets (Morash 2002: 230). Once a fight broke out, Mac Anna escorted McCann from the hall. Ironically, the focus of the protest, similar to that of *The Playboy of the Western World* sixty-three years before, was the representation of Irish womanhood – specifically, the representation of Nationalist MP and activist Bernadette Devlin, who was actually in prison for her political activities as the play was being produced. The actress playing the inspiring public speaker Devlin took the stage at a point in the play and sang, 'I'll tell me ma when I got home / The prods won't leave the tagues alone / They pulled my hair and stole my comb / and left me whingin' on my own . . .' (qtd in Morash 2002: 230).[11] McCann's response to these lines as he climbed on to the stage was 'The caricature of Bernadette Devlin is a disgrace . . . the people here are total hypocrites' (Hunt 1979: 211).

Christopher Morash notes that 'the response to McCann's disruption of *A State of Chassis* revealed the gulf between liberals in the South and working-class republicans in the North' (2002: 230). Once again, the national politics assumed of the national theatre were in conflict with the expectations of content and behaviour among the Abbey's middle-class audience base and directorship, who saw the theatre as a site for thought and reflection rather than action. One respected the performance by not interfering with it – whether by unwrapping candies during the show or climbing onstage to stop the performance. Since 1950, when there had been a minor disturbance over *Design for a Headstone*, the Abbey theatre had not experienced a major audience intervention of a production as it had in its earlier days. In the months and years after *A State of Chassis*, however, it became clear that Irish theatre indeed needed to develop an activist poetics that addressed the issues of Ireland's working classes North and South, and of the new and past crises being brought to the fore by the Troubles, as well as the rapid socio-political change occurring in the Republic.

The Abbey went on to produce other plays dealing with the Troubles, but those works, while thought-provoking, did not necessarily advocate radical action. They did, however, show how second-wave writers like Tom Kilroy and Brien Friel were moving into new territory with their work, challenging the aesthetic, cultural, and political codes of their country in order to reassess Ireland's past and present histories. Brian Friel's *Freedom of the City*, performed at the Abbey in 1973, pushed the Troubles play outside the already stale format of looking only at the impact of the Troubles on a small group within a domestic setting, and instead put his characters in a diverse and public forum that challenged the characters, and likewise the audience, to think about the situation as more than a simple, intractable battle between religious 'tribes', but a conflict deeply affected by class, gender, economics, and politics.

From the mid-1970s, an explosion of new forms of staging and writing began to appear, many of which sought to re-evaluate the historical narratives that affirmed particular beliefs about Irish culture and identity. Margaretta d'Arcy, a Northern Irish actress and playwright, and her husband, the English-born John Arden,[12] co-wrote several plays that employed Brechtian techniques to offer socialist perspectives on issues of great significance to Ireland, such as the role of the Church in government, globalism, and land distribution, and the history of nationalist resistance to imperialism in the nineteenth century. Their most ambitious project, a drama about the life of Irish socialist revolutionary leader John Connolly, *The Non-Stop Connolly Show: A Dramatic Cycle of Continuous Struggle in Six Parts*, was performed at Liberty Hall in Dublin, the headquarters of the Irish Transport and General Workers' Union – an organization founded by James Connolly. Sponsored by the ITGWU and Sinn Fein, the Irish nationalist political party with close ties to the IRA. The drama took twenty-four hours to perform, and included a cast of over thirty professional and amateur players. That same year, Belfast playwright Stewart Parker triumphed at the Dublin Theatre Festival with *Spokesong: or The Common Wheel*, an imaginative, musical, comic drama about the Troubles, with music written by Belfast composer Jimmy Kennedy.[13] Taking place over a period between the 1890s and the 1970s, Parker's play simultaneously celebrates and grieves for the troubled city of Belfast through the lens of a love story between a bicycle-shop owner and a teacher named Daisy. And, in 1977, Tom Kilroy's play *Talbot's Box* reconsidered the life of Matt Talbot, an unskilled labourer, recovering alcoholic, and Catholic ascetic, in an innovative staging at the Abbey Theatre that questioned contemporary notions about identity and history and the role of the Catholic Church in contemporary life in the Irish Republic.

These plays joined avant-garde work being produced throughout Europe and North America during this period. The appearance of such work was more than simple fashion, however. It was also a response to a revisionist historical approach, taking root in Irish cultural thought, that claimed that the Irish Republic would have evolved without the war for independence, and that Northern Ireland should remain outside the Irish Republic. Resistance to this attitude informed much drama and writing of these years, and inspired a literary magazine, *The Crane Bag*, which sought a productive means of engaging with history and the present through art, and of simultaneously dealing with the serious issues confronting both the Republic and Northern Ireland by 'formulating the idea of a fifth province of the imagination, a second centre for the country independent of the centre of power' (Heaney 1982: 8). In the 1980s, in the context of that imaginary space, some of the most dynamic, imaginative, and influential political theatre emerged in Ireland since its first years.

Part IV
Re-imagining Ireland, 1980–2007

Introduction to Part IV

In the 1890s, the Irish cultural revival sought to create images of Ireland and the Irish counter to British imperialist stereotypes. The founders of the Irish Literary Theatre narrowed that definition somewhat in calling for a theatre that would transcend 'the questions that divide us', acknowledging a range of identity positions among the Irish people. But by the 1940s, the dominant Irish political discourse increasingly described the citizens of the twenty-six counties as a far more united community than it was. Patrick Hanafin, Barry Collins, and others see this shift occurring through Ireland's ideologically conservative Constitution of 1937, which 'attempted to make by the invocation of the rural ideal, a hybrid of Irish nationalism, Catholicism and, most importantly, Gaelic romanticism. In this move, the historical legitimacy of the new state could be defined through the constitution by an appropriation of diverse symbols from an imagined past, a golden age of Gaelic unity and moral certainties' (Collins and Hanafin 2001: 53). By the late 1970s, an overwhelming number of historical events and demographic trends, including the Troubles, a rising interest in women's rights, lowering numbers attending Roman Catholic services or entering Church vocations, and the Republic entering the European Economic Community, made abundantly clear that this narrow and singular understanding of the Irish people was not only oppressive, but untenable, and that it ultimately served to exacerbate conflicts raised by cultural and political differences, especially between the Republic and Northern Ireland (Brown 2004; Kiberd 2001).

Irish theatre in both the Republic and Northern Ireland responded to this crisis by creating new work intended either to create an imaginative space inclusive of all Irish difference, or to address the particular needs and concerns of a smaller, overlooked social group. The most famous examples of both these approaches, interestingly, emerged out of Northern Ireland. The Field Day Theatre, founded in 1980 by playwright Brian Friel and actor Stephen Rea, became a laboratory for embodying through performance the historical and critical renegotiations of Irish history and identity in play by Irish cultural scholars like Richard Kearney and Seamus Deane. Martin Lynch and other Belfast playwrights, on the other hand, chose the format of community theatre to empower local groups to have their voices heard, and to advocate for change. Class, religion, sexuality, and women's rights issues were given unprecedented focus in Irish theatre in the 1980s. And, a little ironically, these 'minority discourses' were given unprecedented support by the governments of Northern Ireland and the Republic.

In the 1970s, the Abbey Theatre, the Gate Theatre, and the Lyric Theatre, Belfast, were the only theatres receiving major government support. Garry Hynes's Druid Theatre Company, which was offering innovative, high-quality performances in Galway, was initially denied government aid, but was offered a small amount of funding from Bord Failte, or the Irish Tourist Board. But, from the 1980s, increased arts funding would impact the Irish stage in important ways. In 1982, the Aosdana, an honorary body of 150 (later 200) artists, was established in the Republic, offering 'five-year annuities for artists resident in Ireland who depended solely on their creative work' (Brown 2004: 346). The Irish Film Board was established in 1981 to promote and provide financial support for Irish film. And new, small professional theatre companies, like Charabanc (Belfast, 1983), Rough Magic (Dublin, 1984), Blue Raincoat (Sligo, 1990) and Corcadorca (Cork, 1991) began to emerge. The creation of these small professional companies was crucial to theatrical innovation in Ireland, because it made available to avant-garde playwrights and pro-ducers the degree of skill and resources necessary to try out non-traditional dramaturgies that would be beyond the abilities of many amateur com-panies. By the 1990s, Irish theatre's rebellion against tradition that had been at play since the 1950s turned into full revolution, deconstructing the ubiquitous peasant kitchen plays and all they represented, and finding inspiration at home and abroad in the avant-garde work of theatre companies like Théâtre de Complicité (London), and Théâtre du Soleil (Paris). This exploration of new forms had been in play in Ireland since the 1950s, but by the 1990s it was fully de rigueur.

At the same time that Irish theatre was taking on new forms, a questioning of Irish norms likewise exploded in everyday life, thanks to a series of political and social scandals. In 1992, it was revealed that Eammon Casey, Bishop of Galway, had secretly fathered a child in the 1970s, and helped support the child with Church funds. This scandal, however, was quickly overshadowed by revelations of sexual abuse by priests that had often been covered up for years by the Church. The Irish government, too, experienced its share of scandal. In 1992, it was revealed for the first time that

Taoiseach John Hughey, famous for both a luxurious personal lifestyle and government policies based on frugality (in 1987 he cut £485 million from the budget (Brown 2004: 353)), took huge bribes while in office, after falling deeply into debt. Revelations of tax evasion among Ireland's upper classes also emerged. In 1993 a tax amnesty for evaders willing to report their crime 'brought in about £200 million . . . with £1.3 billion written off' (Brown 2004: 378). And the 'Miss X' abortion case, in which a teenaged, pregnant rape victim who had threatened suicide was forced to remain in Ireland rather than obtain an abortion in England, showed the extremes to which the government could exploit current laws to invade its citizens' personal lives and dictate their behaviour.

It is not surprising therefore that new legislation in the Republic put personal rights over moral platitudes. In the early 1980s, failed attempts to legalize abortion, decriminalize homosexuality, and allow divorce in the Republic seemed to affirm the conservative Catholic nature of the population, although resistance against these causes showed that dissent was in the air. By the 1990s, homosexuality was decriminalized, divorce became legal (although difficult) and, while abortion remained illegal, access to information about abortion was made available for the first time.

Along with these shifts towards allowing for a more diverse and permissive society came tremendous changes in the national economy. The economy grew an average of 7 per cent each year of the 1990s, and consumer spending rose from £23 billion in 1995 to £40 billion in 2000. Indeed, this fantastic prosperity, termed popularly 'the Celtic Tiger', likewise created growth in population and housing. The population rose by 8 per cent from 1996 to 2002, with a population that year of 3,917, 377 (Brown 2004: 383). Many of these new Irish were immigrants from other countries, including a large refugee population. In 2007, 10 per cent of Ireland's workforce was made up of foreign nationals and, in Lady Gregory's hometown of Gort, one third of the population was from Brazil (BBC, 'Ireland's New Multicultural Mix', 18 May 2007).

Perhaps the most important change in Irish culture in the 1980s and 1990s, however, was the progress made towards peace in Northern Ireland – progress that required all parties involved to re-imagine both past claims and future possibilities. Preliminary steps in the 1980s, such as the Anglo-Irish Agreement (1985) that allowed the Republic of Ireland a 'consultative' role in Catholic affairs in Northern Ireland, made small progress and often increased the resolve of unionist groups, largely because of the Republic's claim in its Constitution to sovereignty over the six counties making up Northern Ireland. Real progress began in 1995, when Irish Prime Minister

John Bruton agreed to modify the claim to sovereignty in the Constitution in exchange for British Prime Minister John Major's accession to allow the reunification of Northern Ireland with the Republic if the majority of the people of Northern Ireland so chose. The following year, United States Senator George Mitchell began negotiations among the groups that, two years later, resulted in the Good Friday Agreement, voted in by strong majorities in both Northern Ireland and the Republic of Ireland. A decade later, while conflict does continue, it appears that peace, if not reunification, is at hand. The last British troops stationed in Northern Ireland withdrew in June of 2007.

One of the outcomes of the Republic's Northern Irish negotiations was a legislative – and perhaps ideological – reconception of Irish identity. In the original Constitution, Article 2 declared: 'The national territory consists of the whole island of Ireland, its islands and the territorial seas.' With the passing of the Good Friday Agreement, this language was changed to, 'It is the entitlement and birthright of every person born in the island of Ireland, which includes its islands and seas, to be part of the Irish Nation. That is also the entitlement of all persons otherwise qualified in accordance with law to be citizens of Ireland. Furthermore, the Irish nation cherishes its special affinity with people of Irish ancestry living abroad who share its cultural identity and heritage.' A geographic notion of identity is replaced by a statement that actually extends the notion of identity beyond physical borders, reaching out to the Irish diaspora, as well as to those of Irish and non-Irish ancestry closer to home.

This section explores some of the ways Irish theatre in the last decades of the twentieth century sought to re-imagine Irish identity through performance. Among other topics, chapter 7 examines two of the most important theatre groups in Ireland's history, Field Day and Charabanc, and their strategies for creating new ways to examine old problems. Chapter 8 considers how the radical social and economic shifts in Irish culture led to what is sometimes called a 'third wave' of Irish theatre, as playwrights and theatre companies addressed the rapid socio-political change of this era, and contributed to an unprecedented diversity of representational strategies to describe Ireland's rapidly diversifying culture.

Theatres Without Borders:
Irish Theatre in the 1980s

On 23 September 1980, Brian Friel's *Translations*, a drama about language, history, colonization, and partition, received its world premiere in Derry, Northern Ireland, one of the most politically divided cities on the island. Friel set the play in Donegal during the 1824 Ordnance Survey, when British soldiers made an official map of Ireland and, in the process, renamed its towns and landmarks from Irish to English. In an ironically comic scene in the play, Owen, an Irishman in Donegal helping the British army to translate the names of all landmarks from Irish to English, instructs his father, Hugh, a polyglot schoolmaster, on how to manoeuvre through the new 'English' landscape. When asked where the priest lives, Hugh, who has lived in the community all his life, replies, 'At Lis na Muc, over near . . .' (418) only to be interrupted by his son. Owen 'corrects' his father, replying to him, 'No he doesn't. Lis na Muc, the Fort of Pigs, has become Swinefort . . . And to get to Swinefort you pass through Greencastle and Fair Head and Strandhill and Gort and Whiteplains. And the new school isn't at Poll na gCaorach – it's at Sheepsrock. Will you be able to find your way?' (418). In response, 'Hugh *pours himself another drink*' (418), silenced briefly by the way the colonizer's new map is literally shifting the ground beneath his feet.

This exchange between father and son on the brink of a moment of rupture in Irish history – the eve of the establishment of the English lan-guage schools, rising emigration, and the increasing Anglicization of the Irish people – is also emblematic of the historic effect of colonialism on the Irish people. Hugh and Owen, father and son, share the same physical place, but different ideological spaces. The landscape – of Donegal, of language, of fact – alters according to whose map one uses, whose ideol-ogy one attempts to navigate. At the end of the play, Donegal has been mapped by two cultures, and two languages – that of the colonizer and that of the colonized. An imperial map has left a colonial identity on the landscape that the Irish characters in the play are compelled to inhabit, even as they violently resist colonization.

Audiences at the premiere of *Translations* at the Guildhall, Derry, were well used to navigating multiple ideological maps in their community. The very name of their city pointed to this legacy. Londonderry was the official, British name of this ancient city from the early seventeenth century until 1978, when a Catholic-majority City Council returned the city's name to Derry.[1] Its historical importance as a British stronghold in the seventeenth century, and the more recent memories of sectarian violence and the death of thirteen unarmed protesters during a civil rights protest on 'Bloody Sunday', 1972, likewise showed how the city was a contested site between nationalists and unionists – a city of contested landscapes. Indeed, for the Catholic and Protestant citizens of Derry who were in the audience during that opening night, their very attendance was a kind of performance – an almost ritualistic gathering in their city's historical seat of power to view the dramatization of a defining moment in their shared histories. To add to the meaning of the production, it was the first professional play rehearsed and performed in Derry in 200 years (Morash 2002: 233).[2] Derry theatre-goers that night did not have to go to Belfast or Dublin to see a professional production by their nation's most celebrated playwright. The theatre came to them. Despite what could easily be read as a pro-Republican theme, the drama received a standing ovation and rave reviews in Derry, as it did when it proceeded to tour in small towns and large cities across Northern Ireland and the Republic (Richtarik 2001: 51–3).

Since the 1960s Irish theatre, while maintained largely by a tremendous number of excellent amateur theatre groups throughout the island, had defined itself hierarchically mainly through the major theatres at the island's two urban centres – Dublin's Abbey and Gate theatres, and the Lyric in Belfast. The Abbey, as the nation's national stage, was blessed not just with funding but also an institutional authority, regardless of how lacklustre its performances might have been. *Translations*, and its producing company, the Field Day Theatre Company, moved outside of this historical 'mapping of the theatrical landscape'. Its very rootlessness freed it to move in and out of the communities it wished to serve, transgressing boundaries of urban/rural, North/South, Catholic/Protestant, Nationalist/Unionist. And, by transgressing such borders, the company hoped also to transcend them. Indeed, Field Day was quickly recognized as one of the most important of several theatre companies in the 1980s that aimed to transgress the ideological habitus of Irish historical and political thought through performance.[3] This chapter will explore the range of artistic, ideological, and physical border crossings attempted by a number of playwrights and theatre companies in Ireland throughout the 1980s. Beginning with a close look at Field Day, it will then relate that company's work to the community theatre movement[4] in Belfast and the important work of the all-woman company Charabanc. This chapter also considers several significant plays outside the community theatre tradition that worked along similar lines in order to challenge perceived notions of Irish history, give voice to under-represented communities within Ireland, or make connections between Ireland's colonial experience and that of other nations. And in all cases, it will consider how, in the process, these playwrights and companies stretched Irish theatre's artistic boundaries, re-evaluating, commenting on, or breaking free of the peasant kitchen realist style that continued to inform much Irish drama.

Playing in the Fifth Province: Field Day

The Field Day Theatre Company, one of the most influential Irish performance companies of the last fifty years, began as a proposal for a one-time collaboration between Brian Friel and Irish actor Stephen Rea.[5] Both were interested in developing a play to perform on tour before local, small-town audiences. This 'popular' and 'parochial' agenda, as Marilynn Richtarik describes it, created an opportunity for these artists to develop a theatrical event designed to stir up conversation within local communities about national issues (2001: 11–12), creating a theatre experience for local Irish audiences, rather than a production in a major theatre space hoping to catch the eye of producers from London or New York. To gain funding from the Arts Council of Northern Ireland, they needed to become 'an establishment', and so they created and called themselves the Field Day Theatre Company.[6] After *Translation's* tremendous success, they incorporated a board of directors: poets Seamus Heaney and Tom Paulin, cultural critic Seamus Deane, and broadcaster David Hammond. Hammond was the only one of the new members of the board with experience in theatrical production. The board did, however, boast of some of the most prominent writers in Northern Ireland. It also was split evenly between Catholic and Protestant members, although none of the members were unionists.

Despite Field Day's casual administrative start, the project quickly bloomed into a highly productive organization with a straightforwardly postcolonial agenda. In addition to an annual play, the company began publishing pamphlets on political and cultural themes.[7] Leaders of Irish arts and intelligentsia, like Tom Kilroy, Richard Kearney, Stewart Parker, and Joe Dowling, supplied their talents to the group. And, in a slight departure from Rea's and Friel's original vision, there were also contributions from non-Irish artists and critics interested in looking at Ireland through a postcolonial lens, such as Athol Fugard, Edward Said, and Terry Eagleton.

The organization's emphasis on writing and writers, diversity of project types, loose structure, and frequent use of guest artists, meant that the theatre company did not develop a signature design aesthetic or acting style. Their focus was on their message. Seamus Deane remarked that they were seeking through their work 'a more ecumenical and eirenic approach to the deep and apparently implacable problems which confront the island today' (Introduction, *Ireland's Field Day*) by 'deconstructing the [essentialized and romanticized] mystique surrounding Irish writing of the past two centuries' ('Heroic Styles', 1985: 58). The group adapted Richard Kearney's metaphor of the 'fifth province',[8] which Friel called in 1983 'a place for dissenters, traitors to the prevailing mythologies in the other for provinces' (Gray, 'Field Day five years on', in Richtarik 2001: 245). Some critics of the group, like Edna Longley, however, were finding that Field Day's claims to a transcendent objectivity did not rightfully acknowledge the board members' own nationalist-leaning politics (246–7).

This was an important conversation, but one which raised a now century-old question in Irish theatre about the politics of performance, as well as a phenomenological question about the production of meaning through the stage. Deciphering the politics of a pamphlet is relatively easy, since the message (words) and its vehicle of transmission (text) are more or less stable. Meaning was created in Field Day performances, on the other hand, differently with each performance event by text, actors, space, audience, and context. A production of *Translations* at the Derry Guildhall necessarily created a different meaning from a production at the Enniskillen High School or at the Dublin Theatre Festival. Local audiences who attend community theatre productions, as 7:84 Theatre Company of Scotland's production of *The Cheviot, the Stag, and the Black Black Oil* proved when it toured throughout Scotland in the 1970s, inevitably bring a point of view. But, through the mercurial experience of touring, they also serve to open conversation in and across communities. Still, especially for those interested in Field Day outside of Ireland, it is important to note that their message, while pluralist in some ways, was neither comprehensive nor objective in its points of view. Frank McGuinness remarked in 1985:

I'm a bit worried about the neglect of diversities other than the Catholic-Protestant/Nationalist-Unionist ones in Field Day: the diversities between the needs of men and the needs of women, between the ends not simply of rich and poor, but within the middle class, and of the homosexual and the heterosexual. I feel a sense of comfort about Field Day; it is in danger of repeating itself. (Qtd in Richtarik 2001: 250)

To assess the great accomplishments of Field Day in theatre, despite the company's limits, it is necessary to consider some of their work. Along with the dramatic masterpiece, *Translations*, Field Day produced several other, very different, plays by Friel, including his 'translation' from English into an Irish-English idiom of Chekhov's *Three Sisters* (1981), and *The Communication Cord* (1982), a farcical look at the present middle-class Irish's uneasy relationship with images of Ireland's past. The company then brought in new playwrights, actors, and directors to include a diversity of voices, all of which served to perform new ways of thinking about Irish history and identity.[9]

A common trope in several of the plays was to adapt a classic text into an Anglo-Irish idiom, starting with Friel's adaptation of Chekhov's play. Friel viewed the experience of Chekhov's Russian elite, slowly pushed out of their houses into an unfamiliar modernity, as having a kinship with the Irish experience. 'Maybe because the characters in the plays behave as if their old certainties were as sustaining as ever – even though they know in their hearts that their society is in melt-down and the future has neither a welcome nor even an accommodation for them. Maybe a bit like people of my own generation in Ireland today' (Pine 2006: 104). Tom Paulin's *The Riot Act* (1984), on the other hand, turned to Greek tragedy, using *Antigone* as a metaphor for the current stalemate among government leaders as well as sectarian factions that continued to choose retributive justice over the possibility of ending war through mercy.[10] By choosing to adapt the Greek play *Philoctetes* into *The Cure at Troy*, Seamus Heaney, likewise, chose a Sophoclean play rich with the malaise of exhaustion from entrenched warfare, in which the need for forgiveness and unity become the way to peace.[11]

Tom Kilroy examined the intersections of language, identity, and history provocatively in his 1986 Field Day play *Double Cross*. Set in the First World War, and based on actual persons and events, the play considers the roles of two Irishmen who were leaders of war propaganda in Europe while the Irish Free State remained neutral. Brendan Bracken, Churchill's Minister of Propaganda, played a kind of stage Englishman in the First World War, promoting a British nationalist ideal designed to raise the spirits of the

British during the Blitzkrieg. The other Irishman, William Joyce, worked on Germany's side, serving as a radio announcer known as 'Lord Haw-Haw' who, like 'Tokyo Rose' in the Pacific, broadcast disinformation and propaganda across the border into England. Since their home country is neutral (and, while the majority favoured the Allies, many in the populace supported Germany in the spirit of 'England's difficulty being Ireland's opportunity'), the men are not necessarily betraying their citizenship per se, despite being on opposite sides of the war. Yet, as masters of propaganda, who rely on their 'Britishness' to gain the trust or attention of the English people, both men must wrestle with the secret of their Irish ancestry, and struggle with their personal alienation from their true cultural heritage in the face of the 'stage English' facade on which they make their living. This sense of the men's common existential crisis was foregrounded in performance with Stephen Rea, an actor readily identified by audiences on both sides of the border as an artist committed to promoting Irish arts and identity, playing both Bracken and Joyce, the 'closeted' Irishmen acting the part of the colonizer rather than the colonized. Like Kilroy's earlier drama, *Talbot's Box*, *Double Cross* interrogates the fluidity of identity, while questioning the spiritual cost of sacrificing a culturally grounded sense of self for the immediate material gains of 'passing' within a more dominant culture.

Stewart Parker's Field Day play offering, *Pentecost* (1987), offered perhaps the most emotionally moving of the fourteen plays Field Day produced between 1980 and 1995. The play is set in a Victorian, working-class home in Protestant Belfast in 1974, and it is the last home on the street not to be burned out in rioting. The house is haunted by Lily, the recently deceased owner of the home, who at seventy-four was as old as the century in which she died. The house is now inhabited by four young persons taking refuge from experiences of personal and public violence in their lives. Marian, who is still grieving over the death of her baby and is separated from the child's father, Lenny, develops a special relationship with the house and the ghost. The house is full of remnants of Ulster Protestant life: '*The kitchen*', the stage directions tell us, '*in particular is cluttered, almost suffocated with the furnishings and bric-a-brac of the first half of the century, all the original fixtures and fittings still being in place*' (Parker 1988: 171).

While transporting such a detailed set must have been a nightmare for the stage managers of *Pentecost* while it was touring, the plethora of everyday objects on the set serve in performance as an archive of Lily's experiences, which Marian – as if compelled – soon begins to pore over and analyse, until she understands the owner of these objects well enough to call up her ghost. By sharing Lily's stories with her friends, Marian manages to create for all the characters an opportunity to make peace with the ghosts in each of their lives. At the close of the play Marian releases her grief for her dead son and shares a brief moment of closeness, and perhaps reconciliation, with her estranged husband, before she makes a declaration of purpose to her friends:

> Personally I want to live now. I want this house to live. We have committed sacrilege enough on life, in this place, in these times. We don't just owe it to ourselves, we owe it to our dead too . . . our innocent dead. They're not our masters, they're only our creditors, for the life they never knew. We owe them at least that – the fullest life for which they could ever have hoped, we carry those ghosts with us, to betray those hopes is the real sin against the Christ, and I for one cannot commit it one day longer. (Parker 1988: 245)[12]

Pentecost was first performed in Derry, than travelled across Northern Ireland and the Republic, as well as England, and won the Harvey award at the Dublin Theatre Festival. While some were critical of the play, Tom Maguire notes the excitement that the play generated as 'the audience experiences a utopian sense of resolution in the moment of performance, even if it was not fully motivated by the plot or narrative' (Maguire 2006: 96). Instead of recounting political stalemates, or the genealogies of violence experienced by the characters in the play and their ancestors, Parker offers a symbolic resolution. Stephen Rea remarked that Parker 'was the first Northern writer to reduce such a vision of a harmonious possibility on the other side of violence' (Rea 2000: xii). The boldness of this choice is apparent when comparing *Pentecost* with another classic Irish ghost play, W.B. Yeats's *Purgatory* (1938). Yeats's *Purgatory* dramatized a perpetuation of violence among fathers and sons in an abandoned big house. This bleak drama of a tragic perpetuation of patriarchal violence, in which a father kills his son, as his ghostly father looks on, might seem an apt metaphor for Ireland's political crisis in the 1980s. Parker, writing in the 1980s about one of the most violent periods of sectarian violence in Belfast, imagines a ghost play that dramatizes a mother figure and daughter figure befriending one another, reconciling with the past, and fighting for a better future.

The Field Day Theatre Company more or less discontinued its theatre projects in 1995, although its members and contributors remain leaders in theatre and film. But Field Day continues as a dominant force in Irish criticism and cultural studies, largely because of its ambitious publishing projects, which have been supported institutionally and financially by foundations and universities in Ireland, England, and the United States. Since the 1990s, Field Day has produced fourteen cultural studies texts in its Critical Conditions Series, published by Field Day and distributed by Cork University Press and Notre Dame University Press. While geared more to academic than general audiences, this series remains one of the most influential in Irish studies globally. But the most impressive of these was *The Field Day Anthology of Irish Writing* – a bold assertion of the century-old anti-colonial argument that Irish literature was worthy of study in its own right and not merely a branch of the British canon.[13] Deane went so far as to call the project of creating the anthology a 're-invention of the Irish literary tradition', playing on Eric Hobsbawm's remarks on the ways in which national identities are solidified by invented notions of cultural heritage and tradition. Published in 1992 after years of work, and edited by Deane with the aid of a team of editors, the anthology weighs five pounds and is 4,106 pages long.

The range and collection of writings in *The Field Day Anthology* is indeed impressive. *The Field Day Anthology's* size, support among Irish and American academics, and relationship to Field Day and its deeply respected members seemed to give it the implicit claim that it had the authority to speak for all Irish and to represent fairly all Anglo-Irish writing. However, not all critics saw the project as a pure and unproblematic act of resistance against British imperialism. To publish a pamphlet is to reveal a perspective. To write an anthology is to declare a canon, with all the hegemonic rights and privileges therein. Marilynn Richtarik notes that:

> the polemic slant of the anthology (which itself does in fact contain a mass of heterogeneous material, much of which would challenge Deane's central thesis) achieves one of Field Day's aims (exposing the colonial dimension of 'Irish writing') at the expense of another (encouraging Northern Protestants to identify themselves with Ireland). In this, the anthology is emblematic of the Field Day movement as a whole. (2001: 261)

The most egregious oversight for many critics, however, was the paucity of women included in the anthology. Field Day, 'suitably embarrassed' (Richtarik 2001: 266) by this oversight, commissioned a fourth volume of Irish women's writing. Edited by Angela Bourke, with a team of leading women scholars, the extra volume promised in 1992 appeared a decade later as a two-volume set with 3,250 pages. And included in this new collection is the work of a community theatre that worked simultaneously and on very similar lines to Field Day, Charabanc Theatre Company.

How the Other Half Plays: Charabanc Theatre Company

Despite actor Stephen Rea's founding and principal role in the organization, the Field Day Theatre Company was very much a writer's theatre, committed to developing and producing alternative strategies for understanding Irish history and identity through performance. Charabanc, Northern Ireland's other great community theatre success story in the 1980s, was founded on more pragmatic terms. Five professional actresses established the group as a defiant gesture against Northern Irish casting codes, with their near absence of roles for women beyond traditional physical and gender stereotypes. The original members of the company, Marie Jones, Maureen Macauley, Eleanor Methven, Carol Moore, and Brenda Winter established the group in 1983, with a small loan from Jones's husband, Ian McElhiney (Harris 2006: xiii). As Maria DiCenzo put it, 'they were tired of playing someone's mother or girlfriend' (1993: 178).[14] When they learned that Northern Irish producers were beginning to cast women's roles with English actresses, rather than using local women actors, Charabanc's founders realized that they needed to put their future in their own hands. Although founded out of frustration, desperation, and defiance against Northern Ireland's theatre establishment, Charabanc ultimately produced some of the most engaging discussions of the Troubles and of Northern Irish history in the 1980s, while also providing a closer look at women's vital roles in the history of the region and its politics.

Charabanc originally contacted Martin Lynch to write a play for the company. By the early 1980s, Lynch was a leading Belfast playwright who was also active in community theatre, creating plays for specific communities about local topics from the 1970s onwards (Grant 2001: 33). His first play at the Lyric Theatre, *The Interrogation of Ambrose Fogarty* (1982), a politically charged look at interrogation policies in Northern Ireland, 'played to ninety-four percent capacity over its four week run' (Grant 2001: 34), and helped bring more working-class patrons into the theatre. Lynch recalled from their first meeting with Charabanc his recommendation that they, and not he, write about the experiences of Belfast women. 'This produced an instant silence,' Lynch recalled, 'followed by laughter' (Harris 2006: xvii). It was decided that the women would write their own texts with Lynch's aid.

The company chose as their topic the Belfast Linen Workers' strike of 1911 – an event vital to the labour movement across Ireland. Organized by socialist leader and future hero of Easter 1916, James Connolly, this strike involved 2,000 working-class Belfast women from both Protestant and Catholic backgrounds walking off their jobs and crippling one of the region's most important industries. The strike was a pivotal moment in Irish workers', women's, and nationalist histories. The company members researched the event through newspaper accounts (of which there were surprisingly few) and interviews, and included quotes from those interviews in dialogue. The dramatic structure of the piece included monologues, and the women played men's roles. And the performance was kept entertaining, despite its serious political subject matter, with ample humour and the use of popular songs.

Despite some professional criticism, *Lay Up Your Ends* was very successful among audiences. Between May and October of 1983 'it was seen by 13,515 people in 96 performances in 59 different venues' (DiCenzo 1993: 180), inspiring the company to continue their work. Their next play, *Oul Delf and False Teeth* (1984), considered Belfast life in the late 1940s, discussing such issues as sexuality and contraception. And another Charabanc play, *Gold in the Streets* (1986) presented the lives of three generations of Northern Irish women emigrating from Northern Ireland.

Charabanc's most popular performance, and most eloquent statement about the effect of violence on working-class communities, and the ways in which the length of the struggle had normalized the abnormal experiences of deprivation and war encountered every day by Northern Irish women, was *Somewhere Over the Balcony* (1987). This play describes the often absurd ways a group of working-class Belfast women attempt to maintain a sense of family and home from the epicentre of economic, social, sectarian, and government violence. While other Charabanc plays re-examined women's experience in light of Belfast history, this play was set in the contemporary moment. In a kind of deconstruction of the traditional urban tenement drama made popular by Sean O'Casey in the 1920s, *Somewhere Over the Balcony* takes a profound and subversive look at life for a group of friends in Belfast's Divis Flats which, at the time, was one of the largest – and most violent – housing projects in Europe. This drama forces its audience to examine the absurd levels of terror, violence, and restriction for individuals living in this community, by seeing how the war penetrates the private lives of a group of women living in the flats.

The women in the flats have lost one of the principal comforts of the domestic sphere – privacy – as doors, windows, and even walls have been removed from the tenement in which they live.[15] In addition to near-constant observation by their neighbours, they also must deal with British soldiers watching and taping them from the surveillance towers that surround the flats. Using Brechtian dramaturgy, Charabanc employed minimal props, presentational acting, and comic yet strident analytical songs to point out just how abnormal 'normal life' in working-class Belfast really is.

The play follows three friends, Rose, Ceely, and Kate, as they struggle to create a sense of normality despite such distractions as hunky British soldiers jogging on surveillance towers, German peace tourists, bombs, helicopters, arrests without cause, and a standoff between the British soldiers and an IRA man trying to marry his bride before she goes into labour with their child (the wedding is stalled because the British have surrounded the church to arrest the best man). The absence of a naturalist set gives the audience only sound effects (helicopters, cameras, bombs), the actors' bodies, and a few props to imagine the busy, violent world these women inhabit.

Throughout the play, we see the women resist violence, surveillance, and control through such tactics as running an underground radio station, staring back at the surveillance tower with binoculars, selling bin lids to tourists at exorbitant prices,[16] and making 'sexy poses' for the officers (usually including rude gestures). But their greatest mode of resistance is their insistence on survival, on the right to a normal life in a world far from normal. By exposing the juxtaposition of such everyday events as taking out the trash, playing bingo, sitting on a toilet, or watching television amid the constant threat of surveillance, arrest, and physical harm, this darkly comic play shows the deep abnormality of life in the Divis Flats. Despite the laughter, this absurd and funny play screams for the achievable need for better housing, more privacy, and the cessation of social and political violence. In the programme notes for *Somewhere Over the Balcony*, Charabanc remarked:

> When outsiders ask us what it is like to live in Northern Ireland we tend to say that it is quite normal really. We say that people just go about their business, live their lives, get on with it. We say this to dispel images of constant gun-battles, riots, explosions and the rest. And to some extent it's true. But when violence becomes long-term, institutionalized and with no foreseeable end, when people have lived all or most their lives in a 'war-zone' everything changes – especially the definitions of what is normal.

The parameters of sanity shift and the idea arises that violence has reached an acceptable level. (1987: n.p.)

Instead of theorizing about the causes of sectarian violence on society, *Somewhere Over the Balcony* addresses in its dark, comic way the true cruelty of sectarian violence, the banality about it developed by those who have grown up experiencing it, and the transformative power of a few women to make a kind of meaning amid the everyday violence, to resist that violence creatively, and to try, although they do not always succeed, to create a safe home.[17]

Despite Charabanc's mission to create strong roles for women actors, and to represent women's private and public experiences onstage, the company balked at being termed a feminist theatre company, preferring that their plays be read as statements about power and politics, rather than exclusively discussed as explorations of gender. Imelda Foley remarks that this hesitancy to be termed a feminist troupe stemmed at least partially from their populist leanings:

> While Charabanc's work challenges the social marginalization of women and women's issues, and celebrates 'the lives of women', there is almost a neurosis about the possibility of the company's own marginalization if the term 'feminist' were adopted. [Charabanc member Ellen] Methven revealingly states: 'If we said we were feminist or socialist or any "ist" – it would completely alienate those people back in the community centres in Northern Ireland. So, what's the point of saying it?' (2003: 40)

From a critical and theoretical perspective, Charabanc's plays are irrefutably feminist; but, like feminist performers engaged in other political or human rights movements, like the Black Arts Movement in the United States during the 1960s, the artists preferred not to divide an audience who might construe the term feminist as separatist, and ignore the politics of empowerment for women as well as men in their work. As Methven told an American reporter eager for Charabanc to claim themselves a feminist group, 'We don't want to start that sort of war here, of all places' (Foley 2003: 41). Regardless of what Charabanc chose to call their plays, however, their significance in adding rich and original women's voices to the contemporary Irish stage, and placing women's issues into the theatre discourse, is indisputable.

In its twelve-year history, Charabanc produced twenty-two productions, which they brought to small venues and large theatres throughout Ireland. Additionally, 'they toured the USSR, Germany, and Canada; four times to the USA, and one to Cardiff' (Harris 2006: ix). Their work gave a space not only for women actors on the stage, but also for representations of women in Northern Irish history onstage. They addressed present problems with a mix of polemicism and humour. But they did not generate the same kinds of critical respect – or government funding – granted other community groups. Indeed, the first anthology of their plays was published in 2006 – eleven years after their demise.[18] Yet the spirit of Charabanc continues in the engaged and engaging work the company and its collaborators continue to pursue, as well as in the new theatre regarding gender in Ireland that their plays helped to inspire. After the break-up of the company, Marie Jones attained international success with her play *Stones in His Pockets* (1996), and her collaborations with Pom Boyd and Dubbeljoint Productions. Other members, like Eleanor Methven, are working steadily in Irish and English theatre, film, and television.

Gender and the Troubles in Northern Irish Theatre in the 1980s

Just as women like Maud Gonne, Con Markiewicz, Alice Milligan, and Maire Nic Shiubhlaigh stepped to the fore during the nationalist political crises at the beginning of the century, the era of the Troubles, too, had its share of strong women leaders. Civil rights fighter and MP Bernadette Devlin, journalist Nell McCafferty, IRA soldier Mairead Farrell, and Nobel Prize-winning founder of Peace People, Mairead Corrigan Maguire, offer a glimpse at the many kinds of involvement by women in the Troubles, and the different public stances they took. Charabanc's plays, like those of other playwrights interested in women's experiences in Northern Ireland, made it impossible for audiences to be satisfied only with traditional 'Troubles Plays' that made the domestic space an apolitical sphere, with women as victims but not participants in the ideological struggle surrounding them.[19] The male and female characters in plays by Northern Irish playwrights such as Anne Devlin and Christina Reid show women's pivotal role in the construction, continuation, and sometimes the resistance of political ideology during the Troubles in both the private and public spheres. To achieve this, these playwrights did not abandon the domestic sphere as a dramatic setting, but rather they politicized it.

Anne Devlin's *Ourselves Alone* (1985) considers the impact of the Troubles, around the period of the 1981 hunger strikes, on three Belfast Republican women. Donna is the common-law wife of Liam, an IRA soldier who is the father of her child. She lives with Liam's two sisters, Josie and Frieda, in a house in Andersonstown, a working-class Republican neighbourhood.

All three women feel trapped by their community, especially in relation to the sense of duty placed upon them by their families. Frieda, the youngest and most rebellious of the three, constantly seeks to break out through her music (she sings Republican songs at a local IRA pub) or by changing her appearance. When Josie admonishes her to be herself, Frieda responds, 'When did I ever have a chance to be myself? My father was interned before I was born. My brother's in the Kesh[20] for bank robbery. You mention the name McCoy in this neighborhood, people start walking away from you backwards. I'm fed up living here, this place is a hole' (Devlin 1986: 21). Donna, likewise, finds herself under the constant scrutiny of her neighbours, who marshal her sexual activity while her husband Liam is in prison for his Republican activities. Although she remains faithful, Liam accuses her of adultery when he returns, based purely on gossip. Josie has an affair with an IRA spy, and sees a chance to move away from her sectarian life in Andersonstown. But when he is revealed to be a traitor and she becomes pregnant, her brother, Liam, and her father argue over whether or not she should abort the pregnancy. Josie's father wins the argument and insists she have the baby, and she is forced to return to her father's house and raise her child there. At the end of the play, as the women are about to move away from one another, they recall an evening in their youth when they snuck away from a group discussing politics on the strand to swim naked together in the surf. This recollection offers the women the memory of a momentary transgression and escape from their roles and responsibilities within their community – one that it is doubtful they will achieve again.

The title of the play, *Ourselves Alone*, carries the obvious valence of the Republican motto and name of the Republican political party Sinn Fein, Irish for 'ourselves alone'. But instead of that phrase calling for a uniting of the nation, the phrase for Josie, Donna, and Frieda evokes instead a sense of isolation from the patriarchal centres of power within the IRA (even Donna, who has a significant role in the organization, finds herself often left out of meetings and events), and alienation from the world beyond Andersonstown. This dream-like final image – a memory of swimming in a phosphorescent sea – reflects the women's past experience of freedom and sisterly bonding, and hints that perhaps such a bond can transcend spiritually their current physical separation (Cerquoni, in Sihra 2007: 67). But in the immediate situation, Josie and Donna remain trapped between duty to the men in their lives and to their national cause. Only Frieda, has – Stephen Dedalus-like – achieved the freedom to escape these duties and live outside this status quo.[21]

Christina Reid looks at the impact of violence on the women left to protect and maintain the domestic sphere from a Unionist perspective in her drama, *Tea in a China Cup* (1983).[22] This play reflects on the lives of three generations of Northern Irish Protestant women – Maisie, Sarah, and Beth – whose experiences have been shaped by the three great wars that have rocked Belfast in the twentieth century: the First World War, the Second World War, and the Troubles. During all three military crises, the women have seen it as their duty to protect their family home, and they have had to grieve the loss of male family members fighting in the First World War and the Second World War. In the set design, time passing is shown partly by the women placing on the wall the portrait of each male family member who has joined the army. Underneath these portraits rests the family china cabinet, holding the Belleek tea set that reflects the matrilineal inheritance of the women of the family. 'Both the portraits and the china chest reflect family tradition, but the portraits represent the patrilineal and public aspect of the family history, while the china cabinet represents the family's matrilineal and domestic history' (Trotter 2000: 174). At the end of the play, after matriarch Sarah's death, her daughter Beth sells the home and its contents. While the estate appraiser remarks that the soldier's portraits are almost worthless on the economic market – 'Old wartime photos, cheap frames . . . there's a lot of them about' (Reid [1983]: 1997b: 64) – perhaps commenting on how cheaply soldiers' lives had been valued, she does regret that a teacup is missing from the family's prized Belleek set. Beth assures that it had been broken long ago, and shows little remorse at the loss in an apparent eagerness to finish the sale and move away from the house, the city, and the political crisis. After the valuer leaves, however, Beth gingerly removes the missing teacup from her bag, smiles, and walks off the stage, singing one of her mother's favourite songs.

While a different choice from that made by Marian in Parker's *Pentecost*, Beth in Reid's *Tea in a China Cup* ultimately makes a life choice that reflects an agency previously reserved for men within the Irish literary and theatrical canons. In 1984, Reid wrote about *Tea in a China Cup* that:

> It's about women generally, and how they uphold traditions and beliefs which are positively harmful and damaging to themselves, because they've had it instilled in them that it's safer to do this, that this is what women should do, and no matter how unhappy women's lives are, they tend to re-create the same thing for their daughters, they're not truthful to their daughters. (qtd in Foley 2003: 65)

While it is true that women have also played significant roles in the political public sphere by speaking out for male family members (from 'The Mothers' at *The Plough and the Stars* performance in 1926, to the McCartney sisters of Belfast demanding justice for their brother who was beaten to death by the IRA in a pub in 2005), Reid imagines a space in Irish politics in which women can speak for themselves and of themselves. As one of Reid's characters puts it in her 1989 play, *The Belle of the Belfast City*, 'They say there are no women in Ireland. Only mothers and sisters and wives' (Reid [1989] 1997a: 209). By breaking out of their matrilineal expectations, opportunities for new modes of personal fulfilment, political activism, social organization, and even cultural reinvention arise.

Frank McGuinness and Political Metatheatre

Another important Northern Irish playwright engaged in examining the intersections between nationalism and gender in the 1980s was Frank McGuinness. Like Friel, McGuinness was born in the area of County Donegal that is actually north of Northern Ireland and part of the province of Ulster, but ruled by the Republic. So, like Friel, that experience appears to have supplemented the interest in border crossing that informs his work. While Friel settled in the North, however, McGuinness chose to attend University College Dublin and work in the Republic. His first dramatic success, *The Factory Girls* (1982), a comic yet politically earnest drama about a group of women going on strike in a Northern Irish linen factory, appeared at the Peacock, directed by Patrick Mason, a future Abbey Theatre director with whom McGuinness would develop an important working relationship.

The play that put McGuinness's work on the map, however, was his 1985 drama, *Observe the Sons of Ulster, Marching Toward the Somme*. Originally conceived as a play for Field Day, *Observe the Sons* remains one of the most bravely imaginative contemporary Irish plays to date in its complex portrayal of Ulster Protestant identity, and Irish masculinity, during the First World War. McGuinness, a man born into a Catholic background from the Republic, chose to imagine and stage the experience of six men fighting in 'the almost exclusively Protestant 36th Ulster Division, 6000 of whose members had been massacred at the battle of the Somme [in the First World War] in 1916' (Morash 2002: 260). While, as earlier chapters of this book have shown, Ulster Protestants have a long lineage of plays about the Northern Irish experience, McGuinness's play is rare in its thoughtful representation of the diversity of backgrounds among the Northern Irish characters, and the sensitivity with which their individual stories are portrayed. Most controversially, McGuinness, a gay man himself, includes a loving same-sex relationship in the play between two of the soldiers, which is more or less accepted by their comrades in arms.

McGuinness sets this play up as a ghost play, with Pyper, the only survivor of the battle in 1916, now an old man, haunted in his bed by the memory of his fallen allies. Finally, as all six ghosts have entered, including Pyper's younger self, he calls them to 'Dance. Dance' (McGuinness [1985] 1996: 101), and the play shifts into flashback, carrying us back to 1916. The following sections of the drama – titled 'Initiation', 'Pairing', and 'Bonding' – follow the development of these six individuals into a band of soldiers. Towards the climax of the play, as they prepare for what they know will be a losing battle, the men choose to pass the time, and celebrate their Ulster history, by re-enacting the story of the Battle of the Boyne.[23]

Here the play shifts into meta-theatre, as the audience watches a 'play-within-a-play', by observing the men offer up this sacred Northern Irish Protestant myth. McGuinness's use of meta-theatre here works on several aesthetic and political levels. Its 'play-within-a-play' structure reminds the audience of the theatricality of the performance generally, and calls them to think critically about the relationship between the roles the characters have taken on in the meta-drama, and the roles they play within their culture. It also remarks upon how deeply embedded the story of the Battle of the Boyne is as a founding myth of identity for the soldiers. The relevance of this battle, in fact, turns the re-enactment into a kind of ritual, as the characters re-enact, even if parodically, the battle that defined their identity as Orangemen, warriors, and fighters. Like the annual Orange Marches, these 'sons of Ulster' continue to claim an Irishness that may have been foreign, or even repugnant, to many of the audience members at the Peacock Theatre during the play's first performance. But McGuinness shows it as a complicated and ubiquitous cultural signifier, essential to understanding Northern Irish identity. Indeed, as Nicholas Grene has noted:

> In *Observe the Sons of Ulster* McGuinness seeks an understanding of the psychological, spiritual and political ethos of Protestant Unionism of which it has been all too common among Irish nationalists . . . McGuinness reminds us that there are other places in Ulster besides the one city, and other types of people beyond shipyard workers . . . The sons of Ulster in his play are chosen from a variety of different trades and distributed across the province. (Grene 1999: 247)

Even their class, religion, and sexual identities are diverse. Their joining together to perform this common legend, therefore, elevates the experience to a kind of ritual, enacting a victorious past battle on the way to a fight with less obvious ideologies and an uncertain outcome.

The results of the soldiers' re-enactment of the Battle of the Boyne, despite the audience's awareness of the upcoming disastrous battle, are comic, with 'actors' grumbling over their parts and squabbling about the 'script'. Anderson, taking the role of director among the men, reminds the man playing King James that he cannot improvise his part, and that he must lose. 'And remember, King James, we know the result, you know the result, keep to the result' (McGuinness [1985] 1996: 182). A mishap in performance causes Pyper, playing King William's horse, to trip, sending 'King William', the historic winner, toppling to the ground, reversing the historical 'result' and foreshadowing the battle to come.

Still, the men prepare themselves for battle, trying to shake off the bad omen as they exchange orange sashes (symbols of their ethnicity), and enacting a different ritual as Pyper, until now an atheist, offers up a prayer. His words begin as statements of love for his comrades and for the landscape of home, but ultimately turn into a shared chant for Ulster, '*reaching frenzy*' (80). The chant dies down as the Elder Pyper appears again and speaks to his younger, ghostly self. As the Elder Pyper repeats the now-totemic word, 'Ulster', Younger Pyper urges his older self to make peace with the past and work for the future: 'The house has grown cold, the province has grown lonely . . . You'll always guard Ulster . . . Save it . . . The temple of the Lord is ransacked . . . Dance in this deserted temple of the Lord' (80). In reply to this last urging from his younger self, Elder Pyper accepts the challenge to stop replaying the trauma, but instead to honour the dead, forgive his own survival, and move on, when he replies with the simple word, 'Dance' (80).[24]

The 1980s was a decade rife with performative statements of Republican, Unionist, and imperialist ideological commitment in the real world, with often deathly consequences. Traditional theatre pales against the drama of the hunger strike, the dirty protest, bombing in Eniskillen, or the false imprisonment of the Guildford Four, not to mention the social violence of diminishing rights for Northern Irelanders throughout the decade. Yet to dismiss Irish theatre in the 1980s as mere entertainment, or escape from the real-world battles, is to ignore the work of dozens of theatre artists who pushed beyond aesthetic, ideological, sectarian, and physical borders to bring forward art that challenged the traditional understandings of Northern Irish identities, cultures, and politics. Towards the end of his life, Yeats famously questioned the efficacy of his own political art through his poem, 'The Man and the Echo', in which he asked 'Did that play of mine send out/Certain men the English shot'? While it is generally agreed that one cannot draw a straight line between *Cathleen ni Houlihan* and Easter 1916, it is fair to say that the communal experience of performance can offer a space for cathartic and critical renewal, for individuals as well as communities. The plays and polemics of Irish theatre in the 1980s may not single-handedly have brought on the peace talks in the late 1980s, but they did open up an imaginative space for considering ways to move beyond past traumas and towards forgiveness, reorganization, and new possibilities. In the words of Richard Kearney, 'Politics is far too grave a matter for the politician. Art is far too potent a medium for the artist. Beyond this entrenchment is a place where the two can meet' (Kearney 1982: 7).

8

A New Sense of Place: Irish Theatre since the 1990s

In Dermot Bolger's *The Lament for Arthur Cleary* (1989), an Irishman recently returned to Dublin after working abroad as a labourer for years finds himself pulled between his memories of home and the radical changes that have taken place within Dublin – and himself – in the years between. 'It's all smaller, different when you return. Look at it ... O'Connell Street. Just some honky-tonk provincial plaza' (Bolger [1989] 2000: 21). In Martin McDonagh's *The Beauty Queen of Leenane*, a youth obviously more interested in Australian soap operas than the idyllic beauty celebrated in Irish literature for a century outside his door complains of the local landscape: 'All you have to do is look out your window to see Ireland. And it's soon bored you'd be. "There goes a calf"' (McDonagh 1996: 53). In Gary Mitchell's *In a Little World of Our Own* (1997), a Unionist worries over his neighbourhood's growing integration. 'Used to be a time when taigs were shit scared of walking anywhere near Rathcoole. They just wouldn't do it. And now, they seem to be turning up all over the place' (Mitchell [1997] 1998: 5). And, in Marina Carr's *Portia Coughlan* (1996), a woman refuses to leave even for a brief time the landscape from which she gains her sense of identity: 'Oh I'm sure I'd live through what other folks calls holidays, but me mind'd be turnin' on the Belmont River' (Carr [1996] 1999b: 207). Time and again in contemporary Irish theatre, characters express wonder, rage, nostalgia, or disappointment at the ways their local and national communities are changing, the increasing mobility of populations, and the ways in which globalization is affecting not just the nation but also the neighbourhood. All of these changes create for the characters dizzying conflicts, realizations, resentments, and liberations at a personal level.

Much Irish theatre in the 1980s sought out ways to transcend traditional understandings of the nation and national conflicts, and to find innovative solutions to deeply entrenched problems from an imaginative, unifying space of open discourse and intellectual inquiry. While the pursuit of new understandings of Irish identity continued in the 1990s, these queries also responded to the tremendous political, demographic, and social changes occurring across Ireland thanks to the Celtic Tiger economy, progress towards peace in Northern Ireland, and a tremendous influx of immigrants into the Republic of Ireland from Europe and the developing world.

These plays in fact represent personal responses to a new understanding of Ireland as a rapidly changing social and economic entity, defined not only by geographical boundaries, but also by its relationship among its own diaspora communities, rates of export and import, cultural influence, and policies of migration. On a geographer's map, Ireland remains an island. But, from a cultural standpoint, the Republic of Ireland and Northern Ireland are deeply connected to each other, and to cultures and communities around the world. This fact is reflected by the trend in Irish theatre away from seeking answers to questions about national identity at the macro level, towards seeking a sense of commonality in community and purpose, and finding ways to understand the true diversity of Irish experience both within and without the nation's traditional geographical borders.

Perhaps inspired by the terrific success of community theatres like Field Day and Charabanc, as well as the phenomenally successful Druid Theatre Company, government interest in supporting local professional theatres has flourished since the 1990s, with theatre networks growing as rapidly as the national infrastructure. This growth has increased the diversity of aesthetics performed in Ireland, and supported the creation of new work more specific to local communities. Christopher Morash notes that 'If there is any one dominant trend that can be identified in Irish theatre since the beginning of the 1990s, it is that the expansion and diversification of theatre culture has lifted from any one writer or company the burden of representing the entire nation, a responsibility felt so heavily by the Abbey theatre throughout the twentieth century' (2005: 336).[1] These multiple images of Ireland, created out of a range of aesthetic strategies by theatre companies across the island, allow for a more complex picture of the culture that makes unprecedented room for dissent as well as idealism, and creates a space for the stories of people on the margins as well as those in the centre.

This chapter will tour some of the major themes that have emerged in Irish theatre since the 1990s, and a few of the playwrights and companies that have helped shape these theatrical trends, and Irish theatre generally, over the last two decades. Considering the scores of new playwrights and dozens of new theatre and performance companies that have emerged in the last two decades, it would be impossible to give close examination to all of them; thus, this chapter will look at the way Irish theatre has responded to – and been shaped by – particular cultural concerns that have emerged in Ireland over the last two decades. First, it will consider how contemporary playwrights are addressing transformations in urban Irish life, such as the way in which growing gentrification is displacing many traditional urban dwellers from their neighbourhoods to make room for new urban professionals, as well as a rise in crime, drugs, and other concerns. It will then look at how theatre is addressing the changes in population by reconsidering Ireland's relationship to its diaspora, and representing asylum seekers and other immigrants onstage. The chapter then turns to representations of rural Ireland on the contemporary stage, and considers how the tradition of presenting an idealized Irish west onstage is being revised and satirized by contemporary playwrights. These revisionist representations of the idealized west, however, bring forward other attempts to come to terms with the ghosts of Irish history,[2] from plays in which ghosts haunt the present, to plays that critique commonly held assumptions about particular moments in Irish history. Finally, the chapter will overview some of the developments in the independent theatre movement, with a focus on site-specific theatres.

In its overview of the range of aesthetics, companies, and dramas that have emerged on the Irish stage in the last seventeen years, this chapter will focus on two approaches. First, it will consider how Irish theatre is representing the rapid changes in the physical landscapes of Ireland thanks to urbanization, gentrification, and globalization, through not only plot and dialogue, but also scene design, and even the employment of site-specific performance. Second, this chapter will consider how Irish theatre since the 1980s has engaged with Ireland's political, cultural, and theatre histories by creating plays that consciously echo the themes, tropes, stage designs, and even dialogue of Ireland's rich theatrical legacy.

This interest in reviewing and reassessing the past, while looking for ways to represent new developments in Ireland, has led to exciting and varied theatrical strategies. Enda Walsh and Stella Feehily create images of a radically changing working-class Dublin, easily recognizable to a 1990s Dublin youth but unrecognizable to Padraic Colum or Lady Gregory. Martin McDonagh fills his plays with intertextual references to classical Irish drama (along with some strong peppering of allusions to English theatre and American theatre and film). Conor McPherson's monologues, such as *This Lime Tree Bower*, or dialogue-rich dramas, such as *The Weir* (1997) and *Shining City* (2004), carry on the tradition seen in plays like Brian Friel's *Faith Healer* and Tom Murphy's *The Gigli Concert* of using storytelling to raise the ghosts of political and personal history. And playwrights like Sebastian Barry and Donal O'Kelly continue the mission taken on by Frank McGuinness in *Observe the Sons of Ulster*, where he writes about minority perspectives of Irish identity historically overlooked in the early years of the Irish revival, when the goal was to create a united anti-colonial narrative of resistance to British rule.

Along with this new writing have come several important revivals (and reappraisals) of Irish drama, like the Gate Theatre's Beckett Project (1995), and the Druid Theatre Company's Druid/Synge Festival (2005) as well as adaptations of Irish literary works, such as Conall Morrison's adaptation of the Patrick Kavanagh novel, *Tarry Flynn* (1997). Indeed, to explore Irish theatre since the 1990s is to explore a theatre taking part in an active reinvention of its traditions to make room for a greater diversity of representations of Irish experiences and identity positions, and finding new ways to represent the tremendous changes occurring in contemporary Irish life.

Performing the Irish City

The tremendous growth in Ireland – and especially Dublin – in the 1980s and 1990s led to wide increases in housing development in suburban and 'exurban' areas. As Dublin grew more expensive, traditionally working-class neighbourhoods became gentrified with drastically increased rents, so that middle-class and working-class families were forced to move farther and farther outside the city. These events led to displacement of long-term working-class residents of some neighbourhoods, and homelessness and drug use increased. It is this group of old Dubliners in the new Dublin that Jimmy Murphy represents in his 1997 play, *A Picture of Paradise*. *A Picture of Paradise* starts with the crash of a window heard on a dark stage, followed by anxious, whispering voices: the audience is clearly seeing two desperate figures breaking into a flat. The flat is not being invaded by burglars, however, but squatters. Angela, a middle-aged woman, and her son, armed with a torch that does not work and plastic bags filled with family belongings, are sneaking into a corporate housing flat. They are soon joined by the father of the family, Sean, a former chef now illegally parking cars in empty lots.[3] A friend and fellow car parker, nicknamed 'The Lord', joins the party as the family starts to settle in. 'The Lord's' entrepreneurial spirit poignantly marks his own hand-to-mouth existence juxtaposed against the rapid growth in wealth of fellow Irishmen who can afford to drive cars from the suburbs or exurbs to their Dublin jobs. 'Forget fast food and Left Banks,' the Lord insists. 'Soon the whole city'll become one gigantic car park, there'll be work for everyone' (Murphy [1997] 2003: 112).

In the exposition of the play, we learn that these individuals were actually once secure in a middle-class lifestyle until personal events derailed their lives. The Lord, once a musician, can no longer work after the trauma of his family dying in a fire at home one night when he went drinking with his band after a gig. Sean, a chef, developed a skin disease that made him anathema in kitchens. After years out of work, he has grown more comfortable than he wants to admit with the life of a homeless man. And Angela's gambling addiction causes her to lose any savings the family manages to gather together by gambling it away on the next 'sure thing'.

The son, Declan, has an opportunity to escape his family's cycle of poverty, thanks to a cache of funds he has acquired to attend a computer course, but his codependent relationship with his parents makes the change difficult. When his parents pressurize him to loan them his money so they can get back on their feet (a scenario that it is implied has played out in the family before), Declan realizes that his only escape is a complete break. He takes the money for his education to buy a plane ticket to Belgium, where he will become an expatriate labourer. At the end of the play, Declan has gone, Sean has left for a homeless shelter, and Angela and the Lord share a bottle of wine, looking at a picture of a tropical island given to Angela by Sean on her honeymoon – the titular picture of paradise – and toast to the better days that are sure to come.

Murphy's drama poignantly illustrates the ways in which Angela's and Declan's optimistic view – that the 'rising tide' of the Celtic Tiger economy would lift all boats – fed into their own denial of economic failure. Scenographically, Murphy, with the aid of designer Barbara Bradshaw for the play's Peacock Theatre debut, related the family's demise to that of similar tenement dramas throughout Irish theatre history. At the end of the first Act, the family is thrown out of the flat they had just broken into and, in the second Act, they are living amid their furniture, clothing, and other accoutrements of domestic life, literally in the street outside the apartment bloc. It is not just the family, but also the familiar theatrical setting of the family room from a tenement flat, that have been evicted only to be set up instead outside the tenement that formerly housed them, under a Dublin street lamp in the middle of the night. The metaphor for the family's physical and spiritual displacement in Celtic Tiger Dublin could not be clearer. In 1990s Dublin, not only the working-class family, but even the working-class family play, has been tossed out of the tenement and into the street.[4]

While *A Picture of Paradise* shows city life for Dublin's displaced working classes, Dermot Bolger's *The Passion of Jerome* (1999) ponders the spiritual costs of urban development on those making the most profit from it. Jerome Furlong, a yuppie advertising executive in his mid-forties, uses his drug-dealing brother's subsidized flat in the Dublin suburb of Ballymun for trysts with a co-worker in her early twenties. The play begins with Jerome and his lover making love in the sparse flat (his brother, an artist, has not moved in) and remarking on the neighbourhood's strangeness when compared to their more sophisticated Dublin haunts. Jerome remarks of the flat, 'you were never in Ballymun before in your life, even on safari' (Bolger 1999: 7), comparing it stereotypically to a developing nation, even though it is minutes from home. The working-class exurb also has the benefit of economic and social segregation for the adulterous couple. Unlike the Caribbean, where 'you'll always meet somebody you sat beside in the National Concert Hall,' Jerome comments, 'Ballymun is Antarctica, shoals of shuffling penguins and a few mad scientists studying them' (7). Such a comparison, likewise, implies that Jerome thinks of himself as practically a different species from the struggling poor in the Ballymun flats.

Jerome's careless arrogance about the exoticism of Ballymun is undermined when he encounters the ghost of a child who died in the flat, and he develops stigmata. Although Jerome is an atheist, the stigmata destroys his aloof attitude towards community in both his Dublin and Ballymun lives, and connects him to a tradition of religious belief, personal responsibility, connection, and healing that he does not want, and that is defined by friends and strangers in different ways. His mistress thinks his bleeding is self-inflicted after Jerome's first experience snorting cocaine. A child of the high-tech, Celtic Tiger generation, she has little patience for this throwback to Catholic beliefs from the previous generation. 'Religion is a dangerous thing,' she warns. 'I'm glad we did French and computers instead. We never felt the need to tie ourselves up in chains . . . Things like that don't happen, they're only metaphors' (Bolger 1999: 64). A woman living in the Ballymun flat, however, sees Jerome's stigmata as a miracle and asks

Jerome to pray over her dying granddaughter, which he eventually does, giving some spiritual solace to the grandmother – and himself – although he does not heal the child.

But in the course of the play miraculous transformations do occur. In reaching out to Rita's granddaughter, Jerome is reminded of unselfish acts of kindness. The experience with the dying child also reminds him of the death of his own daughter eight days after her birth and, although his marriage ends, he does finally begin to deal with that experience and grieve that loss with his wife. At the end of the play, with his stigmata healing and the ghost of the child in the flat disappeared, Jerome quits his job, and in doing so finds the sense of personal fulfilment he had lost years earlier. When his brother asks him about his drastic life changes, Jerome replies, 'I don't know. I should feel scared. But there's a presence, beating within the beat of your own heart. I'd forgotten that it used to be there when I was a child. I don't deserve to feel it, a puny scared-shitless nobody like me' (Bolger 1999: 87). Jerome has moved from a mid-life crisis of conspicuous consumption and power games, to a space of considering a more purposeful existence: 'To start again as myself' (88).

A Picture of Paradise and *The Passion of Jerome* reflect the Abbey Theatre's interest in addressing Celtic Tiger Dublin, while also holding on to the realist dramaturgy and liberal, middlebrow sensibilities of much of its audience. Other contemporary dramas, however, offer more aggressive and disturbing portraits of urban Ireland, where drug use and crime skyrocketed in the 1990s.[5] One of the most shocking of these new playwrights is Dubliner Mark O'Rowe, whose fast-paced play, *Howie the Rookie* (1999), shocked and excited at its debut at the Edinburgh Festival, then went on to be performed at the Bush Theatre, London (a space that favours new Irish work), and has been performed since in Ireland and the United States. In the spirit of *Trainspotting*, the play consists of two monologues, offered by Howie Lee and Rookie Lee, and tells of their enigmatic and violent love/hate relationship with each other and with their neighbourhood. The first monologue describes how Howie helps Peaches beat up Rookie because Rookie accidentally gave Howie scabies.

> Someone has to pay for The Peaches' sufferin' an shame an' The Rookie, me namesake in Lee-ness, was the last person before him, he tells us, to sleep on that mat. One night after a party, he asked Ollie could he kep in his place, the neck, the dirty *neck* on him. Ollie couldn't say no, 'cos Ollie's bent an' The Rookie's sexy, thought he'd get him into the sack, give him

a ridin', but straight Rookie, *hetero* Rookie, chose the mat . . . If he caught it, he would've said something, he would've warned us and he didn't . . . Which means he infected the boys. (O'Rowe 1999: 15)

The second monologue describes how Howie befriended Rookie after the beating in order to enlist his help in a new personal vendetta. Both monologues end in descriptions of surreal deaths, but the adrenaline-filled journey to those surprising and difficult endings is dotted with the young men's constant engagement in competitions for male dominance, or casual attempts at sexual conquest, described in a rich, popular-culture-addled slang. While O'Casey may have turned to the tropes of melodrama and the music hall to paint his pictures of Dublin's underclass, O'Rowe, like other playwrights of his generation, turns to the cinema, the popular mode of expression for his postmodern protagonists.

Cork-based playwright Enda Walsh also plays with language to capture the spirit of contemporary youth culture in his dramas, for example, in *Disco Pigs* (1996) and *Sucking Dublin* (1997). One of the founders of Cork-based Corcadorca theatre company, Walsh's theatre work reflects an interest in capturing and relating to the lived experience of contemporary urban Irish. In an almost Joycean manner, Walsh uses language to capture the passions and energies of the urban landscapes his characters inhabit. In *Disco Pigs*, for example, two Cork youths – nicknamed 'Pig' and 'Runt' – who have grown up together and are now lovers describe their ramblings through Cork in their own personal language, their own 'Pig English', to spell out the obvious allusion. Fellow Cork playwright Johnny Hanrahan has remarked that:

> with *Disco Pigs* [Walsh] has represented Cork in a way that brings it more fully alive than anything else ever written about it. Everybody who saw it felt the power of Walsh's scalding poetry, the harsh beauty of his autistic characters' rage. . . . But I actually think that much of the power of *Disco Pigs* derives from its bodying forth of the full complexities of life and language in Pork Sity. (Hanrahan 2001: 96)

Walsh similarly captured the spirit of Dublin's disenfranchised youth at about the same time with his play *Sucking Dublin* – a drama about five youths dealing with the trauma of one of their group. This work actually emerged out of workshops by Walsh and members of the Abbey Theatre's Theatre-in-Education team as part of a youth outreach initiative, and was a moving enough expression of Dublin life to win, in conjunction with *Disco Pigs*, the Stewart Parker Award for Theatre in 1997.

From the perspective of the Irish theatre tradition, one of the most shocking things about the 'in-yer-face theatre' representations of the grittier side of urban Irish culture in works by Walsh, O'Rowe, and others is an apparent absence of interest among its characters in a sense of identity beyond their immediate desires or their loose alliances with similarly disenfranchised souls. But the alienation felt by Pig and Runt is really not that different from the growing despair of the more recognizable Irish characters in Murphy's play. Indeed, these new plays serve to expose the costs of gentrification and rapid development on not only Ireland's physical landscape, but also on the sense of identity and community among its citizens. These plays remind audiences of the humanity, imagination, and struggle of those outside Dublin's 'muesli belt', whose fortunes have not risen with the rising tide of Celtic Tiger economics. Other contemporary plays strive to make visible the marginalized lives of those Irish for whom national identity is a matter of life or death – immigrants and asylum seekers.

Closing the Circle: New and Old Images of Migration

Migration has been a dominant theme of Irish culture for over one and a half centuries, but in the 1990s Ireland and its theatre began to address the concept of migration in new ways. On 3 December 1990, Mary Robinson became the first President of Ireland, and during her tenure she was a tremendous advocate for human rights and for international relations between Ireland and other nations. Famously, she was noted for her sentimentally stated but politically shrewd interest in building bridges with Ireland's diaspora communities, and inviting emigrants to 'close the circle' and return home. She even had a candle always burning in the window of Áras an Uachtaráin, the President's official estate, to lead the emigrants home. It is true that a large percentage of immigrants to Ireland in the 1990s came from the United States. But the Irish theatre, taking up this issue, used the idea of the returning emigrant as a way to challenge historical and current challenges within the nation. This was certainly the case in two emigrant plays that framed the decade's offerings on the Abbey Theatre's main stage, Brian Friel's *Dancing at Lughnasa* (1990) and Tom Murphy's *The House* (2000).

Both dramas might be termed memory plays, in that an emigrated character returns to a home of women who, for economic or social reasons, are left behind. In *Dancing at Lughnasa*, a young boy, the love child of one of five unmarried sisters, remembers growing up in a house with his mother and four aunts. Although seen through the naive eyes of a child, it is clear to the audience that this house was filled with both love and longing, and hints at the resentments and injustices experienced by these women without men in a patriarchal state with little use for women who were not mothers or wives. When their brother, a missionary priest, returns from Africa, his sisters expect a kind of new respect within the community, but their brother's radical ideas that relate too closely to the beliefs of the people he was sent to civilize may have cost the only professional sister, a schoolteacher, her job. Likewise, the boy's father occasionally drops by the house on his business travels, but these visits ultimately serve to foreground the ways in which the responsibility for children born out of wedlock in this period fall very differently on the mother than the father. The women do experience moments of glorious transcendence, however, dancing to the Marconi radio. And it is these moments of joy that the narrator tries to recapture in the memories of these women and of his youth. But the play also ponders, at least implicitly, how the lack of mobility for these women – physically, economically, and socially – limited their lives.[6]

Tom Murphy's *The House* offers a less sentimental but equally poignant picture of the difficulty of returning from abroad to one's home. Set in the 1950s, a young man named Christy returns to his hometown for an annual vacation along with a crowd of other emigrants, who are at first welcomed by the community, but later resented. Christy is obsessed with a house full of women (the deBurca family) but his attempts to rescue them from financial trouble have catastrophic consequences. Both plays, therefore, represent the physical, temporal, and social gaps that restrict the Irish emigrant's homecoming, and perhaps hint at reasons besides economic need why some emigrants may have left in the first place.[7]

Along with growing numbers of Westerners moving to Ireland, the Irish government and the Irish theatre were also aware of a tremendous number of refugees and asylum seekers trying to find freedom, a home, and work in Ireland. After decades of Ireland dealing with the problem of a shrinking population due to emigration, suddenly thousands wanted entrance into Ireland and the EEC. The desire to recover an ethically and spiritually (although not necessarily religiously) grounded sense of self among Irish in the midst of the migration crisis is a central theme in Donal O'Kelly's *Asylum! Asylum!* (1994), by playwright, actor, and activist Donal O'Kelly.[8] O'Kelly's play dramatizes the dilemma the Irish nation confronted in how to address the wave of immigration when the nation had only recently turned around its own emigration problem through the genre of a domestic problem play. The relationships among the members of the indigenous Irish family, and their responses to the story of one asylum seeker, become in the drama an indicator of the historical and ethical issues surrounding Ireland's response to immigration.

As in Bolger's *The Passion of Jerome*, O'Kelly's play creates a Dublin simultaneously familiar and unfamiliar, 'Irish' and 'foreign'. In the first scene, Bill, a 'just-retired sacristan' (O'Kelly [1994] 1996: 114) meets his son Leo and his friend Pillar, immigration officers, in a local pub. The bar, however, has been decorated in a more cosmopolitan style, which leads Bill to remark that the place is 'done up as if it was a clearing in the jungle' (114). The sense of local culture in the pub is further displaced by Pillar's choice of drink. Pillar recommends to Leo that he drink not a local pint but order a 'Grolsch – by the neck' (115). When Leo asks Pillar what Grolsch is, he is assured that it is 'Continental stuff,' and 'Strong. Very strong.' Leo orders the Grolsch, reflecting his desire to consider himself more European than Irish.

Leo's posturing is informed at least partly by his desire to get a job with Interpol and move to 'Europe. The centre. No future here. We're only an off-shore rock. Clinging on for dear life. A lump of wet moss. We're pathetic' (118). And his desire to reject his Irish identity in favour of a European one deeply informs his exchanges with Joseph, a Ugandan refugee seeking admittance into Ireland. In order for Leo to 'escape' Ireland for Europe by joining Interpol, he must show his toughness towards asylum seekers by keeping Joseph out of Ireland (and Europe) and denying him refugee status. Leo's sister, Mary, however, becomes Joseph's solicitor, and fights to allow him to remain.

Ultimately, the plot takes a typical turn with Mary and Leo on opposite sides of Joseph's campaign – Mary insistent on his right to refugee status, and Leo insistent that he is lying. It is clear, however, that Leo's ambition has hardened him to the point that Joseph is not an asylum seeker but an object – an obstacle to his promotion that he must conquer for his own gain; and he exploits Joseph's situation and his stories accordingly. Ironically, Leo actually passes an interview to get into Interpol by posing as an asylum seeker, and telling one of Joseph's own childhood stories so convincingly that he passes with flying colours: 'I acted it so well they told me . . . this was unanimous . . . they told me they'd have granted me asylum on the spot. These guys were the toughest enforcers around. I was able to soften them' (135). Leo's ambition and cynicism has made him completely unaware of his exploitation of Joseph's tragic experiences, and he wins his ticket out of Ireland through the traumatic experiences of another man.

Only after Leo actually witnesses violence by Europeans against refugees, during a riot while he is on duty in his new position in Germany, does he realize the impact of his job on individuals and society. But by then Joseph's request for asylum has been denied and he has been deported. The last scene, however, ends with a glimmer of hope for Irish refugee policy, if not necessarily for Joseph. Bill and Mary sit in a police interrogation room, arrested for their role in trying to help Joseph escape. Pillar tells them they are free to go and charges have been dropped, largely, he implies, to keep the incident out of the press. Mary and Bill silently look at each other, then, smiling, refuse to leave, thus committing themselves to fight for Joseph's return.

Bill and Mary's act of civil disobedience at the end of the play moves the story from a personal tale about a single refugee to a statement about the need for reform of laws for refugees and asylum seekers. They refuse to sell their ethics, or to forget Ireland's own historical experiences of exploitation, violence, and coerced and forced migration, to purchase a sense of belonging to the economic powerhouse of the new, united, Europe.

Since the debut of O'Kelly's play, immigration has continued to grow in Ireland, creating a far more diverse culture than has existed on the island previously. This development has led to emigrants and first-generation Irish becoming involved in theatre as actors, directors, and playwrights. The impact of these new voices in Irish theatre are just beginning to be felt, but promise a new wave of Irish theatre on the near horizon.

Re-inventing Rural Ireland: Marina Carr and Martin McDonagh

Just as images of urban life were being reconsidered in Irish theatre in the 1990s, so were representations of Irish rural life. The idealized west had been debunked decades before (although it did continue to rise like a vampire in Bord Failte advertisements and American films), but two playwrights of the 1990s – Marina Carr and Martin McDonagh – in their very different ways revived an interest in pondering Ireland's rural roots, and both continue that work today.

Marina Carr's haunting images of the Irish midlands offer what some critics claim to be the richest images of Irish language, spirit, and life since the work of John Millington Synge. Carr's first play, *Low in the Dark* (1989), offered a poetic, Beckettian look at gender, sexuality, religion, and repro-duction with an almost punk sensibility and the rhythm of a classic farce. It was the 1994 Peacock Stage production of her matrilineal drama, *The Mai*, however, that presented her almost surreal poetic style to the public, and captured her rich, psychologically complex, and poetic characters. In many of Carr's plays mundane, materialistic individuals are juxtaposed by deeply passionate figures – usually women – in touch with a sense of history, desire, purpose, or love that can make them behave obsessively, cruelly, selfishly, and tragically. They are a far cry from the long-suffering obedient women who have inhabited so much of Irish drama. In *The Mai*, Carr follows four generations of 'proud mad women', each generation of whom reflects a different moment in Irish women's history.[9] The true theme of the play, however, is the eponymous character's destructive love for her adulterous husband.

By the Bog of Cats (1998), with its subtext from *Medea*, as well as use of images from Irish myth, continues to be considered the most emblematic and well conceived of Carr's plays to date. The stirring quality of its first production at the Dublin Theatre Festival on the Abbey main stage, directed by Patrick Mason and with Olwen Fourere in the leading role, only confirmed for many the brilliance of the text. In the play, Hester Swayne is a traveller whose former lover and father of her daughter, Carthage Kilbride, is about to marry a local woman. As in the original Greek tragedy, Hester is furious at this sense of betrayal, although Carthage dismisses her rage, and the bride's father warns Hester not to impede the marriage.

Other elements of the play, however, drift away from the Euripidean source into a more Irish, feminine, and psychological territory. For instance, Hester's death is foretold in the first scene when 'The Ghost Fancier', a symbol of death, comes too early in the day for Hester, thinking that the dawn light during which he arrives is actually dusk. The other sign of Hester's impending death is that, on her entrance onstage in the play, she is dragging behind her a dead black swan. Hester and the bird had played together since Hester's childhood, but she found it frozen in a bog hole that morning. The death of the swan, frozen into the bog it was unable to fly away from, reflects Hester's own psychic entrapment within this com-munity. Having been abandoned by her mother on this spot years before, she remains by the bog of cats, awaiting her mother's return.

Other characters in the play evocative of the Medea myth are presented as well. The Tiresias figure in Carr's play is a middle-aged woman named Catwoman who wears cat fur, keeps mice in her pockets, and has mouse fur in her teeth. Also, Carr includes the legend that Medea killed her brother in her adapation of the drama. Before Hester's death, the ghost of her brother, murdered by Hester, makes a matter-of-fact appearance to reminisce with Hester about their mother.

But underlying these grotesque elements of the play, and Hester's pain over her partner's betrayal, lies a much deeper pain – Hester's abandonment by her own mother. Thus, her murder of her own daughter is not so much out of revenge against Carthage and his new bride as it is out of a desire not to abandon her daughter to the same loneliness and pain she has felt for her own mother for decades. Margaret Llewellyn-Jones remarks that, despite the outsider status of Hester and other Carr heroines, 'the imaginative intensity of all Carr's tragic heroines stands out against the drab pettiness of mundane, narrow-minded rural communities, thus embodying a critique of both female stereotypes and society' (Llewellyn-Jones 2002: 88).

Carr's plays also deconstruct images of rural Ireland through their juxtaposition of the traditional symbolism of the rural Irish west with pre-modern Irish myth and the everyday accoutrements of postmodern Ireland. Carr's world is full of ghosts, legends, and omens, but also cars and televisions. In her chilling adaptation of the Faust myth, *Ariel* (2002), a murdered girl whose body has been left in a lake calls to her brother from the world of the dead – on his mobile phone. Like Lady Gregory's writings that acknowledged the relationship between Irish and Anglo-Irish, ancient and modern, Celtic and Catholic, in the communities of which she wrote, Carr's plays imagine the Irish countryside as a hybrid landscape, where tradition and innovation, belief and reason, the abject and the oppressive, cohabitate.

Marina Carr seeks the deep heart's core of her rural protagonists, and looks for ways in which this core has been shaped and misshaped by family, memory, culture, and history. Martin McDonagh's plays, likewise, are interested in Irish country life; but instead of seeking his characters' hearts, he observes comically the strategies of religion, culture, manners, violence, and denial they employ to avoid any true spiritual introspection. McDonagh himself even denies much introspection in his writing, insisting at the beginning of his fame that his influences were from film and television, and that he had seen or read very few plays.[10] Yet, thanks in no small part to the guiding hand of the

Druid Theatre Company's director Garry Hynes, and some of the best actors in Ireland, McDonagh's *Leenane Trilogy*'s debut performances in the mid-1990s were hailed as masterful postmodern re-evaluations of the rural Irish play, similar to the way Quentin Tarrantino's United States gangster films have been honoured for toying with American cinematic traditions.

The *Leenane Trilogy* follows a group of interrelated individuals in the Irish west. (Leenane is a real town in Connemara, County Galway). Although this community is in the heart of the idealized Irish west celebrated by artists and cultural nationalists at the start of the century, McDonagh's Leenane, however, is a violent community bordering on anarchy. In the first play, a mother ruins her middle-aged daughter's one chance to marry and escape both Leenane and her codependent relationship with her mother. In the second play, the history of a murder is literally uncovered by a group of cemetery workers who are exhuming bodies from the local graveyard and crushing the bones to make room to inter the new dead. And, in the third play, two middle-aged brothers fight over their father's inheritance after one brother shot him in 'questionable circumstances'. At least one murder is revealed and goes unpunished in every play of the trilogy – it is a small wonder that Father Walsh (or is it Welsh? None of the characters can remember his name) ultimately commits suicide, over-whelmed by his spiritual impotence in the community, and hoping that his death will inspire better behaviour among his parishioners. (It does not.)[11]

Within Ireland, some critique has been raised that new representations of rural Ireland stem from anxiety over rapid urbanization and economic growth in Celtic Tiger Ireland. Vic Merriman, in his provocatively titled 1999 essay, 'Decolonisation Postponed: The Theatre of Tiger Trash', states that McDonagh and Carr's plays 'implicate audiences in particular stances toward the poor, the past, Irishness' (313). The *Leenane Trilogy* is filled with old themes from Irish theatre: mother/daughter relationships, emigration, anxiety over inheritance, brotherly feuds, presented to the audience in the familiar and friendly forms of melodramatic farce – characters behaving badly, unlikely coincidences, under-reaction to violent excess and over-reaction to trivial events. For a nation with as diverse and accessible a theatre scene as Ireland's, the threat of McDonagh's farcical west inform-ing contemporary Irish opinions about rural Ireland, or overpowering other imaginings of rural Ireland, is negligible. However, the universality of this kind of humour in Western cultures, plus an international delight in Irish flavour in popular entertainment, has made McDonagh's work – for better or worse – the most recognized, and most talked about, contemporary theatre outside Ireland.

Restaging Irish History

Since the time nationalist activists performed anti-imperialist pageants in Gaelic League feisianna in the 1890s, Irish theatre has served to create a counter-narrative to dominant discourses about significant events in Irish history. This tradition has continued into the twenty-first century, but with a difference. While earlier in the twentieth century political performance sought to celebrate moments of national resistance and community, contemporary playwrights seek to shed light on more ambiguous historical moments and events, or minority Irish discourses. One of the masters of this form is Sebastian Barry.

Due perhaps in part to his Nonconformist religious heritage, Sebastian Barry's plays are particularly sensitive to characters existing in the interstice between the polarized identity positions that often arise in Irish nationalist ideology. 'Against the simple narrative of Irish history as a long tale of colonization and resistance,' Fintan O'Toole writes, 'Barry releases more complex stories in which it is by no means clear who is the native and who the foreigner' (1995: xi). In *The Only True History of Lizzie Finn* (1995), for example, a dancing girl working in England marries an Anglo-Irishman named Robert and becomes the lady of an Anglo-Irish manor. After attempting to fit into that aristocratic role, the couple decide to reinvent themselves by moving to Cork. In *White Woman Street* (1992), Trooper, an Irishman in the United States, undergoes outlaw adventures in the American west while dreaming of the gorse back in Ireland. By a coincidence, the events of the play happen during the general period of the Easter Rising, which appears in the play as a brief mention in an old newspaper. And in his most famous play, *The Steward of Christendom* (1995), Barry imagines the haunted memories of an Irishman who had served as a member of the Dublin Metropolitan Police, 'defending' Dublin against the strikers in the Dublin Lockout of 1913 and, later, the nationalists fighting in the Irish Revolution. The play is set in 1932, with Barry now an elderly man committed in a hospital. He still loves Queen Victoria, and is proud of his service, but he is haunted by his troubled relationships with his daughters. Lear-like, Barry must let go of a self-identity couched in his position of authority, while trying to make peace, at least with himself, over his treatment of his children. In each play, Barry explores the dissolution of an established power structure through the experiences of a character who is perhaps a minor figure in the drama of history, but whose very sense of self is deeply affected by the change.[12]

While dramas focusing on the effects of Irish history on a single figure or a small group continue to be seen in plays like Brian Friel's *The Home Place* (2005), other playwrights and theatre companies have chosen to reassess or even rewrite Irish history through performance. One of the most outlandish of these plays is *Improbable Frequency* (2004), a musical about the Irish Free State during 'the Emergency' (i.e., the First World War), imagining that the physicist Erwin Schrödinger (who did live in Ireland during this time) was working on a secret weapon for the Allies on Irish soil, thus threatening Ireland's neutrality in wartime. Written by Arthur Riordan with music by Bell Helicopter, an Irish music/sound team who work internationally on theatre and film, this irreverent farce imagines to an absurd degree both what Ireland may have been like during the Emergency – a neutral (?) Ireland surrounded by a world at war. Michael West, in collaboration with the Dublin comedian troupe Corn Exchange, turned to re-imagining Ireland's theatre history in *Dublin by Lamplight* (2004), a play that turns the Fay brothers' attempt to create a national theatre into a comic melodrama. The play shows little basis in fact (Yeats and Gregory are conspicuously absent), but a great deal of humour and in-jokes for anyone who has ever performed on an amateur stage.

While quite different in form and purpose, these plays have in common an interest in disrupting traditional historical narratives about Ireland's political or cultural histories in order to undermine historical platitudes and assumptions, and create a space for considering new perspectives, to make the stage a space for imagining possibility, no matter how improbable. And in making space to reconsider and reconcile the past, perhaps these plays also create opportunities for audiences to think about imaginative responses to the rapid changes occurring in Ireland today.

Performing Community

Much Irish theatre has been committed to representing, inventing, or reinventing national identity through performance, which has meant that even plays set in obviously regional locations, like the Aran Islands, Belfast, Dublin, Kerry, or even Friel's imaginary city of Ballybeg, serve as signifiers of national concerns. One of the offshoots of the rise of independent theatres in the late 1980s to the present day, however, has been a growing movement to represent local histories and celebrate local communities. As discussed in the previous chapter, Irish theatre in the 1980s saw a rise in interest in, and funding for, small professional theatre companies and community theatres over the previous tradition of nearly exclusive patronage to the island's three major theatres – the Abbey, the Gate, and the Lyric. By the mid-1990s, the Irish government was supporting community theatre groups across the island, in both major cities and small communities, (Cloake 1996: 173) and funding for community projects remains a high priority for arts-granting institutions in the Republic and in Northern Ireland. These grants supported projects such as Passion Machine in Dublin that gave novelist Roddy Doyle and playwright Paul Mercier a space for creating a new urban dramaturgy. Rough Magic Theatre (founded 1984 in Dublin) likewise boasts a splendid repertoire and a leading reputation for discovering and nurturing new talent, and for creating a space for cutting-edge work. Corcadorca (founded 1991 in Cork) took advantage of its city's historic landscape to create incredible events of site-specific theatre, including a Passion Play winding through the streets of the city like a medieval rite, and a production of *The Merchant of Venice* that played upon the city's own history of once having its own canals. Barrabas, the Company (founded 1993 in Dublin) employs clowning and circus traditions in its devised work. While it performs in both traditional and site-specific spaces, it makes a point of engaging directly with its audiences in all contexts. Smashing Times (founded 1991 in Dublin) uses Boal exercises to train local citizens into performers for its productions that discuss class, race, and other issues pertinent to its working-class communities (Moynihan and Kennedy 2004). And Macnas (founded 1986 in Galway) engages wide sections of the community in its performance events, such as its annual parades in connection with the Galway Arts Festival. The size of Macnas productions is remarkable – their 2000 parade included 474 performers, 175 of whom were children.

The proliferation of these new companies in just a decade has been tremendous. And these companies' emphasis on the visual, the local, and the 'liveness' of performance, along with an ability to reflect and address immediate issues from within the community, have helped establish younger and more economically and racially diverse audiences for Irish theatre (McMullan 1996: 35). As Anna McMullan points out, 'performance has the potential to mediate between the traditions of the past and the contemporary scene, between national and international concerns, expanding the signifying potential of the stage, opening up new possibilities of

collaboration between text and performance, performance and audience'
(35–6). While the immediacy, intimacy, and emphasis on spectacle over text
make these community performance events often harder to record and
analyse than more traditional theatre, their influence on how Ireland, and
Irish theatre, started to see themselves in the 1990s – a trend continuing
today – is telling. A century ago, local performers created images of an
Irish identity onstage to resist the essentialized image of their culture and
personality proliferating on the stages abroad. While the Irish National
Theatre Society centralized the aesthetics that emerged from these local
events, the national theatre was ultimately shaped by the local. Today, Irish
communities continue to perform for themselves images of who they are,
what their problems are, how they are changing, and what they want to
become. And, just as in the Gaelic League days, it is through the conversations between the local and the national that new images of Ireland and
Irishness will begin to emerge.

Conclusion: What is an Irish Play?

On 3 October 2007, a new version of one of the most influential plays in modern Irish theatre, *The Playboy of the Western World*, opened as part of the Dublin Theatre Festival at the Abbey Theatre. One hundred years after the original production received its controversial reception at Ireland's national theatre, Roddy Doyle and Bisi Adigun had updated the drama to reflect contemporary anxieties surrounding Irish identity, and presented it on the same stage. Doyle and Adigun's adaptation takes into account the drastically new demographic make-up of twenty-first-century Ireland, with a majority of its population living in the cities, and the image of Ireland once reflected by the idealized peasant increasingly being supplanted by characters who are working-class urbanites. Directed by Jimmy Fay, this new *Playboy of the Western World* featured Irish actors easily identified for their film and television careers, most notably Angeline Ball and Eileen Walsh. And Christy's father was played by Olu Jacobs, one of Nigeria's most celebrated film actors. Doyle and Adigun have moved the setting of the play from 1907 to the present, and from the west coast of Ireland to a pub in West Dublin. And Christy Mahon, the exotic stranger with a secret to tell, is now a Nigerian immigrant. These updates allowed the production to comment transparently on contemporary crises in Irish culture – namely, the fate of immigrants into the country, and the rise in urban violence. A favourite scene in the new production shows Christy beating up a thug (in lieu of winning a pony race in the original) while the local girls film the incident on their mobile phones. But placing the production in the context of *The Playboy* permits this new adaptation to claim its lineage among national plays seeking to, in Christopher Murray's terms, hold the 'mirror up to nation' (Murray 1997) in a moment of cultural crisis – to show what can be lost and what gained in the wake of a decade of unprecedented economic growth, with an influx of men and women from around the world wishing to make Ireland their home.

Earlier in 2007, the Druid Theatre Company produced its own *Playboy of the Western World* as part of the Tokyo International Arts Festival. The Druid's production offered a more 'faithful' rendition of Synge's play, and echoed director Garry Hynes's important production of the play in the mid-1980s, with Mick Lally and Marie Mullen revising their roles as the Old Mahon and the Widow Quin, respectively. The Druid Theatre has had *The Playboy of the Western World* at the forefront of its repertory since producing the play in 2004, and again as part of the ambitious *Druid/Synge* project – a cycle of all six of Synge's plays. After performing *Druid/Synge* in Galway and Dublin in 2005, the company took *The Playboy* and their other Synge plays to the Guthrie Theatre, a company with intimate Irish ties, and helped open the Guthrie's new $125 million facility, before moving on to Broadway. While not as transparent a statement about contemporary Irish culture as the Abbey's 2007 production, the Druid Theatre's work with *The Playboy* reflected the Druid's general interest in capturing the past and present voice and spirit of the Irish west. In *Druid/Synge*, for example, traditional settings of *The Playboy* and *Riders to the Sea* were juxtaposed with contemporary settings for *The Well of the Saints* and *The Tinker's Wedding*, showing how the tension between individual desire and community expectations in rural Ireland continues into the new century. Likewise, Druid has given voice to contemporary images of Irish life through the work of playwrights like Frank McGuinness and Martin McDonagh.

These two revivals of this quintessential 'revival' play, borne out of a single dramatic source but on opposite ends of the island, display the variety of directions in which Irish theatre is proceeding as it enters the new millennium. On the one hand, artists and audiences continue to find meaning in the century's canonical works, and these plays often tour in other countries, or are produced by theatre companies abroad. On the other hand, much contemporary theatre seeks to break away from the tropes of the classic Irish play by commenting ironically upon them, like McDonagh's *Leenane Trilogy* or Doyle and Adigun's adaptation of *The Playboy* (2007), or by ignoring them in favour of new performance models that address new issues, like Enda Walsh's *Sucking Dublin* (1997) or Stella Feehily's *O Go My Man* (2006).

While these new approaches to performance and politics raise concern among some that Irish theatre is losing its identity, it is an inevitable and necessary development. In 2000, Fintan O'Toole noted that, when writing about Irish suburbia, one finds that 'the great tradition of Irish writing is silent on the subject . . . so you can slip out from under its shadow. No one has ever mythologized this housing estate, this footbridge over the motorway, that video rental shop. It is, for the writer, virgin territory' (O'Toole 2000: ix–x). But it is through these new developments on the Irish landscape, among others, that the nation's people are experiencing the nation and imagining its future. And it is contemporary theatre's responsibility to inscribe these places, the people who inhabit them, and the ideals that emerge from them, into Irish theatre history by presenting them onstage.

In *The Landscape of History*, John Lewis Gaddis reminds us that the detail and diversity of an historical moment, like a point in a landscape, becomes more obscure the further away the observer finds herself from it. It is easy from a century's distance to reduce the range of ideologies and identity positions, circulating in the nationalist movement at the turn of the twentieth century, into the simplistic and incorrect binary of W.B. Yeats's Anglo-Irish modernism versus an amorphous mob of melodramatists and propagandists. Likewise, it is easy to forget the artistic and economic importance of England, France, and the United States to Irish theatre's survival in its first decades, not to mention Ireland's influence on the theatre traditions of other countries. By the same token, when looking at contemporary Irish theatre from the point of view of the seat in the theatre or the article in today's newspaper, one may more readily miss the ways Ireland's most radical new theatres actually continue a tradition of using the stage to counteract stereotypical images of the nation and its people by offering new perspectives on the nation's history, and establishing truthful and diverse images of the present. The Gaelic League feis and the Macnas parade are closer than they appear. The contemporary turn towards avant-garde performative strategies is a reminder of the experiments in poetic and dance drama, from W.B. Yeats, to Austin Clarke, to Samuel Beckett. Yet the fascination with language and history persists in playwrights like Sebastian Barry, Brian Friel, and Conor McPherson.

In fact, the question of what defines an Irish play has preoccupied practitioners, critics, and historians both in Ireland and among its diaspora communities since the first years of the Irish revival, largely because of the theatre movement's roots in cultural nationalism. In retrospect, the answers to the question have transcended ideologies, identity positions, and even geographic borders. But all perspectives on the question share an interest in theatre that is dynamically engaged in reflecting on the cultural past and present and helping to construct Ireland's cultural and political future. As the Irish nation, and Irish culture, continue to develop increasingly complex relationships within and without their geographical borders, and inside and outside of its diaspora communities abroad, so will Irish theatre.

Notes

Chapter 1 Imagining an Aesthetic: Modern Irish Theatre's First Years

1 The nineteenth century saw the theatre increasingly become a forum for discussing social issues, from the melodramatic, middle-class morality of the temperance play, to the critiques of bourgeois morality found in the naturalist theatre of Hauptmann and Ibsen. For the Irish, Ole Bull's success with developing theatre in Norway to describe political issues, and that theatre's role in developing a Norwegian national identity was a model for creating an Irish national theatre.

2 For an informative and insightful description of some early Irish language plays and their producers, see Karen Vandevelde, 'The Gaelic League and the Daughters of Erin', *The Alternative Dramatic Revival in Ireland* (2005).

3 The classic discussion of Yeats's invention of self as nationalist and artist in connection with the theatre is James W. Flannery's *W.B. Yeats and the Idea of a Theatre* (1976). More contextualized readings of Yeats's political and artistic development in the 1890s are Richard Ellman's classic biography, *Yeats: the Man and the Masks* (1979), and the first volume of R.F. Foster's biography, *W.B. Yeats: The Apprentice Mage* (1997).

4 Although overlooked for decades, revisionist readings of Gregory's life and involvement in the dramatic movement as a playwright and administrator over the past decade have contributed more complex and complete readings of her indispensable contributions to Irish theatre. Along with her own, published, recollections of her life in the theatre, *Our Irish Theatre* (1913), see, e.g., recent reassessments of Gregory by Paige Reynolds (2007) and Colm Toibin (2002).

5 Moore was so energized by his experience with the Irish Literary Theatre that he moved back to Ireland in 1901, and lived there until 1911. His memoirs of his Ireland years, *Hail and Farewell* ([1914] 1985), offer a wry and gossipy look at these formative years of the Irish dramatic movement, and the people in it. Moore remarked about his book that, 'One half of Dublin is afraid it will be in the book, and the other is afraid that it won't.'

6 The Rebellion of 1798 was a foiled attempt by the United Irishmen to gain Irish independence from England. France, being at war with England and seeing the political advantage of England fighting two enemies at once, offered naval support for the Rebellion. French ships landed at Killala in August of 1798, and captured the town from the British. The town remained under Franco-Irish rule for thirty-two days until the British regained power and executed its leaders. The aftermath of the Rebellion led to the dissolution of Grattan's parliament, and the establishment of the Act of Union in 1800, officially making Ireland part of the United Kingdom. The memory of this Rebellion would be fresh in the minds of the first audience of *Cathleen ni Houlihan*, thanks to the widespread commemorations of the centennial of the Rebellion just a few years before.

7 Regrettably, she shared not only a child with Millevoye, but anti-Semitic beliefs, as well. See Levitas (2002).

8 For an examination of other playwrights in the peasant play tradition, see chapter 2.
9 These included her important translations of Irish legends, *Cuchulain of Muithmemne* and *Gods and Fighting Men*, and her memoirs of the early days of the movement, *Our Irish Theatre* (1913).
10 In her Introduction to *J. M. Synge: Collected Works* (1982a), Ann Saddlemyer notes that, for Synge's production of *Riders to the Sea*, 'Michael Costello of Inisheer forwarded *pampooties*, the traditional Aran footgear and replied to Synge's queries, "I herewith enclose patterns of the flannel usually worn by the native men here . . . The kind of thick flannel was spun on the woollen wheel by hand and woven in Aranmoore."'
11 In fact, she had financed the Avenue Theatre productions of Yeats's *Land of Hearts Desire*, Shaw's *Arms and the Man*, and Todhunter's *Comedy of Sighs* in 1894.
12 See Ann Saddlemyer, *Theatre Business: The Correspondence of the First Abbey Theatre Directors*.
13 It should be noted that *Sinn Fein* was edited at this time by Arthur Griffith, an early member of the Irish National Theatre Society who resigned from the company, enraged by Yeats's refusal to perform Padraic Pearse's play, *The Saxon Shillin'*, which had originally been published by his newspaper, *Sinn Fein*.
14 The actual line in the text does not refer to Mayo girls but 'chosen females'. Fay was so nervous, however, that he 'fluffed probably the most famous line of his career, making the insult even worse by making it more specific' (Morash 2002: 132).

Chapter 2 Realisms, Regionalisms, and Revolutions

1 When being interviewed by a reporter for *Le Gaulois* about his French play, *Salome*, Wilde said of the English, 'Here people are essentially anti-artistic and narrow-minded. Though I have English friends, I do not like the English in general. There is a great deal of hypocrisy in England, which you in France very justly find fault with. The typical Briton is Tartuffe, seated in his shop behind the counter. There are numerous exceptions, but they only prove the rule' (qtd in Ellman 1987: 373).
2 Education would remain a vital theme for Shaw throughout his life.
3 Sally Peters remarks on the difficulty in even categorizing Shaw's prolific output over seven decades of work. 'Not only was he the author of some five dozen plays,' she writes, 'his mountain of writings includes five completed novels, a number of short stories, lengthy treatises on politics and economics, four volumes of theatre criticism, three volumes of music criticism, and a volume of art criticism. Add to that total over a hundred book reviews and an astonishing correspondence of over a quarter of a million letters and postcards' (1998: 3).
4 The Land Wars in the 1880s were not military struggles per se, but acts of civil disobedience and resistance to laws that allowed landlords to charge exorbitant rents and to evict tenants with little recourse. The Wyndham Act broke up the landlord's monopoly, and in fact made it possible for small farmers like Martin and Murtagh to purchase the farms their families had been working for generations.
5 'Familism' is the social custom of placing the needs of one's family over individual desire. In Ireland, this translated into the custom of handing down small farms to one child, who would not marry until he inherited the land. This tradition delayed marriage – in the nineteenth century, the Irish people married later than any other group in Europe – and spurred the children who did not inherit the land towards emigration.
6 See Frazier (1990: 139–40).
7 In 1915, Ervine became manager of the Abbey and imposed such strict and hierarchical rules on the actors that they rebelled and many, including Arthur Sinclair and Kathleen Drago, were dismissed (Cronin 1988: 8). Ervine quit the post a year later, joined the British

army in the First World War and, after the war, turned from peasant realism to drawing room comedies for London's West End (Cronin 1988: 9). Later in life, he would return to Irish themes in his playwriting and prose. Regardless, his animosity towards Irish nationalism as produced at the Abbey was profound.

8 In fact, while he was deputy editor for the nationalist newspaper *Nationality* in 1918, he was involved in a fight with British soldiers who had invaded the press, and later died of a hemorrhage from the incident. He was given a hero's funeral (O'Grady 1997: 271).

9 Of course, this movement did not spring out of nothing: in the early 1900s, Cork could already boast of a long and rich theatre tradition. As Christopher Morash points out, Cork, along with Dublin and Belfast, was part of the traditional theatre tour circuit in Ireland, so its audiences were exposed to a range of high and low theatre forms from England and Europe. In fact, Cork had its own national theatre society, founded in 1904 on a rocky foundation, but resurrected as the Cork Dramatic Society in 1908.

10 Robinson was raised in a unionist home with a Protestant minister father, but the family was apparently open to new ideas, especially considering their ready acceptance of Lennox's working at the national theatre.

11 Robinson was one of several Anglo-Irish playwrights whom Yeats took under his wing to make manager of the theatre. Robinson served the post well, although he was the individual responsible for infuriating Horniman for the last time and losing her subsidy for the theatre when he failed to close the theatre for the death of Edward VII. He led the theatre through the crises of the war for independence and the Civil War, and continued to be an influential playwright and theatre manager well into the mid-twentieth century.

12 On the ULT's production of *Cathleen ni Houlihan*, the play that, more than any other, generated Dublin's interest in a national theatre movement, Gerald MacNamara remarked that 'The Belfast public was not taken by Cathleen ni Houlihan. Ninety-nine percent of the population had never heard of the lady – and cared less; in fact someone in the audience said that the show was going "rightly" till *she* came along' (Bell 1972: 4).

13 *Uladh* ran four numbers from 1904 to 1905, funded largely by donations from its founders (Danaher 1988: 6).

14 One hears in Connla's remarks a hint of resentment at his own treatment at the hands of the NTS. Cousins's first play, *The Racing Lug* (1902), was one of the first productions of the INDC, but his later work was mysteriously dismissed by Yeats and was not performed at the Dublin theatre.

15 *Suzannah and the Sovereigns* actually began as a party sketch put on during the Christmas season in the Morrows's home (Bell 1972: 29).

16 In fact, MacNamara gave Dublin nationalism – or at least its national theatre – a similar treatment with *The Mist that Does Be on the Bog*, a parody of J.M. Synge's language, with not-so-subtle jabs at Yeats and Gregory, in 1909. In the spirit of good-humoured satire rather than mud-slinging, however, the ULT opened the drama at the seat of Syngean dialogue, the Abbey Theatre (MacNamara 1988b: 58).

Introduction to Part II

1 Casement's anti-colonial sensibilities were developed while working as a diplomat in the Congo. There, he wrote about the atrocities against the people brought on by Belgium, and was awarded a British knighthood in 1911. He helped found the Irish Republican Volunteers in 1913, and even travelled to Germany in 1914 and 1915 as part of a failed plot to bring prisoners of war of Irish extraction back to Ireland to

fight in the coming insurrection. He was hanged by the British government in 1916.

2 Many Irish writers have addressed Ireland's involvement in the First World War in their work, most famously W.B. Yeats's poem, 'An Irish Airman Foresees his Death', and Frank McGuinness's drama, *Observe the Sons of Ulster Marching Toward the Somme*.

3 For a concise reading of the events leading up to the Easter Rising, and the event itself, see Foster (1989: 471–93).

4 See Peter De Rosa's *Rebels: The Irish Rising of 1916* (1990) for a detailed yet accessible account of the event.

5 See Maire Nic Shiubhlaigh, *The Splendid Years* (1955), pp. 140–86.

6 Ireland is made up of four provinces (Ulster, Leinster, Munster, and Connacht) in which there are thirty-two counties. The six counties which remained part of the United Kingdom according to the treaty were: Antrim, Down, Armagh, Londonderry, Fermanagh, Tyrone. Since partition was based on demographics rather than geography, the northernmost part of the Republic of Ireland is actually north of Northern Ireland.

7 See Robert Kee, *The Green Flag*, vol. III (1972), p. 155.

8 See Clair Wills, *That Neutral Island: A History of Ireland During the Second World War* (2007).

9 This kind of behaviour was often loved by audiences, and even seemed to some to signal their virtuosity and star status, especially in the musical theatre. US performers like Al Jolson, Ethel Merman, and Zero Mostel were (in)famous for such actions from the 1920s through the 1960s. But playwrights and directors often grew frustrated by the way that actors' onstage behaviour influenced the tone of the works performed, especially social dramas and tragedies, and the overall professionalism of the theatre.

10 At the same time, Irish theatre was now undeniably international in its scope and its influence. In the 1920s, Dudley Digges worked closely with the highly influential Theatre Guild in the United States, and tours and lectures by Irish theatre playwrights and performers began to influence America's Little Theatre movement. In the 1930s, Una O'Connor and Sara Allgood were favourite actors of Alfred Hitchcock, and Barry Fitzgerald often worked with Hollywood directors like Howard Hawks and, later, the Irish-American director John Ford.

Chapter 3 The Abbey Becomes Institution, 1916–1929

1 For more on the Abbey's growing international cache in the 1910s, see Reynolds 2007.

2 Early examples of theatre addressing violent social change include Padraic Colum's *The Saxon Shilin'* (1903) and Maud Gonne's *Dawn* (1904). Both one-act works of agit-prop were published in Arthur Griffith's nationalist newspaper *Sinn Fein*. The early movement was more cagey about performing plays urging violent revolution, with a few exceptions such as Yeats's and Gregory's *Cathleen ni Houlihan*. The commercial melodrama houses, however, revelled in patriotic dramas celebrating early Irish revolution. See Herr (1991); Watt (2004).

3 Many of the leaders of the Easter Uprising, including Pearse, MacDonagh, and Maloney, were pillars of the theatre movement – so much so that signers of the proclamation involved in the theatre included Pearse, Thomas MacDonagh, Joseph Plunkett, and James Connolly. Abbey theatre performers who fought included Maire Nic Shiubhlaigh, Nelly Bushell, Peadar Kearney, Barney Murphy, Helena Molony, and Arthur Shields (Moran 2007 16).

4 Pearse also founded St Ita's, a school for girls, but was mostly engaged in his work at St Enda's.

5 W.B. Yeats, 'A People's Theatre: An Open Letter to Lady Gregory' ([1919] 1923).

6 While not officially a part of the Theatre of Ireland, which dissolved in 1913, many of the Theatre of Ireland's leading actors went on to support and work in this less politically charged yet still important company.

7 For information on Seumas O'Kelly and the Theatre of Ireland's urban dramas, see Nelson O Ceallaigh Ritschel (2000).

8 Temperance dramas, such as *The Bottle*, were immensely popular tools in the Victorian period for reforming working-class citizens away from alcohol, and towards more middle-class behaviours. While these dramas did address an important social issue – the effect of alcoholism on individuals and families – they rarely looked at the larger social factors that led to such high rates of alcohol and drug use among the nineteenth-century working class.

9 For an excellent reading of the big house in Irish drama, see Doyle (2003).

10 An Comhar Damuiochta, led by Piaras Beaslai, Gearoid O Lochlainn, and others, based itself on the model of the Dublin Drama League, and actually received its own grant from the government of £600 a year in 1924, months before the Abbey. See Welch (1999: 85–6, 91).

11 Protesters included Hanna Sheehy-Skeffington, Padraic Pearse's mother, Tom Clarke's widow, and Abbey Theatre playwright Dorothy Macardle.

12 For more on the cult of true womanhood as it was represented on the stage, see Bruce McConachie, 'How Her Blood Tells', *Melodramatic Formations* (1996).

13 Sean O'Casey, Letter to Lennox Robinson, 5 April 1928 (Robinson Papers, Southern Illinois University).

14 Sean O'Casey, Letter to Lennox Robinson, n.d. (Robinson Papers, Southern Illinois University).

Chapter 4   New Voices of the 1930s and 1940s

1 The Gate was not only a site of daring, but also one of whimsy. One of the ways they flouted their cosmopolitanism upon the opening of their new theatre was to write the words 'men' or 'women' on the theatre's public toilets in eight different languages.

2 True, the Abbey performed Yeats and Shaw during this period, as well as newer playwrights whose dramas, while conservative in structure, had the potential to question the status quo. But they grew increasingly unlikely to seek out a work's potential to challenge an audience in performance.

3 See Jill Dolan, 'Building a Theatrical Vernacular: Responsibility, Community, Ambivalence, and Queer Theatre', *The Queerest Art: Essays on Lesbian and Gay Theater* (2002), pp. 1–8.

4 Michael Mac Liammóir, *All For Hecuba: An Irish Theatrical Autobiography* (1967), p. 67. This design echoes the aesthetics Yeats espoused for the Abbey in its first decade. See Karen Dorn, *Players and Painted Stage* (1984).

5 For more information on the craze and controversy surrounding representations of *Salome* in the early twentieth century, see Erdman (2004); and Krasner (2001). The most notorious of these Salomes was the portrayal by Maud Allen in London in the 1910s.

6 See *Scene Change: One Hundred Years of Theatre Design at the Abbey*, the catalogue for the 2004 exhibition at the Irish Museum of Modern Art. The catalogue is edited by Helen O'Donoghue (2004).

7 Qtd in John Cowell, *No Profit but the Name: The Longfords and the Gate Theatre* (1988), p. 96.

8 In a publisher's note, the editor, George Jean Nathan, remarked that the play 'was produced by the Abbey Theatre on March 16th, and was the occasion of a half-column notice in *The Times* newspaper on the following Friday. "With 'Katie Roche'" wrote the *Times* critic "Miss Deevy definitely takes a high place among contemporary Irish playwrights"; and he goes on to remark that, "it is almost impossible to give an idea of the quality of this really fine play." Our own view (after reading the script) coincided with that of the *Times* critic, and we felt that the band of regular purchasers of our Famous Plays Series would welcome the inclusion of this play, even though it cannot yet be called famous.' [George Jean Nathan]. 'Publisher's Note', *Famous Plays of 1935–6* (1936) n.p.

9 See Cathy Leeney, 'Interchapter I: 1900–1939', *Women in Irish Drama: A Century of Authorship and Representation*, ed. Melissa Sihra (2007), p. 156.

Chapter 5 Irish Theatre in the 1950s

1 Blythe's work championing Irish language theatre was indeed important to that branch of Irish's drama's development. As early as 1929, Blythe encouraged development of *An Taibdhearc*, the Galway Irish language company founded partly by Mícheál Mac Liammóir. And, by 1950, the National Theatre had produced thirty-six Irish language dramas (Murray 1997: 142).

2 Blythe's hard-headedness, his strict adherence to the bottom line, and his refusal not only to give in to criticism, but even to respond to it, has made him a very easy figure to vilify. Since he headed the Abbey Theatre for twenty-six years, longer than any director in its history, and since those twenty-six were some of its dullest years, criticism towards him must not be entirely undeserved. Still, Hunt, Mac Anna and other of his contemporaries acknowledged his efforts to keep the theatre intact during a very difficult period in its history. Peter Kavanagh, writing angrily at the end of the 1940s, 'to vindicate the ideals of the original founders of the Abbey Theatre' (1950: xi) gives Blythe no such leeway, citing such events as the ideology-driven board of directors choosing Blythe over Lennox Robinson, and the removal of Starkie from the board of directors.

3 And the sense of Irishness in the work was pointedly clear among the Irish accents in its English language production at the Pike Theatre in Dublin in 1955. While the Pike Theatre production was not confronted with the English Lord Chamberlain's censoring of particular references to bodily functions and other lines, it did receive a slight 'Hibernicization' from its director, Alan Simpson, who changed the now-famous line 'Nothing to be done', with a more Dublinese 'It's no good' (Morash 2002: 199), and *The Stage* remarked that Vladimir delivered his lines in an 'authentic O'Casey voice' (qtd in Morash 2002: 202).

4 Alan Simpson seems to have agreed with this reading, for in his Pike Theatre production of the play he had Lucky dressed in tattered remnants of Georgian era livery.

5 Although in late middle age by the 1950s, MacMaster continued to play leading Shakespearean roles like Othello, Shylock, and even Hamlet in country Irish towns (Pinter).

6 For a discussion of the Pike's production of *Waiting for Godot*, see chapter 5.

7 See Murray in Watt et al. (2000) for more on the controversy surrounding *The Drums of Father Ned*.

8 Joan Dean quotes a letter about his withdrawing his dramas to Carolyn Swift in February of 1958: 'As long as such conditions prevail in Ireland I do not wish my work to be

performed there, either in festivals or outside them. IF no protest is heard they will prevail forever. This is the strongest I can make. I have therefore to cancel the permission I gave you to present *All that Fall* and *Endgame*. I hope you will forgive me' (2004: 164). That final sentence points to how difficult a decision this was for Beckett, and the cost of his decision on his supporters and friends, Swift and Simpson. When he lifts his ban in 1960, he takes a lighter tone: 'I have decided it is now time I fell off my high Eire moke' (Dean 2004: 164).

Chapter 6   Irish Theatre's Second Wave

1 Not all actresses, however, were enamoured by Big Maggie. Phyllis Ryan wrote, 'Siobhan [MacKenna] had reservations about John B. Keane's plays; "I want to understand those Kerry Amazons he writes about – I want to be sure they exist." Ryan quips in response to MacKenna's anxiety that "had [MacKenna] ever played 'Big Maggie', what a revelation that would have been" ' (Ryan 1970: 269).

2 In an ironic turn, Pinter actually learned his writing trade largely in Dublin, where he toured with Anew MacMaster's company – the same company that had trained Mac Liammóir and Edwards years before.

3 The difference between Murphy's dramaturgy and that of his second-wave cohorts may be most obvious in comparing his dramas of emigration to those of his counterparts. While Keane's *Many Young Men and Twenty* and Friel's *Philadelphia Here I Come!* tinge their social commentary with a rather sentimental look at their characters, Murphy's *A Crucial Week in the Life of a Grocer's Assistant* paints what Seumas Kelly called a 'wickedly squalid picture' (Lanters 1997: 233) of the factors leading to widespread emigration.

4 The revolutionary who disappears but remains a spiritual and perhaps physical presence is common in works about social revolution, from John Steinbeck's Tom Joad in *The Grapes of Wrath* to the Donnelly twins in Friel's *Translations*.

5 Murphy of course was himself an artistic exile in the 1960s. His eventual success on the Irish stage, however, led him to return to Ireland and even Seumas on the board of the Abbey.

6 While perhaps not intended by Friel, 'California, Here I Come', like other Jolson hits, played on a sense of displacement and longing for a return to home or homeland felt by many of his audience members, who were immigrants or recent descendants of immigrants, or who had migrated to the city from rural areas. For a closer examination of how American popular theatre – especially minstrelsy – responded to the stresses of migration for its audiences, see Lott (1995).

7 The latter interpretation probably was the favoured one for most audiences when the production moved to Broadway in 1966, where it ran for 326 nights (Farquharson 1997: 98). Ultimately, it also received six Tony award nominations, including nominations for best play, best director (Hilton Edwards), and best actor (Patrick Bedford and Donal Donnelly, public and private Gar, respectively, were both nominated). Although Friel's work, especially the dramas written after 1968, take on serious socio-political concerns, at the same time his entertaining examinations of memory, nostalgia, and history appeal to both politically alert and nationally sentimental audiences. His popularity as a playwright in the United States and other countries has opened the door for other playwrights to be produced abroad. Still, the fact that Friel's plays have been produced on Broadway – the commercial heart of the American theatre – twelve times since 1966, and no Murphy play has been produced on Broadway, speaks to the theatrical and cultural assumptions surrounding Irish theatre – the desire for entertainment, beautiful or clever language, and rural settings – that have appealed to US audiences of Irish theatre since the Abbey's first tours to North American shores.

8 This is especially remarkable when considering that, initially, Northern Irish officials promoted supporting theatre as a forum not to engage with the crisis, but to escape it through entertainment. For an insightful account into the politics of theatre funding in Northern Ireland, see Byrne (2001).

9 The Ulster Group Theatre was still in existence in the 1970s, but performed almost exclusively light musical theatre.

10 The other, the Arts Theatre Trust, was commissioned to establish 'the mobile educational drama unit Interplay Theatre . . . By March 1973 Interplay had given 254 performances to 68, 782 children' (Byrne 2001: 11).

11 This satire of Devlin is clearly gendered, making her appear a childish, 'whinging' woman. Additionally, to touch or dishevel a woman's hair onstage, or to have a woman appear onstage with dishevelled hair, is a traditional symbol of sexual violation. Devlin's song, therefore, makes it appear that her foray into the public sphere is a threat to herself and others.

12 Arden is more famous outside Ireland for his work in London in the late 1950s and 1960s, especially his Brechtian drama about British imperialism and army conscription, *Serjeant Musgrave's Dance* (1959).

13 Born in Omagh, Kennedy served as lyricist for such popular songs from the 1930s and 1940s as 'Red Sails in the Sunset', 'South of the Border (Down Mexico Way)', and 'Istanbul (Not Constantinople)'.

Chapter 7   Theatres Without Borders: Irish Theatre in the 1980s

1 Friel was used to negotiating the ideology of Irish border geography in his own life. He was born in Donegal in the Republic, but educated in Londonderry, Northern Ireland, just a few miless away from his home.

2 The premiere cast included Liam Neeson, Stephen Rea, and Brenda Scallon.

3 The notion of bringing professional theatre to small or disenfranchised communities had already been successfully executed with such groups as 7:84 theatre in Scotland a decade before, and was practised in Northern Ireland by practitioners like Martin Lynch.

4 To clarify, while 'community theatre' usually refers to amateur performances by local groups in the United States of America, the term evolved in the UK and Ireland in the 1970s to mean professional theatre being devised and staged for local communities. This usage, however, has caught on in the United States with groups like Cornerstone Theatre, based in Los Angeles, California. See Kuftinec (2003).

5 Known best to most outside Ireland for his work in film, Rea has been one of the leading actors in Irish theatre for over three decades, including prominent roles at the National Theatre, London, the Abbey and Gate Theatres, and, of course, his work with Field Day.

6 The Arts Council of Ireland also funded Field Day, making their work, inadvertently, a kind of collaboration between Northern Ireland and the Republic.

7 The Field Day pamphlets served as a vehicle for circulating some of the critical and theoretical premises of Field Day to a wider audience than the readership of academic journals, or even a culturally engaged journal like the *Irish Review*. The first six pamphlets were collected into a book, *Ireland's Field Day* (Deane 1985b).

8 Kearney's thought that Irish artists, historians, and critics could escape the essentialist dichotomies informing much thinking about Irish identity by writing from a 'fifth province', an imaginary space in the mind that would transcend the four geographical provinces of the island of Ireland, Ulster, Leinster, Munster, and Connacht. See chapter 6.

9 A brief list of Field Day Theatre collaborators includes Joe Dowling, Jim Sheridan, Patrick Mason, and Clare Davidson.

10 The Antigone myth, with its civil war setting and call for forgiveness, was an especially popular play for adaptation during the Troubles. The most recent major version, by Seamus Heaney, was performed as part of the Abbey Theatre's centenary. See Roche (1988).

11 A chorus from this play has established for itself a life of its own as a poem of the possibility of reconciliation, of a time when 'hope and history rhyme'. Among its many appropriations is its use in Easter services in Christian churches, and inclusion in speeches by US politicians Bill Clinton and Joe Biden.

12 Marian's friend Ruth, responds to her words by reading a passage from Acts of the Apostles sharing a similar sentiment. Not only do the Catholics and Protestants in the play discuss life, death, history, and violence; they also discuss religion.

13 The argument for Anglo-Irish literature's cultural autonomy was made very eloquently in several Field Day pamphlets, including Tom Paulin's 'A New Look at the Language Question' (1983), Heaney's poem about his work being anthologized in a collection of British rather than Irish poetry, 'An Open Letter' (1983), and Edward Said's 'Yeats and Decolonisation' (1988).

14 Company member Eleanor Methven remarked, 'In the first five years of my professional life, I played nothing but Noras and Kathleeens. I did a fine line of them. I was told in no uncertain terms never to cut my hair or the work would dry up' (Harris 2006:16).

15 It should be remembered that Northern Irish citizens had very few rights to privacy, and could be held in prison without being accused for a crime for seventy-two hours.

16 Women during the Troubles would beat bin lids, or the lids of trashcans, on the ground or on walls to alert the IRA of the arrival of the police or the army. They might also be used to protect oneself in a riot. Thus, the play jokes, they would fetch a high price from an earnest German 'peace tourist'.

17 One of the characters' children falls off an unprotected balcony to their death, leaving the mother haunted by the experience and overly protective of her remaining children, whom she forces to wear metal pots and pans on their heads.

18 Although Charabanc's work was anthologized only in 2006, *Somewhere Over the Balcony* appears in *Postcolonial Drama* and, a little ironically, in the *Field Day Anthology of Women's Writing*.

19 In *Celtic Revivals* (1973), Seamus Deane argued that 'The medium through which politics is viewed (in Northern Irish troubles plays like *The Flats*) is the one in which politics does not operate, the apolitical family unit.' While it is true that the domestic sphere is often seen as a kind of safe haven for male characters against the seemingly limitless dangers outside the family fold, the gender politics in the Troubles plays can be quite complex indeed, with women playing important ideological roles as a means of manipulating the survival of their men, even if it means the women die in the process. Plays by Reid, Devlin, and others expose those ideological processes in 1970s Northern Irish sectarian cultures.

20 'The Kesh' is a colloquialism for the HM Prison Maze, located about nine miles outside of Belfast at Long Kesh and used to hold IRA prisoners during the Troubles. This prison was the site of the 1981 IRA hunger strikes.

21 Devlin herself chose to live and work outside Ireland after spending the beginning of her career living in Belfast and writing radio plays. *Ourselves Alone* was commissioned by Bill Morrison at the Liverpool Playhouse and debuted there and at the Royal Court Upstairs (Cerquoni 2007: 163). Devlin also responded to this play with a kind

of sequel in 1996, *After Easter*, in which Josie returns home to Belfast from England.

22 Reid, who grew up within a strongly Protestant, working-class background, left school in her teens to join the workforce, but returned 'to full-time education in her mid-thirties, as a mother of three' (Delgado, Intro to Reid 1997). She became a full-time playwright in 1983, after *Tea in a China Cup* won the Thames TV Award and she received a residency at the Lyric Theatre, Belfast (Delgado 1997: vii).

23 The Battle of the Boyne (1690) was an emblematic event in Northern Irish history, during which William of Orange (King Billy) defeated James II for rule over England and Ireland. The event is the inspiration for the Protestant Marches that continue in areas of Northern Ireland in July of every year.

24 A similar benediction occurs at the end of McGuinness's 1989 play *Carthaginians* when a group of characters, each speaking one line, offer up a similar sentiment: 'Forgive the dead. Fogive the dying. Forgive the living. Forgive yourself . . . Bury the dead. Raise the dying. Wash the living' (378–79).

Chapter 8 A New Sense of Place: Irish Theatre since the 1990s

1 Christopher Morash, 'Irish Theatre', in *The Cambridge Companion to Modern Irish Culture*, ed. Joe Cleary and Claire Connolly (2005), pp. 322–38.

2 Neither of these strategies for looking at the nation-state are new. Yeats's *Purgatory* and *The Words on the Window Pane* analysed the Anglo-Irish tradition through ghost characters, and Field Day plays like Brian Friel's *Making History* (1988) re-examined important figures and events in Irish history from new critical perspectives.

3 This was a common job among out-of-work Dubliners in the 1990s. With the increase of private car use and a lack of public parking, entrepreneurs like Sean would make tips finding and holding spaces at construction sites and other semi-legal parking sites.

4 Murphy looks at a similar theme in *The Muesli Belt* (2000) about a working-class Dublin pub holding out against its increasingly gentrifying neighbourhood.

5 Drug use in Dublin, especially heroin, was high enough in economically disadvantaged parts of the city for the government to call it an epidemic, and HIV infections were also high. Much of this activity was attributed to high unemployment rates in the poorer parts of the city.

6 While Breda Grey and other scholars have pointed out that emigration actually was a liberating event for many Irish women, it is also true that many Irish women had negative experiences due to a lack of socialization or education, or were not even given the choice to emigrate. In the play, the narrator recounts that years after the time represented in the drama, two of his aunts emigrated to England to find work, but with limited education and skills (one aunt was learning impaired) they disappeared into poverty.

7 Returning women emigrants in plays set in the 1990s – a decade much friendlier to female emigration than the 1930s of *Dancing at Lughnasa* – did not fare much better. Christina Reid's *The Belle of the Belfast City* (1988), Pom Boyd's *Down Into Blue* (1994), and Anne Devlin's *After Easter* (1994) all feature women emigrants who on one level long for home and family, but on another need to escape the private dysfunction of their families, and the public dysfunction of their communities.

8 It is not surprising that O'Kelly, one of the founders of Calypso productions, and an artist deeply concerned with human rights issues, would be the first playwright to receive a staging of a play on this issue by the National Theatre Society.

9 Hugh Leonard follows a similar plot, although with a very different spirit, in *Love in the Title* (1999).

10 Since making those pronouncements over a decade ago, McDonagh has indeed followed his interest in film, writing an Academy Award winning short film, *Six Shooter* (2005), and writing and directing a feature-length film, *In Bruges* (2008).

11 McDonagh's *Lieutenant of Inishmore* (2001) adds sectarian politics to his anarchic vision of rural Ireland, merging the traditions of the Troubles play, American gangster films, and theatrical farce.

12 Similarly, Tom Kilroy's 1997 play, *The Secret Fall of Constance Wilde*, examines the notorious trial of Oscar Wilde through the lens of his wife and children.

Bibliography

Adams, Bernard (2002) *Dennis Johnston: A Life*. Dublin: Lilliput Press.

Allgood, Sarah (1922) Letter to Lady Gregory. April 1922.

Anderson, Benedict (1992) *Imagined Communities: Reflections on the Origin and Spread of Nationalism*, rev. edn. London: Verso.

Barry, Sebastian (1995) *The Only True History of Lizzie Finn, The Steward of Christendom, White Woman Street*, ed. and intro. Fintan O'Toole. London: Methuen.

Barton, Ruth (2006) *Acting Irish in Hollywood: From Fitzgerald to Farrell*. Dublin: Irish Academic Press.

Beckett, Samuel (2006) *Waiting for Godot*, in *Samuel Beckett, The Grove Centenary Edition, Vol. III, Dramatic Works*, ed. Paul Auster. New York: Grove Press.

Behan, Brendan (1978) *The Quare Fellow*, in *Brendan Behan: The Complete Plays*. New York: Grove Press.

Bell, Sam Hanna (1971) 'Theatre', in Michael Longley (ed.), *Causeway: The Arts in Ulster*. Belfast: Arts Council of Northern Ireland, pp. 83–94.

Bell, Sam Hanna (1972) *Theatre in Ulster: A Survey of the Dramatic Movement in Ulster from 1902 until the Present Day*. Dublin: Gill and Macmillan.

Bolger, Dermot (1999) *The Passion of Jerome*. London: Methuen.

Bolger, Dermot (2000) *The Lament for Arthur Cleary*, in *Dermot Bolger Plays: 1*. London: Methuen, pp. 1–68.

Boyle, William (1905) *The Building Fund*. Dublin: Maunsel and Company.

Brown, Terence (2004) *Ireland: A Social and Cultural History, 1922–2002*. London: Harper Perennial.

Burke, Helen (2003) *Riotous Performances: The Struggle for Hegemony in the Irish Theatre, 1712–1784*. Notre Dame, IN: University of Notre Dame Press.

Byrne, Ophelia (2001) 'Theatre – Companies and Venues', in Mark Carruthers and Stephen Douds (eds), *Stepping Stones: The Arts in Ulster 1971–2001*. Belfast: Blackstaff Press, pp. 1–26.

Cairns, David and Richards, Shaun (1988) *Writing Ireland: Colonialism, Nationalism, and Culture*. Manchester: Manchester University Press.

Carr, Marina (1999a) *By the Bog of Cats*, in *Marina Carr: Plays 1*. London: Faber and Faber, pp. 257–341.

Carr, Marina (1999b) *Portia Coughlan*, in *Marina Carr: Plays 1*. London: Faber and Faber, pp. 187–256.

Carr, Marina (2002) *Ariel*. Loughcrew: Gallery Books.

Carroll, Paul Vincent (1937) *Shadow and Substance*. New York: Random House.

Cave, Richard Allen (2004) 'On the Siting of Doors and Windows: Aesthetics, Ideology and Irish Stage Design', in Sean Richards (ed.), *The Cambridge Companion to Twentieth Century Irish Drama*. Cambridge: Cambridge University Press, pp. 93–108.

Cerquoni, Enrica (2007) 'Women in Rooms: Landscapes of the Missing in Anne Devlin's *Ourselves Alone*', in Melissa Sihra (ed.), *Women in Irish Drama: A Century of Authorship and Representation*. London: Palgrave Macmillan, pp. 160–74.

Charabanc Theatre Company (2006) *Four Plays by the Charabanc Theatre Company: Inventing Women's Work*, ed. Claudia Harris. London: Colin Smythe.

Clark, Brenna Katz (1982) *The Emergence of the Irish Peasant Play at the Abbey Theatre*. Ann Arbor, MI: University of Michigan Press.

Clark, Brenna Katz and Ferrar, Harold (1979) The *Dublin Drama League: 1919–1941*, Irish Theatre Series 9, ed. Robert Hogan, James Kilroy and Liam Miller. Dublin: Dolmen Press.

Clarke, Austin (1967) 'Introduction', in *The Plays of George Fitzmaurice: Dramatic Fantasies*. Dublin: Dolmen Press, pp. vii–xv.

Cloake, Mary (1996) 'Beyond the Theatre Review: The Arts Council and Regional Developments in Irish Theatre', in Eberhard Bort (ed.), *The State of Play: Irish Theatre in the 'Nineties*. Trier: WVT Wissenschaftlicher Verlag Trier, pp. 167–82.

'Cluithcheoiri na hEireann' (1906) n.p.: Dublin.

Collins, Barry and Hanafin, Patrick (2001) 'Mothers, Maidens and the Myths of Origin in the Irish Constitution', *Law and Critique* 12/1: 53–73.

Colum, Padraic (1916) 'Introduction', in *Three Plays*. Dublin: Dolmen Press.

Colum, Padraic (1970) *The Saxon Shillin'*, in Robert Hogan and James Kilroy (eds), *Lost Plays of the Irish Renaissance*. New York: Proscenium Press, pp. 65–72.

Colum, Padraic ([1905] 1990) *The Land*, in Coilin D. Owens and Joan N. Radner (eds), *Irish Drama 1900–1980*. Washington, DC: Catholic University of America Press.

Connolly, James (2007) *Under Which Flag?*, in James Moran (ed.), *Four Irish Rebel Plays*. Dublin: Irish Academic Press, pp. 105–32.

Cousins, James H. (1970) *The Racing Lug*, in Robert Hogan and James Kilroy (eds), *Lost Plays of the Irish Renaissance*. New York: Proscenium Press, pp. 39–50.

Cousins, James H. (1988) 'Irish Drama Arrives', in E. H. Mikhail (ed.), *The Abbey Theatre: Interviews and Recollections*. Totowa, New Jersey: Barnes and Noble Books, pp. 1–3.

Cowell, John (1988) *No Profit but the Name: The Longfords and the Gate Theatre.* Dublin: O'Brien Press.

Cronin, John (1988) 'Introduction', in *Selected Plays of St. John Ervine.* Gerrards Cross, Bucks: Colin Smythe.

Cullingford, Elizabeth (1981) *Yeats, Ireland and Fascism.* London: Macmillan.

Cullingford, Elizabeth (2001) *Ireland's Others: Gender and Ethnicity in Irish Literature and Popular Culture.* Notre Dame, IN: University of Notre Dame Press.

Cullingford, Elizabeth (2002) *Ireland's Others: Ethnicity and Gender in Irish Literature and Popular Culture.* Notre Dame: University of Notre Dame Press.

Curtis, L. Perry Jr (1997) *Apes and Angels: The Irishman in Victorian Caricature.* Washington, DC: Smithsonian Institution Press.

Danaher, Kathleen (1997) Gerald MacNamara (1865–1938) in Bernice Schrank and William W. Demastes (eds), *Irish Playwrights, 1880–1995: A Research and Production Sourcebook.* Greenwood Press, Westport, Connecticut, pp. 69–79.

Danaher, Kathleen (ed.) (1988) *The Plays of Gerald MacNamara. Journal of Irish Literature* 17: 2–3.

Dean, Joan Fitzpatrick (2004) *Riot and Great Anger: Stage Censorship in Twentieth-Century Ireland.* Madison, WI: University of Wisconsin Press.

Deane, Seamus (1973) *Celtic Revivals.* London: Faber and Faber.

Deane, Seamus (1984) 'Introduction', *Selected Plays: Brian Friel.* Dublin and Washington, DC: Colin Smythe; Catholic University of America Press, pp. 11–22.

Deane, Seamus (1985a) 'Heroic Styles: The Tradition of an Idea', in Seamus Deane (ed.), *Ireland's Field Day.* London: Hutchinson.

Deane, Seamus (ed.) (1985b) *Ireland's Field Day.* London: Hutchinson.

De Burca, Seamus (1983) *The Queen's Royal Theatre Dublin, 1829–1969.* Dublin: S. de Burca.

Deevy, Teresa (1935) *The King of Spain's Daughter*, in *Theatre Arts Monthly* XIX/6 (June 1935): 459–66.

Deevy, Teresa (1936) *Katie Roche*, in *Famous Plays of 1935–6.* London: Victor Gollancz, Ltd, pp. 607–701.

Delgado, Maria (1997) 'Introduction', *Christina Reid: Plays 1.* London: Methuen Drama, pp. vii–xxii.

De Rosa, Peter (1990) *Rebels: The Irish Rising of 1916.* New York: Fawcett Columbine.

Devlin, Anne (1986) *Ourselves Alone*, in *Ourselves Alone with A Woman Calling and The Long March.* London: Faber and Faber.

Dicat, Sinn (1906) *Sinn Fein*, 15 December, p. 3.

DiCenzo, Maria R. (1993) 'Charabanc Theatre Company: Placing Women Center Stage in Northern Ireland', *Theatre Journal* 45: 175–84.

Diviney, Kay S. (1997) 'Padraic Colum (1881–1972)', in Bernice Schrank and William W. Demastes (eds), *Irish Playwrights, 1880–1995: A Research and Production Sourcebook.* Westport, Greenwood Press, CT: pp. 69–79.

Dolan, Jill (2002) 'Introduction: Building a Theatrical Vernacular: Responsibility, Community, Ambivalence, and Queer Theatre', in Alisa Solomon and Framji Minwalla (eds), *The Queerest Art: Essays on Lesbian and Gay Theater*. New York: New York University Press.

Dorn, Karen (1984) *Players and Painted Stage: The Theatre of W.B. Yeats*. Totowa, NJ: Barnes and Noble.

Doyle, Maria-Elena (2003) 'Strangers in Her House: Staging a Living Space for Northern Ireland'. *New Hibernia Review* 7/3: 106–26.

Eakin, David B. and Case, Michael (1995) 'Introduction', in *Selected Plays of George Moore and Edward Martyn*. Gerrards Cross, Bucks: Colin Smythe.

Edwards, Ruth Dudley (1990) *Patrick Pearse: The Triumph of Failure*. Dublin: Poolbeg Press Ltd.

Ellman, Richard (1979) *Yeats: The Man and the Masks*. New York: Norton.

Ellman, Richard (1987) *Oscar Wilde*. New York: Alfred A. Knopf.

Erdman, Andrew L. (2004) *Blue Vaudeville: Sex, Morals, and the Mass Marketing of Amusement, 1895–1915*. Jefferson, NC: McFarland & Co.

Ervine, St John (1988a) *Mixed Marriage*, in John Cronin (ed.), *Selected Plays of St. John Ervine*. Gerrards Cross, Bucks: Colin Smythe, pp. 17–64.

Ervine, St John (1988b) *James Ferguson*, in John Cronin (ed.), *Selected Plays of St. John Ervine*. Gerrards Cross, Bucks: Colin Smythe, pp. 121–96.

Farquharson, Danine (1997) 'Brian Friel (1929–)', in Bernice Schrank and William W. Demastes (eds), *Irish Playwrights, 1880–1995*. Westport, CT: Greenwood Press, pp. 97–107.

Feeney, William J. (1984) *Drama in Hardwicke Street*. Cranbury, NJ: Associated University Presses, Inc.

Fitzmaurice, George (1967) *The Magic Glasses*, in Howard K. Slaughter (ed.), *The Plays of George Fitzmaurice: Dramatic Fantasies*. Dublin: Dolman Press, pp. 1–18.

Fitzmaurice, George (1969) *The Pie-Dish*, in Howard K. Slaughter (ed.), *The Plays of George Fitzmaurice: Folk Plays*. Dublin: Dolmen Press, pp. 41–56.

Fitzmaurice, George (1970) *The Country Dressmaker*, in Howard K. Slaughter (ed.), *The Plays of George Fitzmaurice: Realistic Plays*. Dublin: Dolmen Press, pp. 15–58.

Fitz-Simon, Christopher (2002) *The Boys: A Biography of Micheál Mac Liammóir and Hilton Edwards*. Dublin: New Island Books.

Flannery, James (1976) *W. B. Yeats and the Idea of a Theatre: The Early Abbey Theatre in Theory And Practice*. Toronto: Macmillan of Canada.

Fleming, Deborah (1995) *A Man Who Does Not Exist: The Irish Peasant in the Work of W. B. Yeats and J. M. Synge*. Ann Arbor, MI: University of Michigan Press.

Foley, Imelda (2003) *The Girls in the Big Picture: Gender in Contemporary Ulster Theatre*. Belfast: Blackstaff Press.

Foster, R. F. (1989) *Modern Ireland: 1600–1972*. New York: Penguin.

Foster, R. F. (1997) *W. B. Yeats: A Life. Vol. I: The Apprentice Mage*. Oxford: Oxford University Press.

Fox, Christie (2000) 'Neither Here nor There: The Liminal Position of Teresa Deevy and Her Female Characters', in Stephen Watt, Eileen Morgan and Shakir Mustafa (eds), *A Century of Irish Drama: Widening the Stage*. Indianapolis and Bloomington: Indiana University Press, pp. 193–203.

Frazier, Adrian (1990) *Behind the Scenes: Yeats, Horniman, and the Struggle for the Abbey Theatre*. Berkeley, CA: University of California Press.

Frazier, Adrian (2000) *George Moore, 1852–1933*. New Haven, CT: Yale University Press.

Friel, Brian (1984a) *Philadelphia, Here I Come!*, in *Selected Plays: Brian Friel*. London: Faber and Faber, pp. 23–100.

Friel, Brian (1984b) *Translations*, in *Selected Plays: Brian Friel*. London: Faber and Faber, pp. 377–452.

Friel, Brian (1999) *Dancing at Lughnasa*, in *Brian Friel: Plays Two*. London: Faber and Faber, pp. 1–108.

Gibbons, Luke (1996) *Transformations in Irish Culture*. Notre Dame, IN: University of Notre Dame Press.

Grant, David (2001) 'Theatre – the Playwrights and Their Plays', in Mark Carruthers and Stephen Douds (eds), *Stepping Stones: The Arts in Ulster 1971–2001*. Belfast: Blackstaff Press, pp. 27–51.

Gregory, Lady Augusta Persse (1913) *Our Irish Theatre: A Chapter of Autobiography*. New York: G. P. Putnam's Sons.

Gregory, Lady Augusta Persse (1995a) *The Rising of the Moon*, in Lucy McDiarmid and Maureen Waters (eds), *Lady Gregory: Selected Writings*. New York: Penguin, pp. 363–72.

Gregory, Lady Augusta Persse (1995b) *Spreading the News*, in Lucy McDiarmid and Maureen Waters (eds), *Lady Gregory: Selected Writings*. New York: Penguin, pp. 312–28.

Grene, Nicholas (1999) *The Politics of Irish Drama: Plays in Context from Boucicault to Friel*. Cambridge: Cambridge University Press.

Grene, Nicholas (ed.) (2006) *Irish Theatre on Tour*. Dublin: Carysfort Press.

Hanrahan, Johnny (2001) 'Theatre in Cork/Cork in Theatre', in Dermot Bolger (ed.), *Druids, Dudes, and Beauty Queens: The Changing Face of Irish Theatre*. Dublin: New Island Press.

Harrington, John (2004) 'Samuel Beckett and the Countertradition', in Shaun Richards (ed.), *The Cambridge Companion to Twentieth-Century Irish Drama*. Cambridge, UK: Cambridge University Press.

Harris, Claudia (2006) 'Introduction', in Claudia Harris (ed.), *Four Plays by the Charabanc Theatre Company: Inventing Women's Work*. London: Colin Smythe, pp. ix–liii.

Harris, Susan Cannon (2002) *Gender and Modern Irish Drama*. Bloomington, IN: Indiana University Press.

Hawkins, Maureen S. G. (1997) 'Brendan Francis Behan (1923–1964)', in Bernice Schrank and William W.Demastes (eds), *Irish Playwrights, 1880–1995*. Westport, CT: Greenwood Press, pp. 23–42.

Heaney, Seamus (1991) *The Cure at Troy: A Version of Sophocles' Philoctetes*. New York: Farrar, Straus and Giroux.

Heaney, Seamus (1982) 'Preface', in Mark Patrick Hederman and Richard Kearney (eds), *The Crane Bag*. Dublin: Blackwater Press, pp. 7–12.

Herr, Cheryl (ed.) (1991) *For the Land They Loved: Irish Political Melodrama, 1890–1925*. Syracuse, NY: Syracuse University Press.

Hogan, Robert (ed.) (1967a) 'Pull Back the Green Curtains', in *Seven Irish Plays*. Minneapolis: University of Minnesota Press, pp. 3–27.

Hogan, Robert (1967b) 'Michael Molloy', in *Seven Irish Plays*. Minneapolis: University of Minnesota Press, pp. 29–31.

Hogan, Robert and Burnham, Richard (1992) *The Years of O'Casey, 1921–1926: A Documentary History*. Gerrards Cross, Bucks: Colin Smythe.

Hogan, Robert, Burnham, Richard, and Poteet, Daniel P. (1978) *The Abbey Theatre: The Years of Synge, 1905–1909*. Atlantic Highlands, NJ: Dolmen Press.

Hogan, Robert and Kilroy, James (eds) (1970) *Lost Plays of the Irish Renaissance*. Delaware: Proscenium Press.

Hogan, Robert and Kilroy, James (1975) *The Irish Literary Theatre, 1899–1901*. Dublin: Dolmen Press.

Hogan, Robert and James Kilroy (1976) *Laying the Foundations: 1902–1904*. Atlantic Highlands, Monmouth: Dolmen Press.

Holloway, Joseph (1967) *Joseph Holloway's Abbey Theatre: A Selection From His Unpublished Journal – Impressions of a Dublin Playgoer*, ed. Robert Hogan and Michael J. O'Neill. Carbondale, Illinois: Southern Illinois University Press.

Hunt, Hugh (1979) *The Abbey: Ireland's National Theatre, 1904–1979*. New York: Columbia University Press.

Hyde, Douglas (1894) 'On the Necessity of de Anglicising Literature', in *The Revival of Irish Literature: Addresses by Sir Charles Gavan Duffy, Dr. George Sigerson, and Douglas Hyde*. London: F. T. Unwin.

Hyde, Douglas ([1901] 1991) *The Twisting of the Rope*, in Gareth W. Dunleavy and Janet Egleson Dunleavy (eds), *Selected Plays of Douglas Hyde 'An Craoibhin Aoibhinn' with translations by Lady Gregory*. Gerrards Cross, Bucks: Colin Smythe.

Jeffares, A. Norman and Knowland, A. S. (1975) *A Commentary on the Collected Plays of W. B. Yeats*. Stanford, CA: Stanford University Press.

Johnston, Denis (1983a) *The Old Lady Says No!*, in *Selected Plays of Denis Johnston*. Gerrards Cross, Bucks: Colin Smythe.

Johnston, Denis (1983b) *The Moon in the Yellow River*, in *Selected Plays of Denis Johnston*. Gerrards Cross, Bucks: Colin Smythe.

Johnston, Denis (1992) *Orders and Desecrations: The Life of the Playwright Denis Johnston*, ed. Rory Johnston. Dublin: Lilliput Press.

Jones, Marie (2006) *Somewhere Over the Balcony*, in Claudia W. Harris (ed.), *Four Plays by the Charabanc Theatre Company: Inventing Women's Work*. Gerrards Cross, Bucks: Colin Smythe.

Junker, Mary (1995) *Beckett: The Irish Dimension*. Dublin: Wolfhound Press.

Kavanagh, Peter (1950) *The Story of the Abbey Theatre, From Its Origins in 1899 to the Present*. New York: Devin-Adair.

Kealy, Sister Marie Hubert (1993) *Kerry Playwright: Sense of Place in the Plays of John B. Keane*. London and Toronto: Associated University Presses.

Keane, John B. (1994a) *The Field*, in *The Field and Other Irish Plays*. Niwot, CO: Roberts Rinehart Publishers, pp. 91–168.

Keane, John B. (1994b) *Big Maggie*, in *The Field and Other Irish Plays*. Niwot, CO: Roberts Rinehart Publishers, pp. 169–239.

Kearney, Eileen (1997) 'Theresa Deevy (1894–1963)', in Bernice Schrank and William W. Demastes (eds), *Irish Playwrights, 1880–1995: A Research and Production Sourcebook*. Westport, CT: Greenwood Press, pp. 80–92.

Kearney, Richard (1982) 'Beyond Art and Politics', in *The Crane Bag Book of Irish Studies* (1977–81). Dublin: Blackwater Press, pp. 13–21.

Kearney, Richard (1996) *Postnationalist Ireland: Politics, Culture, Philosophy*. London: Routledge.

Kearns, Kevin C. (2000) *Dublin Tenement Life: An Oral History*. New York: Penguin.

Kee, Robert (1972) *The Green Flag, Volume III: Ourselves Alone*. London: Penguin.

Kiberd, Declan (1995) *Inventing Ireland*. London: Random House.

Kiberd, Declan (2001) *Irish Classics*. Cambridge, MA: Harvard University Press.

Kilroy, Tom (1994) *Double Cross*. Oldcastle: Gallery Books.

Krasner, David (2001) 'Black Salome: Exoticism, Dance, and Racial Myths', in Harry J. Elam and David Krasner (eds), *African-American Performance and Theatre History: A Critical Reader*. Oxford: Oxford University Press, pp. 192–211.

Kruger, Loren (1992) *The National Stage: Theatre and Cultural Legitimation in England, France, and America*. Chicago, IL: University of Chicago Press.

Kuftinec, Sonia (2003) *Staging America: Cornerstone and Community Based Theatre*. Carbondale, IL: Southern Illinois University Press.

Lanters, Jose (1997) 'Thomas Murphy', in Bernice Schrank and William W. Demastes (eds), *Irish Playwrights, 1880–1995*. Westport, CT: Greenwood Press, pp. 231–42.

Laurence, Dan H. (ed.) (1995) *Bernard Shaw Theatrics*. Toronto: University of Toronto Press.

Laurence, Dan H. and Grene, Nicholas (eds) (1993) *Shaw, Lady Gregory and the Abbey: A Correspondence and a Record.*, Gerrards Cross, Bucks: Colin Smythe.

Leeney, Cathy (2007) 'Interchapter I: 1900–1939', in Melissa Sihra (ed.), *Women in Irish Drama: A Century of Authorship and Representation*. London: Palgrave Macmillan.

Levitas, Ben (2002) *The Theatre of Nation: Irish Drama and Cultural Nationalism, 1890–1916*. Oxford: Oxford University Press.

Llewellyn-Jones, Margaret (2002) *Contemporary Irish Drama and Cultural Identity*. Bristol: Intellect.

Longford, Countess (1936) 'Mr. Jiggins of Jigginstown', in Curtis Canfield (ed.), *Plays of Changing Ireland*. New York: Macmillan, pp. 269–320.

Longford, Earl of (1936) *Yahoo*, in Curtis Canfield (ed.), *Plays of Changing Ireland*. New York: Macmillan, pp. 149–94.

Lott, Eric (1995) *Love and Theft: Blackface Minstrelsy and the American Working Class*. Oxford: Oxford University Press.

Lyons, Laura E. (2000) 'Of Orangemen and Green Theatres: The Ulster Literary Theatre's Regional Nationalism', in Stephen Watt, Eileen Morgan, and Shakir Mustafa (eds), *A Century of Irish Drama: Widening the Stage*. Bloomington, IN: Indiana University Press, pp. 34–53.

Mac Anna, Tómas (1988) 'Ernest Blythe and the Abbey', in E. H. Mikhail (ed.), *The Abbey Theatre: Interviews and Recollections*. Totowa, New Jersey: Barnes and Noble, pp. 167–72.

Mac Anna, Tomás and Carleton, Karen (2001) 'Tomás Mac Anna in Conversation with Karen Carleton', *Theatre Talk: Voices of Irish Theatre Practitioners*. Dublin: Carysfort Press, pp. 277–89.

Macardle, Dorothy (1934) 'Experiment in Ireland', *Theatre Arts Monthly* XVIII (February 1934): 126–7.

McConachie, Bruce (1996) *Melodramatic Formations*. Iowa City, IA: University of Iowa Press.

McDonagh, Martin (1996) *The Beauty Queen of Leenane*. London: Methuen Drama in Association with the Royal Court Theatre.

MacDonagh, Thomas (2007) *When the Dawn is Come*, in James Moran (ed.), *Four Irish Rebel Plays*. Dublin: Irish Academic Press, pp. 43–82.

McGinley, P. T. ([1901] 1970) *Lizzie and the Tinker*, trans. Sheila O'Rouke and Fr Patrick Corkell, in Robert Hogan and James Kilroy (eds), *Lost Plays of the Irish Renaissance*. Newark, Delaware: Proscenium Press.

McGlone, James P. (2002) *Ria Mooney: The Life and Times of the Artistic Director of the Abbey Theatre, 1948–1963*. NC and London: McFarland and Company, Jefferson.

McGuinness, Frank (1996) *Observe the Sons of Ulster, Marching Towards the Somme*, in *Frank McGuiness: Plays One*. London: Faber and Faber.

Mac Liammóir, Micheál (1967) *All For Hecuba: An Irish Theatrical Autobiography*. Boston: Branden Press.

McMahon, Timothy (2008) *Grand Opportunity: The Gaelic Revival and Irish Society, 1893–1910*. Syracuse, NY: Syracuse University Press.

McMullan, Ann (1996) 'Reclaiming Performance: The Contemporary Irish Independent Theatre Sector', in Eberhard Bort (ed.), *The State of Play: Irish Theatre in the 'Nineties*. Trier: WVT Wissenschaftlicher Verlag Trier, pp. 29–38.

MacNamara, Gerald (1988a) *Suzanne and the Sovereigns*, ed. Kathleen Danaher, *Journal of Irish Literature* 17: 2–3.

MacNamara, Gerald (1988b) *The Mist That Does Be on the Bog*, ed. Kathleen Danaher, *Journal of Irish Literature* 17: 2–3.

McPherson, Conor (2004) *Plays: Two*. London Nick Hern Books.

McPherson, Conor (2004) *Shining City*. London: Nick Hern Books.

Maguire, Tom (2006) *Making Theatre in Northern Ireland: Through and Beyond the Troubles*. Exeter: University of Exeter Press.

Malone, Andrew E. (1939) 'The Early History of the Abbey Theatre', in Lennox Robinson (ed.), *The Irish Theatre*. London: Macmillan.

Manning, Mary (1936) 'Youth's the Season – ?', in Curtis Canfield (ed.), *Plays of Changing Ireland*. New York: Macmillan, pp. 321–404.

Martyn, Edward (1995) *The Heather Field*, in *Selected Plays: George Moore and Edward Martyn*, ed. and intro David B. Eakin and Michael Case. Gerrards Cross, Bucks: Colin Smythe, pp. 215–68.

Martyn, Edward *Maeve*, in *Selected Plays: George Moore and Edward Martyn*, ed. and intro. David B. Eakin and Michael Case. Gerrards Cross, Bucks: Colin Smythe, pp. 269–98.

Matthews, P. J. (2003) *Revival: The Abbey Theatre, Sinn Féin, the Gaelic League and the Co-Operative Movement*. Notre Dame, IN: University of Notre Dame Press.

Maxwell, D. E. S. (1984) *A Critical History of Modern Irish Drama, 1891–1980*. Cambridge: Cambridge University Press.

Mayne, Rutherford (2000a) *The Drone*, in Wolfgang Zach (ed.), *Selected Plays of Rutherford Mayne*. Gerrards Cross, Bucks: Colin Smythe, pp. 35–90.

Mayne, Rutherford (2000b) *The Turn of the Road*, in Wolfgang Zach (ed.), *Selected Plays of Rutherford Mayne*. Gerrards Cross, Bucks: Colin Smythe, pp. 1–34.

Merriman, Vic (1999) 'Decolonisation Postponed: The Theatre of Tiger Trash', *Irish University Review* 29/2 (autumn/winter 1999): 305–17.

Mikhail, E. H. (ed.) (1988) *The Abbey Theatre: Interviews and Recollections*. Totowa, New Jersey: Barnes & Noble Books.

Mikhail, E. H. (ed.) (1979) *Oscar Wilde: Interviews and Recollections*. London: Macmillan.

Milligan, Alice (1900) *The Last Feast of the Fianna: A Dramatic Legend*. London: D. Nutt.

Mitchell, Gary (1998) *In a Little World of Our Own*, in *Tearing the Loom and In a Little World of Our Own*. London: Nick Hern Books, pp. 2–61.

Molloy, M. J. (1998) *The Wood of the Whispering*, in Robert O'Driscoll (ed.), *Selected Plays of M. J. Molloy*. Gerrards Cross, Bucks: Colin Smythe.

Moore, George (1985) *Hail and Farewell*, ed. Richard Allen Cave. Washington, DC: Catholic University of America Press.

Moran, James (2005) *Staging the Easter Rising: 1916 as Theatre*. Cork: Cork University Press.

Moran, James (ed.) (2007) *Four Irish Rebel Plays*. Dublin: Irish Academic Press.

Morash, Christopher (2002) *A History of Irish Theatre, 1601–2000*. Cambridge: Cambridge University Press.

Morash, Christopher (2005) 'Irish Theatre', in Joe Cleary and Claire Connolly (eds), *The Cambridge Companion to Modern Irish Culture*. Cambridge, UK: Cambridge University Press.

Moynihan, Mary and Kennedy, Paul (2004) 'Laughing Together: Community-based Theatre's Vital Sense of Humour', in Eric Weitx (ed.), *The Power of Laughter: Comedy and Contemporary Irish Theatre*. Dublin: Carysfort Press, pp. 118–28.

Murphy, Jimmy (2003) *A Picture of Paradise* in Sanford Sternlicht and Judy Friel (eds), *New Plays from the Abbey Theatre, 1999–2001*. Syracuse, NY: Syracuse University Press.

Murphy, Tom (1992) *Famine*, in *Tom Murphy Plays: One*. London: Methuen Drama.

Murphy, Tom (2007) *The House* in *Tom Murphy Plays: Five*. London: Methuen Drama.

Murray, Christopher (ed.) (1982) *Selected Plays of Lennox Robinson*. Gerrards Cross, Bucks: Colin Smythe.

Murray, Christopher (1997) *Twentieth-Century Irish Drama: Mirror Up to Nation*. Syracuse, NY: Syracuse University Press.

Murray, Christopher (2000) 'The Drums of Father Ned in Context', in Stephen Watt, Eileen Morgan and Shakir Mustafa (eds), *A Century of Irish Drama: Widening the Stage*. Indianapolis and Bloomington: Indiana University Press, pp. 117–29.

Murray, Christopher (2004) *Sean O'Casey: Writer at Work*. Montreal, Ithaca: McGill- Queen's, University Press.

Murray, T. C. (1998) *Maurice Harte* in *Selected Plays of T. C. Murray*; Richard Allen Cave (comp). Gerrards Cross, Bucks: Colin Smythe, pp. 59–100.

[Nathan, George Jean] (1936) 'Publisher's Note', *Famous Plays of 1935–6*. London: Victor Gollancz Ltd.

[Nathan, George Jean] (1937) 'Erin Go Blah', *Newsweek* X (17 December 1937): 24.

New York Times (1938) 'The Substance of Paul Vincent Carroll', 30 January 1938, Section X, p. 1.

Nic Shiubhlaigh, Maire and Kenny, Edward (1955) *The Splendid Years: Recollections of Maire Nic Shiubhlaigh; As Told to Edward Kenny*. Dublin: James Duffy and Company,

O'Casey, Sean (1998a) *Juno and the Paycock*, in *Sean O'Casey: Plays One*. Dublin: Faber and Faber, London, pp. 1–86.

O'Casey, Sean (1998b) *The Shadow of a Gunman*, in *Sean O'Casey: Plays Two*. London: Faber and Faber, pp. 1–62.

O'Casey, Sean (1998c) *The Plough and the Stars*, in *Sean O'Casey: Plays One*. London: Faber and Faber, pp. 63–162.

O'Casey, Sean (1928) Letter to Lennox Robinson, 5 April 1928. Robinson Papers, SIU.

O'Casey, Sean (n.d.) Letter to Lennox Robinson. Robinson Papers, SIU.

Ochshorn, Kathleen (2006) 'Colonialism, Postcolonialism, and the Shadow of a New Empire: *John Bull's Other Island*', *SHAW: The Annual of Bernard Shaw Studies*, vol. 26. University Park, PA: Penn State University Press, pp. 180–93.

O'Donoghue, Helen and Vaněk, Joe (2004) *Scene Change: One Hundred Years of Theatre Design at the Abbey*. Dublin: Irish Museum of Modern Art/Aras Nua-Ealaíne na Eireann.

O'Flaherty, Gearoid (2004) 'George Bernard Shaw and Ireland', in Shaun Richards (ed.), *The Cambridge Companion to Twentieth-Century Irish Drama*. Cambridge, UK: Cambridge University Press.

O'Grady, Brendan (1997) 'Seumas O'Kelly (*c*.1880–1918)', in Bernice Schrank and William W. Demastes (eds), *Irish Playwrights, 1880–1995: A Research and Production Sourcebook*. Greenwood Press, Westport, CT, pp. 270–78.

O'Kelly, Donal (1996) *Asylum! Asylum!*, in Christopher Fitz-Simon and Sanford Sternlicht (eds), *New Plays from the Abbey Theatre, 1993–1995*. Syracuse: Syracuse University Press, pp. 113–74.

O'Kelly, Seumas (1907) *The Matchmakers*. Dublin: Maunsel and Company.

O'Kelly, Seumas (1909) *The Shuiler's Child*. Dublin: Maunsel and Company.

O'Rowe, Mark (1999) *Howie the Rookie*. London: Nick Hern Books.

O'Sullivan, Seumas (1988) 'How Our Theatre Began', in E. H. Mikhail (ed.), *The Abbey Theatre: Interviews and Recollections*. Totowa, New Jersey: Barnes and Noble Books, pp. 11–14.

O'Toole, Fintan (1995) 'Introduction', in Sebastian Barry, *The Only True History of Lizzie Finn, The Steward of Christendom, White Woman Street*, ed. and intro Fintan O'Toole. London: Methuen.

O'Toole, Fintan (2000) 'Irish Theatre: The State of the Art', in Eamonn Jordan, (ed.), *Theatre Stuff: Critical Essays on Contemporary Irish Theatre*. Dublin: Carysfort, pp. 47–58.

Owens, Cóilín D. and Radner, Joan N. (eds) (1990) *Irish Drama: 1900–1980*. Washington, DC: The Catholic University of America Press.

Parker, Stewart (1988) *Pentecost*, in *Stewart Parker Plays: 2*. London: Methuen, pp. 169–245.

Pearse, Padraic (1960) *The Singer*, in *The Singer and Other Plays*. Dublin: Talbot Press, pp. 3–44.

Peters, Sally (1998) 'Shaw's Life: A Feminist in Spite of Himself', in C. D. Innes (ed.), *The Cambridge Companion to George Bernard Shaw*. Cambridge, UK: Cambridge University Press, pp. 3–24.

Pilkington, Lionel (2001) *Theatre and the State in Twentieth Century Ireland: Cultivating the People*. London: Routledge.

Pine, Richard (1990) *Brian Friel and Ireland's Drama*. London and New York: Routledge.

Pine, Richard (2006) 'Friel's Irish Russia', in Anthony Roche (ed.), *The Cambridge Companion to Brian Friel*. Cambridge, UK: Cambridge University Press, pp. 104–16.

Rea, Stephen (2000) 'Introduction', *Stewart Parker Plays: 2*. London: Methuen, pp. ix–xii.

Reid, Christina (1997a) *The Belle of the Belfast City*, in *Christina Reid: Plays One*. London: Methuen Drama, pp. 177–250.

Reid, Christina (1997b) *Tea in a China Cup*, in *Christina Reid: Plays One*. London: Methuen Drama, pp. 1–66.

Reynolds, Paige (2007) *Modernism, Drama, and the Audience for Irish Spectacle*. Cambridge, UK: Cambridge University Press.

Reynolds, Paige (2002) 'Modernist Martyrdom: The Funerals of Terence Mac-Swiney', *Modernism/Modernity* 9/4: 535–59.

Richards, Shaun (2003) 'Foreword', *Selected Plays of Irish Playwright Teresa Deevy, 1894–1963*, ed. Eibhear Walshe. Lewiston, Queenstown, Lampeter: Edward Mellen Press, pp. iii–xii.

Richtarik, Marilynn J. (2001) *Acting Between the Lines: The Field Day Theatre Company and Irish Cultural Politics, 1980–1984*. Washington, DC: Catholic University of America Press.

Riordan, Arthur and Bell Helicopter (2005) *Improbable Frequency*. London: Nick Hern Books.

Ritschel, Nelson O Ceallaigh (2000) 'The Alternative Aesthetic: The Theatre of Ireland's Urban Plays', in Stephen Watt, Eileen Morgan, and Shakir Mustafa (eds), *A Century of Irish Drama: Widening the Stage*. Indianapolis and Bloomington: Indiana University Press, pp. 17–33.

Roach, Joseph R. (2002) ' "All the Dead Voices": The Landscape of Famine in *Waiting for Godot*', in Una Chaudhuri and Elinor Fuchs (eds), *Land/Scape/Theatre*. Ann Arbor: University of Michigan Press, pp. 84–93.

Robinson, Lennox (1911) *Two Plays: Harvest; The Clancy Name*. Dublin: Maunsel and Company.

Robinson, Lennox (1942) *Curtain Up*. London: M. Joseph Ltd.

Robinson, Lennox (1982a) *The Big House*, in Christopher Murray (ed.), *Selected Plays of Lennox Robinson*. Gerrards Cross, Bucks: Colin Smythe, pp. 137–98.

Robinson, Lennox (1982b) *The Whiteheaded Boy*, in *Selected Plays of Lennox Robinson*. Murray, Christopher (ed.). Gerrards Cross, Bucks: Colin Smythe, pp. 63–118.

Roche, Anthony (1995) *Contemporary Irish Drama: From Beckett to McGuinness*. New York: St Martin's Press.

Roche, Anthony (1988) 'Ireland's Antigones: Tragedy North and South', in Michael Kenneally (ed.), *Cultural Contexts and Literary Idioms in Contemporary Irish Literature*. Totowa, NJ: Barnes and Noble, pp. 221–50.

Roche, Anthony (1994) 'Woman on the Threshold: J. M. Synge's *The Shadow of the Glen*, Teresa Deevy's *Katie Roche*, and Marina Carr's *The Mai*', *Irish University Review* (winter): 142–62.

Russell, George (AE) (1929) *Deirdre*, in Curtis Canfield (ed.), *Plays of the Irish Renaissance: 1880–1930*. New York: Ives Washburn.

Ryan, Fred (1970) *The Laying of the Foundations*, in Robert Hogan and James Kilroy (eds), *Lost Plays of the Irish Renaissance*. New York: Proscenium Press, pp. 23–38.

Ryan, Phyllis (1996) *The Company I Kept*. Dublin: Town House.

Saddlemyer, Ann (1982a) 'Introduction', in *J. M. Synge: Collected Works, Vol. III, Plays, Book I*. Gerrards Cross, Bucks: Colin Smythe.

Saddlemyer, Ann (1982b) *Theatre Business: The Correspondence of the First Abbey Theatre Directors: William Butler Yeats, Lady Gregory and J. M. Synge*. Gerrards Cross, Bucks: Colin Smythe.

Shaw, George Bernard (1962a) 'Preface to John Bull's Other Island', in *Bernard Shaw, Complete Plays with Prefaces, Vol II*. New York: Colin Smythe, pp. 443–502.

Shaw, George Bernard (1962b) *John Bull's Other Island*, in *Bernard Shaw, Complete Plays with Prefaces, Vol II*. New York: Dodd, Mead and Company, pp. 503–611.

Shiels, George (1936) *The New Gossoon*, in Curtis Canfield (ed.), *Plays of Changing Ireland*. New York: Macmillan, pp. 202–68.

Sinn Dicat (1906) 'About the Theatre Abbey', *Sinn Fein*, 15 December, p. 3.

Slaughter, Howard K. (1969) 'Introduction', in *The Plays of George Fitzmaurice: Folk Plays*. Dublin: Dolmen Press, pp. vii–xx.

Smith, Gus and Hickey, Des (1992) *John B: The Real Keane*. Dublin: Mercier Press.

Synge, J. M. (1982a) *The Playboy of the Western World*, in Saddlemyer, Ann (ed.), *Collected Works, Vol. IV: Plays, Book II*. Gerrards Cross, Bucks: Colin Smythe, pp. 51–178.

Synge, J. M. (1982b) *The Shadow of the Glen*, in Ann Saddlemyer (ed.), *Collected Works, Vol. III: Plays, Book I*. Gerrards Cross, Bucks: Colin Smythe, pp. 29–62.

Toibin, Colm (2002) *Lady Gregory's Toothbrush*. Madison: University of Wisconsin Press.

Trotter, Mary (2000) 'Translating Women into Irish Theatre History', in Stephen Watt, Eileen Morgan and Shakir Mustafa (eds), *A Century of Irish Drama: Widening the Stage*. Indianapolis and Bloomington: Indiana University Press, pp. 163–78.

Trotter, Mary (2001) *Ireland's National Theaters: Political Performance and the Origins of the Irish Dramatic Movement*. Syracuse, NY: Syracuse University Press.

Vandevelde, Karen (2005) *The Alternative Dramatic Revival in Ireland, 1897–1913*. Dublin: Maunsel and Company.

Walsh, Enda (1998) *Disco Pigs and Sucking Dublin*. London: Nick Hern Books.

Ward, Margaret (1996) *Unmanageable Revolutionaries: Women and Irish Nationalism*. London: Pluto Press.

Ward, Patrick (2002) *Exile, Emigration and Irish Writing*. Dublin: Irish Academic Press.

Watt, Steven (2004) 'Late Nineteenth-century Irish Theatre: Before the Abbey – and Beyond', in Shaun Richards (ed.), *The Cambridge Companion to Twentieth-Century Irish Drama*. Cambridge, UK: Cambridge University Press, pp. 18–32.

Welch, Robert (1999) *The Abbey Theatre 1899–1999: Form and Pressure*. Oxford: Oxford University Press.

West, Michael with Corn Exchange (2005) *Dublin by Lamplight*. London: Methuen.

Whelan, Gerard with Carolyn Swift (2002) *Spiked: Church – State Intrigue and The Rose Tattoo*. Dublin: New Island Books.

Wilde, Oscar (1994a) 'The Decay of Lying', in *Collins Complete Works of Oscar Wilde*. 3rd edn, New York: Harper Collins, pp. 1071–92.

Wilde, Oscar (1994b) *The Importance of Being Earnest*, in *Collins Complete Works of Oscar Wilde*, 3rd edn, New York: Harper Collins, pp. 357–419.

Wilde, Oscar (1994c) *Lady Windermere's Fan*, in *Collins Complete Works of Oscar Wilde*, 3rd edn, New York: Harper Collins, pp. 420–64.

Wills, Clair (2007) *That Neutral Island: A History of Ireland During the Second World War*. Cambridge, MA: Harvard University Press.

Worth, Katherine (1986) *The Irish Drama of Europe from Yeats to Beckett*. London: The Athlone Press.

Yeats, W. B. ([1919] 1923) 'A People's Theatre: An Open Letter to Lady Gregory', in *Plays and Controversies*. London: Macmillan, pp. 199–218.

Yeats, W. B. (1936) *Autobiographies*. New York: Macmillan.

Yeats, W. B. (1966a) *Cathleen ni Houlihan*, in Russell K. Alspach (ed.), *The Variorum Edition of the Plays of W. B. Yeats*. London: Macmillan, pp. 214–31.

Yeats, W. B. (1966b) *The Countess Cathleen*, in Russell K. Alspach, (ed.), *The Variorum Edition of the Plays of W. B. Yeats*. London: Macmillan, pp. 1–169.

Yeats, W. B. (1966c) *The Hour-Glass*, in Russell K. Alspach (ed.), *The Variorum Edition of the Plays of W. B.Yeats*. London: Macmillan, pp. 576–639.

Yeats, W. B. (1966d) *On Baile's Strand*, in Russell K. Alspach (ed.), *The Variorum Edition of the Plays of W. B. Yeats*. London: Macmillan, pp. 456–525.

Yeats, W. B. (1975) *Uncollected Prose*, vol. 2, ed. J. P. Frayne and C. Johnson. New York: Columbia University Press.

Zach, Wolfgang (2000) 'Introduction', in *Selected Plays of Rutherford Mayne*. Gerrards Cross, Bucks: Colin Smythe, pp. vii–xxvii.

Index